WITHDRAWN

PLAYS OF THE YEAR

Volume 47

'I do not claim that they are the best plays of their period. I submit merely that all are good of their kind, and that they share qualities for which a true playgoer looks.'

Preface to *Plays of the Year*, Volume One, 1949

PLAYS OF THE YEAR

YEAR

EDITED BY
J. C. TREWIN

ABIGAIL'S PARTY
Devised by Mike Leigh

ONCE A CATHOLIC
Mary O'Malley

THE LAST MEETING OF THE
KNIGHTS OF THE WHITE MAGNOLIA
Preston Jones

VOLUME 47

FREDERICK UNGAR PUBLISHING CO. INC.
NEW YORK

Published by
FREDERICK UNGAR PUBLISHING CO. INC.
250 Park Avenue South, New York, N.Y. 10003

ABIGAIL'S PARTY
© *Mike Leigh*

ONCE A CATHOLIC
© *Mary O'Malley*

*THE LAST MEETING OF THE
KNIGHTS OF THE WHITE MAGNOLIA*
© *Preston Jones*

*Printed in Great Britain by
Clarke, Doble & Brendon Ltd.
Plymouth*

FOR WENDY
At a Special Anniversary

CONTENTS

INTRODUCTION
page 7

ABIGAIL'S PARTY
page 13

ONCE A CATHOLIC
page 105

THE LAST MEETING
OF THE KNIGHTS OF
THE WHITE MAGNOLIA
page 209

INTRODUCTION

We have had several plays from Hampstead in this series. Now, for Volume 47, there is a particularly rich double event: ABIGAIL'S PARTY and THE LAST MEETING OF THE KNIGHTS OF THE WHITE MAGNOLIA. None of the small fringe, 'try-out', experimental, or test-tube theatres, whichever description you prefer, has done so much for the London stage since James Roose-Evans founded what was then a theatre-club at the Moreland Hall in 1959. (Three years later it moved to Swiss Cottage.) Today Hampstead is still a stimulating source of new theatre.

The other play, in the middle of this volume, is from the Royal Court: it is superfluous to introduce the theatre that has been a 'quick forge and working-house' in Sloane Square since the days of George Devine in 1956 and the first high fever of the stage rebellion. Mary O'Malley's ONCE A CATHOLIC, which went to Wyndham's in the West End for a long run, is as cheerful as anything the Court has yet discovered.

ABIGAIL'S PARTY first. 'Devised and directed by Mike Leigh', this is a remarkable semi-documentary piece, 'evolved from scratch entirely by rehearsal through improvisation', the kind of thing that needs to be done without flaw. Mr Leigh and his company have provided the answers; and, as we can see, the text will help future social historians when they look back on our time. I call it a semi-documentary because, towards the end of the night, the play breaks from its task of finding an exact rendering of one form of modern speech and behaviour and adds a sudden dramatic climax. Unexpected; yet we realise that the path has been prepared.

The party named in the title remains invisible even though it can be heard. It seems that Abigail, a sophisticated fifteen, is having a teenagers' occasion with a few score guests. We are established next door where her anxious mother has been invited for refuge, and where the hosts and two other friends are suggested with relentless precision. The dialogue, a composite achievement, has been devised for the ear (not all dialogue is). Its speakers were uncannily realised at Hampstead, especially by Alison Steadman; she won two important awards for her bitchily uncompromising portrait of Beverly, the hostess, with a voice like an off-key adenoidal wood-pigeon.

ONCE A CATHOLIC, a determined and out-spoken challenge to tolerance and a sense of humour, manages to be amusing from the first reading of the form register, though we may doubt whether all convent schools are like that of Our Lady of Fatima, allegedly in Harlesden during 1956-7: a period (not to our surprise) when the dramatist, Mary O'Malley, was being educated in Harlesden herself. So luxuriant a growth might do with tactful pruning; yet we can credit these adolescent girls who find their training so much at odds with the lives they are likely to live. All of them are Irish, and practically all of them are called Mary. Our sympathy is with Mary Rooney — the London actress, Jane Carr, had immense charm — a dear soul, wrongfully the convent's scapegoat or black sheep, who aspires to be a nun. Throughout, the writing has a mischievous relish. As a piece of theatre, high-spirited and single-

*minded, the play has conquered and it will go on
conquering.*

*So to our third choice, the second from
Hampstead where Michael Rudman directed it
ingeniously. THE LAST MEETING OF THE
KNIGHTS OF THE WHITE MAGNOLIA is an
ample title for an ample comedy. By an American
dramatist, Preston Jones — who is also an actor
and director — it is part of a Texas trilogy but self-
contained. The three plays, of which this is the
first, are all set in a milieu that has been studied to
the last detail: 'Bradleyville, Texas — population
6,000 — a small dead West Texas town in the
middle of a big dead West Texas prairie between
Abilene and San Angelo. The new highway has
bypassed it and now the world is trying to.'*

*Luckily, the theatre has not bypassed Preston
Jones's triptych (its other panels are 'Lu Ann
Hampton Laverty Oberlander' and 'The Oldest
Living Graduate'). We are concerned with the
helpless Knights of the White Magnolia; the title
of their play tells us the end before we have begun
— not, I think, that anyone will worry. The period
is 1962. We are with the last lodge of a fading
brotherhood, among those curious bodies,
basically social clubs, that hide themselves under
some portentous ritual (the Knights' rule-book
was written by Maynard C. Stempco in 1902):*

*You are now on a journey, initiate Lonnie Roy
McNeil. A journey to seek the Golden Fountain
of Truth that flows deep in the darkness of the
Mystic Mountain . . . During your journey . . .
you will converse with the great heavenly sages,
and as you heed their advice, your reply will be
'Stempco, Stempco, Stempco.' . . . Your first
journey is to the pale blue grotto of the moon.*

And so on. Most of the members turn up for

dominoes and a drink. But when there is the rarity of a new Knight, a raw boy from the back of beyond, all must give way to the initiation ceremony. The required hats, the chapeaux de rituale, *are 'fez-type with ribbons on the back and emblems on the front. A half-moon, a sunburst, a cloud with streamers for the west wind, a lamp for wisdom, a series of fountain-type lines for the truth, and a bolt of lightning for the wizard.' You gather what the Knights are like: they are worth meeting, and their dialogue never falters in its idiomatic zest.*

J. C. TREWIN

Hampstead, 1978.

I am most grateful to my colleague, Sandra Gorman, for her valuable aid and tolerance.

NOTE

Previous volumes in this series have included the following plays from theatres represented in Volume 47:

ROYAL COURT THEATRE

Volume 24: The Keep by GWYN THOMAS.

Volume 26: Jackie the Jumper by GWYN THOMAS.

Volume 35: The Restoration of Arnold Middleton by DAVID STOREY.

Volume 35: Marya by ISAAC BABEL; adapted by Christopher Hampton.

Volume 38: In Celebration by DAVID STOREY.

Volume 39: Uncle Vanya by ANTON CHEKHOV; new version by Christopher Hampton.

Volume 39: Three Months Gone by DONALD HOWARTH.

Volume 40: The Contractor by DAVID STOREY.

Volume 41: Home by DAVID STOREY.

Volume 44: The Changing Room by DAVID STOREY.

HAMPSTEAD THEATRE

Volume 21: Siwan by SAUNDERS LEWIS; translated by Emyr Humphreys.

Volume 29: The Little Clay Cart, attributed to King Sudraka; translated by Revilo Pendleton Oliver; adapted by James Roose-Evans.

Volume 30: How's The World Treating You? by ROGER MILNER.

Volume 33: Country Dance by JAMES KENNA-WAY.

Volume 34: The Happy Apple by JACK PULMAN.

Volume 37: Have You Any Dirty Washing, Mother Dear? by CLIVE EXTON.

Volume 37: The Black Swan Winter by JOHN HALE.

ABIGAIL'S PARTY

devised by
Mike Leigh

ABIGAIL'S PARTY

Hampstead Theatre, London, presented *Abigail's Party* on 18 April 1977, with the following cast:

BEVERLY	*Alison Steadman*
LAURENCE	*Tim Stern*
ANGELA	*Janine Duvitski*
TONY	*John Salthouse*
SUSAN	*Thelma Whiteley*

Devised and directed by Mike Leigh
Designed by Tanya McCallin
Costumes by Lindy Hemming
Lighting by Alan O'Toole

In a later revival at Hampstead Theatre (from 18 July 1977), and also in the television version transmitted as a *Play for Today* on BBC-1 on 1 November 1977, *Harriet Reynolds* appeared as SUSAN.

Abigail's Party was evolved from scratch entirely by rehearsal through improvisation.

CHARACTERS

BEVERLY

LAURENCE, Beverly's husband

ANGELA, a new neighbour

TONY, Angela's husband

SUSAN, another neighbour

The action takes place in Laurence and Beverly's house.

ACT I
Early evening in Spring

ACT II
Later that evening

Time — the present

ACT ONE

Laurence and Beverly's house, the ground floor. Room divider shelf unit, including telephone, stereo, ornamental fibre-light, fold down desk, and prominently-placed bar. Leather three piece suite, onyx coffee-table, sheepskin rug. Open-plan kitchen, dining area with table and chairs. Hall and front door unseen.

Lights up.

(Enter Beverly. She puts on a record (Donna Summer: Love to Love you Baby*). Lights a cigarette. Places a copy of* Cosmopolitan *in magazine rack. Pours a gin-and-tonic. Gets a tray of crisps and salted peanuts from the kitchen and puts it on the coffee table. Sits.*

Pause.

Enter Laurence, with executive case.)

LAURENCE *(kissing her)*: Hullo.
BEVERLY: Hi.

(Laurence puts case on armchair.)

You're late.
LAURENCE: Sorry? *(Laurence turns down music.)*
BEVERLY: I said, you're late.

(Laurence pours himself a scotch.)

LAURENCE: Yes: sorry about that — unavoidable.
BEVERLY: What happened?
LAURENCE: Oh, some clients, they were late.

BEVERLY: Laurence, don't leave your bag on there, please.
LAURENCE: I'll move it in a minute.
BEVERLY: D'you get something to eat?
LAURENCE: No.
BEVERLY: No? I had to throw your pizza away, I'm sorry.

(Beverly gets from fridge two small platesful of home-made cheese-and-pineapple savouries each consisting of one cube of cheese and one chunk of pineapple on a cocktail stick.

Laurence opens desk. Gets case. Opens notebook. Goes to 'phone.

Beverly returns, puts plates on coffee table.)

LAURENCE: Just got to make a couple of 'phone-calls.
BEVERLY: D'you want me to make you a little sandwich?
LAURENCE: No, I must get these out of the way first.
BEVERLY: Laurence, you want to have your bath and get changed: they're going to be here soon.
LAURENCE: Yes.

(Beverly sits.)

Oh, is Mr O'Halligan there, please? O'Halligan. Yes. Well, he's big. He's bald, with red hair. Thank you.

(Pause.)

BEVERLY: Laurence, you're going to get heart-burn.

LAURENCE: Mr O'Halligan? Mr Moss here,
Wibley Webb. Hullo. D'you realise I've been
trying to contact you all afternoon? I know you've
been out! Now where's that key to 15 Clittingham
Avenue? Ah, but you were supposed to have it
back before lunch! That's no good, I need it now.
Will you be in tomorrow morning? Tonight!
Where? Belfast? What time's your 'plane? All
right, train then. A party? I thought you just said
you were going to Belfast! Well what time are you
going to Kilburn? Well, what time are you having
your bath? I'm not asking you to bath in cold
water — I just want the key to 15 Clittingham
Avenue; I've got another client who wants to view
the property. What about you, Mr O'Halligan?
Well Mr O'Halligan, if you'd like to come in on
Monday morning with your deposit, and go ahead
and get in touch with your Building Society, we'll
see how things go. Now what about this key? All
right, I will come and get it! Now!
BEVERLY: Laurence — no!
LAURENCE: Yes, I've got the address. Yes, I know
how to get there. Okay — I'll see you shortly —
Goodbye! *(He hangs up.)* Stupid man.
BEVERLY: Oh Christ, Laurence.
LAURENCE: What?
BEVERLY: How long's all this going to take,
please?
LAURENCE: Oh, yes — I'm sorry. It won't take
long. *(He dials another number.)*
BEVERLY: D'you get those lagers?
LAURENCE: Er, no: I didn't have time.
BEVERLY: Laurence! *(Pause.)* Well, you'd better
get them when you go out, and don't forget,
please.
LAURENCE: Hullo, Mrs Cushing? Laurence Moss
here, Wibley Webb! Yes, Mrs Cushing, we have

run him to ground, and you'll be happy to knov
that I'm now in the throes of retrieving the key!

(Beverly gets herself another drink.)

Not at all, not at all — all part of the service! Ah.
Ah, yes . . . now, when would be best for you?
No, no, I'll fall in with you, Mrs Cushing. How
about tomorrow morning?
BEVERLY: Laurence!
LAURENCE: My pleasure, Mrs Cushing, my
pleasure. Now, what time would suit you best?
No, I'm at your service, Mrs Cushing: he who
pays the piper calls the tune! You name the hour,
and I shall appear! No, really: I insist. What time?
Eight o'clock? Sure, surely.
BEVERLY: Laurence!!
LAURENCE: Early? Not at all, Mrs Cushing — up
with the lark, you know. Don't mention it, Mrs
Cushing, it's my privilege. 'Bye, Mrs Cushing —
see you tomorrow morning! 'Bye now! *(He hangs
up.)*
BEVERLY: You're going to kill yourself, you know,
Laurence.
LAURENCE: Yes. Well it can't be helped.
BEVERLY: It's ridiculous.
LAURENCE: It's not a 9 to 5 job — you know that,
Beverly.
BEVERLY: You can say that again.

(Laurence sits with Beverly.)

You gonna get changed?
LAURENCE: Yes. I'll drink this; I'll get changed;
then I'll go out.
BEVERLY: And don't forget those lagers.
LAURENCE: Beverly; where are the olives?
BEVERLY: In the kitchen, Laurence. Laurence, if

you want olives, would you put them out, please?

(The front door bell chimes.)

LAURENCE *(jumping up)*: They're early, aren't they?
BEVERLY: No they're not. And you've not changed.
LAURENCE: I know that. *(He goes to answer the door.)* Beverly, get the olives.

(Beverly composes herself, then rises, and prepares to receive guests. Meanwhile, offstage:)

ANGELA: Hello, you must be Laurence!
LAURENCE: That's right.
ANGELA: I'm Angie.
LAURENCE: Do go in, won't you?
ANGELA: Thank you. This is my husband, Tony.
TONY: How d'you do.
LAURENCE: Hullo.

(They come in.)

BEVERLY: Hi, Ang.
ANGELA: Hello, Beverly — what a lovely dress!
BEVERLY: Thanks.
ANGELA: Were we meant to wear long?
BEVERLY: No, no, it's just informal, you know, so . . .
ANGELA: This is my husband, Tony.
BEVERLY: How d'you do, pleased to meet you.
TONY: How d'you do.
BEVERLY: He's got a firm handshake, hasn't he?
ANGELA: Yes.
BEVERLY: Yeah, fantastic. Like to go through?
TONY: Ta.
ANGELA: This is the suite I was telling you about.

It's nice, isn't it?

TONY: Lovely.

ANGELA: We've just bought a new three-piece suite, but ours isn't real leather, like this — it's "leather look".

BEVERLY: Oh, the Leather Look? Great.

LAURENCE: Drink?

TONY: Yes, please.

BEVERLY: Laurence, would you like to take Angela's coat, please?

LAURENCE: Surely.

ANGELA: Thanks.

LAURENCE: Pleasure.

(Laurence takes coat out.)

BEVERLY: It's funny, 'cos he's a lot bigger than I thought he was. Yeah . . . 'cos I've seen him across the road, Ang, and I thought he was about the same size as Laurence —

ANGELA: Oh, no . . .

BEVERLY: — but he's not, he's a lot bigger, yeah, great. Would you like a drink?

TONY: Yes please.

BEVERLY: What would you like?

TONY: Barcardi-and-Coke, please.

BEVERLY: Ice and lemon?

TONY: Yes please.

BEVERLY: Great. How about you, Ang?

ANGELA: Have you got gin?

BEVERLY: Gin-and-tonic?

ANGELA: Please.

BEVERLY: Ice and lemon?

ANGELA: Yes, please.

BEVERLY: Great.

(Enter Laurence.)

Laurence, would you like to get the drinks, please? Tony would like Bacardi-and-Coke with ice and lemon, Angela would like a gin-and-tonic with ice and lemon, and I'd like a little fill-up, okay?

LAURENCE: Surely.

BEVERLY: D'you like lager, Tony?

TONY: I'll be all right with Bacardi, thank you.

BEVERLY: No — as a chaser, a little bit later on; because Laurence is gonna get some.

TONY: It'll be okay, thank you.

BEVERLY: Or a light ale. Which d'you prefer?

TONY: Light ale.

BEVERLY: Light ale? Laurence, would you get some light ale as well, please?

LAURENCE: Yes.

BEVERLY: Actually, Ang, it's going to be really nice, because I've invited Sue from Number 9.

ANGELA: Oh, lovely.

BEVERLY: Yeah, so I thought it'd be nice for you to meet her as well. Yeah, 'cos her daughter's having a party. Well, she's only a teenager, so I said, well pop down and spend the evening with us.

ANGELA: That'd be really nice, 'cos I want to meet all the neighbours.

BEVERLY: Yeah, just say hello, Ang, and break the ice.

ANGELA: 'Cos that was what was so nice when you came over, 'cos it really made me feel at home.

BEVERLY: Well, Ang, I know what I felt like when I moved in — I was lonely. So I thought, well, that's not going to happen to you.

ANGELA: Well, you're the friendly type, aren't you?

BEVERLY: Yeah, yeah. It's funny, 'cos as soon as we met, I knew we were gonna get on.

ANGELA: Well, we're alike, aren't we?

BEVERLY: Yeah, yeah.

(Laurence gives them their drinks.)

Thanks.
ANGELA: Thanks.

(Laurence gives Tony his drink.)

TONY: Thank you.
BEVERLY: Cheers, everyone!
ANGELA: Cheers!
BEVERLY: Cheers, Tone!
TONY: Cheers.

(Laurence gets his glass, from the coffee table.)

LAURENCE: Cheers!
ANGELA: Cheers!
BEVERLY: What are you doing, darling? Are you staying, or going?
LAURENCE: Er, I'll stay for a while.
BEVERLY: Laurence has to pop out on business, I'm afraid, so . . . Now: anybody like a cigarette? Laurence would you, please?

(Laurence offers cigarette box.)

BEVERLY: Angela?
ANGELA: No thanks.
BEVERLY: Tony, would you like a cigarette?
TONY: No, thank you.
ANGELA: We've just given up.
BEVERLY: Oh, yeah. Sorry!
LAURENCE: Now, who'd like some olives?
BEVERLY: Not for me. Ang?
ANGELA: No, thanks.
BEVERLY: Tony, d'you like olives?

TONY: No, I don't.

BEVERLY: No, they're horrible, aren't they?

ANGELA: Yes.

BEVERLY: They've got a very bitter taste, haven't they, Ang?

ANGELA: Yes.

BEVERLY: I told you nobody'd like olives, Laurence.

LAURENCE: Not nobody, Beverly: I like olives. And that's twenty-five per cent of the assembled company.

ANGELA: We've met you before, haven't we?

LAURENCE: Really?

ANGELA: He is the one you remember, isn't he?

TONY: Yeah.

ANGELA: D'you remember us? We came looking for a house.

LAURENCE: I can't say I do; of course, we see a lot of clients.

TONY: We saw a lot of estate agents.

ANGELA: Yes, we went to all the ones in the area. We got the house from Spencer's in the end — Anthony Spencer.

BEVERLY: Oh, Anthony Spencer, yeah, yeah.

ANGELA: Well it was Nicholas Spencer who was dealing with us.

BEVERLY: Yeah?

ANGELA: He's very nice. D'you know him?

LAURENCE: Yes, I know him.

ANGELA: Have you seen those boards they have outside?

BEVERLY: Ang, aren't they beautiful?

ANGELA: Yes, they're lovely. With the house and the family and the car and the tree. When I saw them I thought, 'I hope we get a house with one of those boards.' I expect they sell a lot of houses because of the boards. Don't you think so?

LAURENCE: No, actually, I don't.

ANGELA: Oh, don't you? We were very lucky, actually, 'cos we got the price of the house down from twenty-two thousand to twenty-one thousand.

BEVERLY: Really? Oh that is fantastic, Ang, that's really great.

(During following, Beverly offers cheese-pineapple savouries to Angela and Tony. So does Laurence, though superfluously as it turns out. Tony says 'Ta' where appropriate.)

BEVERLY: Is it your first house?

ANGELA: Yes, we were in a furnished flat before.

BEVERLY: Oh, that's a bit grim, isn't it, furnished flat? Yeah.

ANGELA: Yes. Well it was nice for us while we were saving.

BEVERLY: Yeah.

ANGELA: But the trouble is, with it being furnished, it means we haven't got much furniture of our own together yet.

BEVERLY: Yeah, and you feel it when you move, don't you?

ANGELA: Yes.

BEVERLY: Mind you, Ang, your house is smaller than this one, yeah, because I know they are smaller on your side, yeah.

ANGELA: Yes. Mmm. These are lovely.

BEVERLY: Yes, they're dainty, aren't they?

(Beverly has sat down again.)

Your bed arrived yet, Ang?

ANGELA: Oh, don't talk about that — it's a sore point.

BEVERLY: Is it?

ANGELA: Well, it's funny, really . . . 'cos I came back from work today, 'cos I'm not working nights any more, I'm on days.

BEVERLY: Yeah?

ANGELA: And I came home, and I saw this big parcel in the hall, and I saw his face, and he was looking furious, and I thought, What's happened? . . . and you know what? The bed-head had arrived, and no bed.

BEVERLY: No, Ang! Laurence, did you hear that? How many weeks ago is it you ordered that bed, Ang?

ANGELA: Four.

BEVERLY: Four weeks ago they ordered a bed, and it still hasn't arrived. It's disgusting.

LAURENCE: Well, you can't trust anybody these days.

ANGELA: No.

BEVERLY: It's disgraceful. I mean, you've been sleeping on the floor, haven't you Ang?

ANGELA: Yes. Well, we've got a mattress from Tony's mum, but it's not the same.

BEVERLY: No. Well, let's face it, Tone, you can't do much with a bed-head, can you? D'you know what I mean?

(Pause.)

LAURENCE: What line of business are you in?

TONY   ⎫ .Computers.
ANGELA ⎰ 'He's in computers.

BEVERLY: Oh, really, Tone? That's funny, 'cos my brother's in computers, actually.

ANGELA: Is he?

BEVERLY: Yeah, he's a . . . programmes analyst.

ANGELA: Oh yes? Tony's, just an operator.

BEVERLY: I know it's a fantastic job, though, Tone, 'cos my brother, he had to go to college and get exams. I mean, he was studying for years, wasn't he Laurence?

LAURENCE: Oh, yes.

BEVERLY: Did you have to do all that, Tone? — go to college?

ANGELA: You didn't really, did you?

TONY: No.

ANGELA: No.

BEVERLY: I know it is a fantastic job, though, Tone, 'cos my brother, he's got a fabulous house and he gets great wages, y'know? Yeah.

LAURENCE: 9 to 5, is it?

TONY: No, it's not, actually; there's quite a bit of variation.

ANGELA: Shift-work.

TONY: It's a two-weekly system: one week I work from 8 in the morning till 4 in the afternoon, and the following week I work from 4 till midnight. I get every other Saturday off.

BEVERLY: Oh, great. Were you off today, Tone?

TONY: Yeah, I was, actually.

ANGELA: Yes. It's lucky, 'cos if I'm working on a Saturday, he can do all the shopping.

LAURENCE: Oh yes? Where do you shop?

ANGELA ⎫
TONY ⎬ : Sainsbury's.

LAURENCE: Ah, we usually go to the Co-op: I find they have a much wider range of goods there.

BEVERLY: Don't you find shopping boring, though, Ang?

ANGELA: Mmm.

BEVERLY: Oh, I do — I hate it. He takes me down in the car, and I get me wheely, Tone, and I whizz in, and I grab anything I can see, and I bung it in the wheely, he writes me a cheque, we bung it in the car, bring it home, and it's done for the week, d'you know what I mean?

LAURENCE: Beverly is not very organised: she

doesn't believe in making shopping-lists. You
have a car, do you?

TONY: Yeah.

ANGELA: Yes, an Escort.

LAURENCE: A yellow one?

ANGELA: That's it.

LAURENCE: Yes, I've seen it.

BEVERLY: Yeah, it's beautiful, actually.

ANGELA: Beverly was saying you only like Minis.

LAURENCE: No, not at all. I don't only like Minis
— I like lots of other cars. But I find the Mini
economical, efficient and reliable, and the most
suited to my purposes. Of course, I change my car
every year.

BEVERLY: Yeah, but what I say, Ang, is this: What
is the point in changing your car if all you change
is the colour?

LAURENCE: That's not all you change, Beverly; the
design does alter. But then you're not a motorist,
so of course you just don't understand these
things.

BEVERLY: Yeah, okay. I know I failed my test
three times.

LAURENCE: Three times.

BEVERLY: But, I'm his wife, Ang, and I reckon a
wife should have a little say in the choosing of a
car.

LAURENCE: Well, when you've passed your test,
Beverly, then you can have your little say. Until
then, please leave it to me.

BEVERLY: Let me put it to you this way, Ang.
When we chose the furniture, we chose it together;
when we chose the house, we chose it together;
but, when it comes to the car, I'm not allowed to
have a say.

(Laurence goes.)

Don't forget those light ales!

LAURENCE: No — and the lagers, yes!

ANGELA: You going to take your test again?

BEVERLY: Yeah, I'm going to have another try, yeah. Don't get me wrong, Tone, it's not that I can't drive — in fact I'm a good driver, but, let me put it to you this way, when I get to my test my nerves fail me, d'you know what I mean? I mean it was me nerves that failed me the last time, to be honest with you, because you know the way they take you out in threes, Tone, right? I started off behind this bloke — he was a Chinese bloke actually. Now: my bloke had told me to turn left, right? Now, we came to the first Give Way, and the bloke in front slammed his brakes on. Now, I'm going behind him, and I suppose I'm going a little bit too quick with me nerves; so I slam on my brakes, and I went slap in the back of him.

ANGELA: Ah.

BEVERLY: Now, I reckon that prejudiced my examiner against me.

ANGELA: What a shame.

BEVERLY: Yeah, it was, actually. Can you drive, Ang?

ANGELA: No. I'd like to learn, but Tony won't let me. He doesn't think I'd be any good. And it's a shame, 'cos it's so awkward for me to get to work since we've moved.

BEVERLY: Is it, yeah?

ANGELA: And you see, I could use the car when he wasn't working.

BEVERLY: And that would make you completely independent of Tone, wouldn't it?

(Pause.)

D'you pass your test first time, Tone?

TONY: Yeah.

BEVERLY: I thought so, actually — he looks the

type, doesn't he? *(She goes to the bar.)* Who's for another drink? Ang?

ANGELA: Thanks.

BEVERLY: How about you, Tone?

TONY: Ta.

BEVERLY: Yeah? Great.

(Enter Laurence.)

BEVERLY: What's the matter?

LAURENCE: Nothing. Tony, I wonder if you could give me a hand for a moment, please?

BEVERLY: Won't the car start?

LAURENCE: No.

ANGELA: Go on, Tony!

TONY: All right!

(Tony follows Laurence out.)

BEVERLY: Mind you don't go getting dirt on your suit. All right, Tone? *(She concludes pouring drinks.)* Ang.

ANGELA: Thanks.

BEVERLY: Cheers.

ANGELA: Cheers.

BEVERLY: Ang: would you mind if I asked you a personal question?

ANGELA: No.

BEVERLY: Now, please don't be offended when I say this, but, what colour lipstick are you wearing?

ANGELA: A pinky red.

BEVERLY: A pinky red! Now, can you take a little bit of criticism? Please don't be offended when I say this, but, you're wearing a very pretty dress, if I may say so; now, you see that pink ribbon down the front? If you'd chosen, Ang, a colour slightly nearer that pink, I think it would have blended more with your skin tones; d'you know what I mean?

ANGELA: A paler colour.

BEVERLY: A slightly paler colour. Now, can I give you a tip?

ANGELA: . . . yes.

BEVERLY: Now, okay. I can see what you've done: you've just sat down in front of your mirror, and you've put your lipstick on. Now, this is something I always used to tell my customers, and it always works . . . now, next time, just sit down in front of your mirror, and relax. And just say to yourself, "I've got very beautiful lips". Then take your lipstick and apply it, and you'll see the difference, Ang. Because then you will be applying your lipstick to every single corner of your mouth, d'you know what I mean? Will you try it for me next time?

ANGELA: Yes.

BEVERLY: Just sit down in front of your mirror, and relax, and say to yourself —

ANGELA: "I've got very beautiful lips."

BEVERLY: And I promise you you'll see the difference, Ang! Okay?

ANGELA: Thanks.

(The front door bell chimes.)

BEVERLY: Would you excuse me just one minute, Ang?

(Beverly goes out. Angela helps herself to a cheese-pineapple savoury. Meanwhile, starting offstage.)

BEVERLY: Hi, Sue.

SUSAN: Hello, Beverly.

BEVERLY: Come in.

SUSAN: Thank you.

BEVERLY: All right, Sue?

SUSAN: Yes, thank you.

BEVERLY: Come through.

SUSAN: I'm sorry I'm a bit late.

BEVERLY: Now, don't worry, Sue, that's all right. Would you like to slip your jacket off?

SUSAN: Oh, thank you.

BEVERLY: Everything all right, Sue?

SUSAN: Yes, I think so. I hope so.

BEVERLY: Come through and say hello. Ang: this is Sue. Sue, this is Ang.

ANGELA: Hello.

SUSAN: How d'you do.

BEVERLY: Sue's from Number 9.

ANGELA: Oh, we've just moved into Number 16.

SUSAN: Oh, really?

BEVERLY: Yeah, you know the Macdonalds' old house, Sue?

SUSAN: Yes.

BEVERLY: Yeah. Sit down Sue. I'll just pop your coat in the hall. *(going)* Won't be a sec. Make yourself at home, Sue!

SUSAN: Thank you. *(She puts a wrapped bottle on the bar, and proceeds to sit down.)*

ANGELA: We've only been here a fortnight.

SUSAN: Oh, really?

(Beverly returns.)

BEVERLY: Did you bring that, Sue?

SUSAN: Yes.

BEVERLY: Is it for us?

SUSAN: Yes.

BEVERLY: Oh, thank you, Sue!

SUSAN: It's nothing very special, I'm afraid.

BEVERLY: Ah. Isn't that kind, Ang?

ANGELA: Yes.

SUSAN: Not at all.

BEVERLY *(unwrapping the bottle)*: Oh, lovely! 'Cos Laurence likes a drop of wine, actually. Oh, it's Beaujolais. Fantastic! Won't be a sec, I'll just pop it in the fridge. *(She goes to kitchen)*

ANGELA: I'm so pleased to meet you. I want to meet all the neighbours.

SUSAN: Yes.

(Beverly returns.)

BEVERLY: Now, Sue: what would you like to drink?

SUSAN: I'll have a glass of sherry, please.

BEVERLY: Sherry, are you sure?

SUSAN: Yes. Thank you.

BEVERLY: 'Cos we've got everything. There's gin, whisky, vodka, brandy, whatever you'd like. Would you like a little gin-and-tonic, Sue? 'Cos me and Ang are drinking gin-and-tonic, actually.

SUSAN: All right — thank you.

BEVERLY: Ice and lemon?

SUSAN: Yes please.

BEVERLY: Great.

ANGELA: It's a nice drink, gin-and-tonic, isn't it?

SUSAN: Yes, it is.

ANGELA: Refreshing. *(Tony returns during:)* Sometimes I drink lager-and-lime. Say I'm in a pub with my husband, I'll drink that. But I prefer this.

TONY: Can I wash me hands, please?

BEVERLY: Yes, just one second, Tone, while I finish making Sue's drink. Sorry: Sue — this is Tony.

ANGELA: My husband.

SUSAN
TONY   } : How d'you do.

ANGELA: Did you push it all right?

TONY: Yeah. The battery was flat.

BEVERLY: Sue!

SUSAN: Thank you.

BEVERLY: Cheers.

SUSAN: Oh, cheers.

BEVERLY: Now. Tony, hands! Come through. *(She takes him to kitchen.)* Soap and towel there. Okay?

TONY: Ta.

ANGELA: D'you work?

SUSAN: No. No, I don't.

ANGELA: I'm a nurse.

SUSAN: Oh.

ANGELA: At St. Mary's in Walthamstow.

SUSAN: Oh, yes.

ANGELA: Beverly says your daughter's having a party. Is that right?

SUSAN: That's right, yes.

ANGELA: Has it started yet?

SUSAN: Yes. Yes, it has.

BEVERLY: All right, Tone?

TONY: Yes, thank you.

BEVERLY: Come through.

(He comes through.)

Drink's on there. Like to sit down?

TONY: Ta.

BEVERLY: Now then, Sue, let's see . . . would you like a little cigarette?

SUSAN: Oh. No, thank you.

BEVERLY: Are you sure?

SUSAN: Yes. Thank you.

BEVERLY: Perhaps you'll have one a little bit later on. And I know Angela doesn't want one. Now, everybody all right?

TONY: Yes thank you.

ANGELA: Yes, lovely thanks.

SUSAN: Yes. Thank you.
BEVERLY: Yes? Great!

(Rock music starts at Number 9, not especially loud.)

BEVERLY: Aye aye! It's started, Sue.
ANGELA: They've got the record-player going, haven't they? They're going to have fun, aren't they?
BEVERLY: Sounds like it.
SUSAN: I hope so.
ANGELA: How old is she, your daughter?
SUSAN: Fifteen.
ANGELA: What does she look like? 'Cos I might have seen her.
SUSAN: Oh. Well, she's quite tall, and she's got fair hair, quite long fair hair.
ANGELA: She hasn't got a pink streak in her hair, has she?
SUSAN: Yes.
BEVERLY: Yeah, that's Abigail! And she wears those jeans, Ang, with patches on, and safety-pins right down the side, and scruffy bottoms.
ANGELA: Yes, I've seen her.
SUSAN: And plumber's overalls.
BEVERLY: Yeah, plumber's overalls. She makes me die, you know!
ANGELA: I've seen her: she was standing outside your gate with a friend. And you've seen her as well, haven't you? Getting off that motorbike.
TONY: Yeah.
ANGELA: How many people are coming to the party?
BEVERLY: About fifteen, isn't it, Sue?
SUSAN: Well, it was fifteen. Then it went up to twenty, and last night I gathered it was twenty-five.

BEVERLY: It's creeping up, Sue.

SUSAN: I've told her that's the limit. Well, I think that's enough. Don't you?

BEVERLY: Definitely, Sue, yeah, definitely.

ANGELA: Yeah.

BEVERLY: But, this is it with teenagers: okay, they tell you twenty-five; but a friend invites a friend; that friend invites another friend; and it creeps up till you end up with about seventy or eighty. This is it. This is the danger!

TONY: I've just seen a couple of people arriving, actually.

SUSAN: Yes. Nice of them to help you with the car.

TONY: Oh, no — not them: a couple of coloured chaps and a girl roared up in a Ford Capri.

SUSAN: Oh, really? *(Pause.)* Well, there were only half a dozen there when I left . . . When I was asked to leave.

BEVERLY: Yeah, this is it, isn't it? They don't want Mum sitting there, casting a beady eye on all the goings-on, do they?

ANGELA: No. Not when they get to fifteen. When I was fifteen I really wanted a party of my own, and my Dad, he'd never let me. You see, I've got four sisters. Haven't I, Tony?

TONY: Yeah.

ANGELA: And I think he was a little bit worried that I'd invite all my friends, and they'd bring along a few of theirs, and we'd end up with a houseful.

BEVERLY: This is it.

ANGELA: And he was worried about people pinching things, and things getting broken.

BEVERLY: Have you locked your silver away, Sue?

SUSAN: No, I haven't got any. Well, not much, anyway. I've put a few things upstairs; just in case of accidents.

ANGELA: Yes, well it's better to, isn't it? 'Cos it

can easily happen.

BEVERLY: Yeah.

ANGELA: Like that egg-timer. Tony was furious. It was a wedding present.

BEVERLY: Don't get me wrong, Sue: I wasn't meaning that any of Abigail's friends are thieves — please don't think that. But, you don't know who you get at a party. And let's face it: people are light-fingered.

ANGELA: Yes.

(Pause.)

BEVERLY: D'you leave your carpets down, Sue?

SUSAN: Er — yes.

ANGELA: Have you got fitted carpets?

SUSAN: Yes.

ANGELA: Yes . . . we've got fitted carpets. The Macdonalds left them all. They were inclusive in the price of the house.

SUSAN: Oh?

ANGELA: And we're very lucky, because we got the price of the house down from twenty-two thousand to twenty-one thousand.

SUSAN: Really?

ANGELA: I don't know what we'll do about our carpets when we have a party. 'Cos we're having a party soon, aren't we?

TONY: Housewarming.

ANGELA: Yeah. You'll have to come.

SUSAN: Thank you.

BEVERLY: This is it, though, isn't it, with fitted carpets you don't know what to do for the best. Particularly with teenagers. Because let's face it, they're not as careful as, say, we would be, d'you know what I mean, they don't think; I mean, they've got a drink in one hand, a cigarette in the other, they're having a bit of a dance, and the next thing you know is it's cigarette on your carpet, and stubbed out.

ANGELA: Is it your daughter's birthday?

SUSAN: No. She just wanted a party. No particular reason.

BEVERLY: Yeah, well, they don't need a reason these days, do they? Any excuse for a bit of a rave-up — what do they call it, freak out? D'you get that beer, Sue?

SUSAN: Yes. I got four of those big tins, and some Pomagne.

ANGELA: Oh, that's nice, isn't it?

SUSAN: Yes it is.

BEVERLY: It's funny, at that age we used to drink Bulmer's Cider. We used to say, "A glass of cider, and she's anybody's."

ANGELA: I got very drunk on champagne at our wedding. D'you remember?

TONY: Yeah.

BEVERLY: Gives you a terrible headache, champagne, doesn't it?

ANGELA: Yes. In the morning.

BEVERLY: Yeah, shocking. D'you get any spirits, Sue?

SUSAN: No. No, I didn't.

BEVERLY: No. You're very wise. 'Cos they're so expensive, aren't they? And let's face it, if they want to drink spirits, they can bring their own. Particularly the older boys. 'Cos they're working, aren't they? I mean, there will be older boys at the party, won't there?

SUSAN: Oh, yes.

BEVERLY: Yeah. Well, let's face it, Ang, when you're fifteen you don't want to go out with a bloke who's fifteen, do you?

ANGELA: No.

BEVERLY: 'Cos they're babies, aren't they? I mean, when I was fifteen, I was going out with a bloke who was twenty-one.

(Pause.)

How's Abigail getting on with that bloke, by the way, Sue?

SUSAN: I'm not sure: I daren't ask.

BEVERLY: Mind you, I reckon you're better to let her go out with as many blokes as she wants to at that age, rather than sticking to the one. Don't you agree with me, Ang?

ANGELA: Yes. How many boy friends has she got?

SUSAN: I don't know. I don't think she really knows herself.

ANGELA: Footloose and fancy free!

BEVERLY: Actually, Sue, I was just thinking: it might be a good idea if a little bit later on, if Laurence and Tony pop down there. Now I don't mean go in; but, just to check that everything's all right; put your mind at rest. Don't you agree with me, Ang?

ANGELA: Yes, it's a good idea. You don't mind, do you?

TONY: No.

SUSAN: It's very nice of you. But I don't think it'll be necessary.

TONY: Your husband's away, then, is he?

SUSAN: No. We've split up, actually.

ANGELA: Are you separated, or divorced?

SUSAN: Divorced.

ANGELA: When did you get divorced?

SUSAN: Three years ago.

ANGELA: Oh, well: that's given you time to sort of get used to it, hasn't it? We've been married three years — three years in September, isn't it?

BEVERLY: Yeah, me and Laurence have been married three years, actually.

ANGELA: Oh, it's funny — we were all getting

married about the same time as you were getting divorced!

SUSAN: What a coincidence.

ANGELA: Yes! Where is he now? D'you know?

SUSAN: Yes. He lives quite near here, actually.

ANGELA: Oh, that's nice. D'you keep in touch?

SUSAN: Yes.

BEVERLY: Yeah, he pops over to see the kids, doesn't he, Sue?

SUSAN: Yes. He comes every Sunday.

ANGELA: Does he?

SUSAN: For lunch.

ANGELA: Ah, lovely. Is he coming tomorrow?

SUSAN: I expect so.

ANGELA: Ah, that's nice — for the kids.

BEVERLY: Yeah, well, let's face it, Sue, whatever you say about him, he is their father, isn't he?

SUSAN: Yes.

BEVERLY: Mind you, I don't believe in people sticking together for the sake of the kids. To me, that is wrong. I mean, take my parents, for example. Now, you might not believe this Sue, but it's the truth: my parents have not spoken to each other for twenty years, and as long as I can remember, my father has slept in the boxroom on his own.

ANGELA: Yeah, well that's like my father: he's terrible to my mother.

BEVERLY: Is he?

ANGELA: He hardly speaks to her.

BEVERLY: Yeah. You see, it's not fair, is it Ang? I mean, take my mum, right? She's sixty and she's ever so sweet — she wouldn't hurt a fly. But, she's really ill with her nerves. And why? It's a result of all the rows that have been going on.

ANGELA: Yes, well that's like my mum. She's been very ill for five years, seriously ill with a blood disease.

BEVERLY: Ah!

ANGELA: She might die at any moment.

BEVERLY: Really?

ANGELA: But it doesn't make any difference: my dad's still as rotten to her as he's always been.

BEVERLY: Is he? Yeah, you see, it's not fair, is it? I mean, this is the truth: if my father was to drop dead tomorrow, I wouldn't care. 'Cos I hate him. We all hate him. But, he's the kind of bloke, he'll live till he's ninety. Whereas your Mum, bless her, she could do with her good health, and she hasn't got it. Now to me, it's all wrong. I mean, they say The Good Die Young, and I'm afraid it's true.

ANGELA: Yeah, well it's like Tony's dad: he just walked out and left Tony's mum, and you were only about three, weren't you?

TONY: You like living round here, do you?

SUSAN: Yes. It's a very pleasant area.

(Pause.)

ANGELA: What did your husband do?

SUSAN: He's an architect.

ANGELA: Oh, that's a good job, isn't it?

SUSAN ⎱ :Yes, it is.
BEVERLY ⎰ Yeah, it's a good job, architect.

ANGELA: Well paid.

SUSAN: Yes, it can be. It's quite a long training, though.

ANGELA: Yes.

BEVERLY: Has David married again, Sue?

SUSAN: Yes.

ANGELA: Oh, well: it's a good job that he's got a good job, then, isn't it? I mean, if he's got two families to support.

BEVERLY: Have they got any children, Sue?

SUSAN: No. But she wants some. So they're trying. But they don't seem to have had any success so far.

ANGELA: Does she come over on Sundays?

SUSAN: No, he comes on his own.

ANGELA: Oh, but I suppose like, when your kids go over there, it's nice for her 'cos she's got a little ready-made family.

SUSAN: Well, they don't go over there, actually. Well hardly ever.

ANGELA: Don't you get on with her?

SUSAN: No. Well — I hardly know her, really.

ANGELA: Well, I mean . . . if your husband runs off with another woman, well . . . !

BEVERLY (going to bar): Well, let's face it, Ang, you can hardly be the best of mates, can you, d'you know what I mean?

ANGELA: No.

BEVERLY: Now, would anybody like another drink? Ang?

ANGELA: Thanks.

BEVERLY: Sue?

SUSAN: I still have some, thank you.

BEVERLY: Yeah, come on, Sue: I'll just give you a little top-up. That's it. Now, Tone: another drink?

TONY: Ta.

(Beverly pouring drinks.)

ANGELA: I think more and more people are getting divorced these days, though.

BEVERLY: Yeah, definitely, Ang. Mind you, I blame a lot of it on Women's Lib. I do. And on permissiveness, and all this wife-swapping business. Don't you, Tone?

TONY: I suppose so.

BEVERLY: Don't you, Sue?

SUSAN: Possibly.

BEVERLY: I mean, take Peter Sellers for example. Now he has been married at least five or six times.

SUSAN: Four, actually.

BEVERLY: Is it four, Sue?

ANGELA: Well, look at Elizabeth Taylor and Richard Burton.

BEVERLY: Now to me, their relationship is ridiculous. I think they make a mockery of marriage. I think it's disgusting.

ANGELA: They only do it for the publicity.

BEVERLY: I mean, with these film stars, I reckon half the time the attraction is purely physical.

ANGELA: They did it in the jungle.

BEVERLY: Yeah. I mean, to a filmstar, getting divorced is like going to the lavatory, if you'll pardon my French. But to us, it's a big wrench, isn't it, Sue?

SUSAN: Yes, of course.

ANGELA: Yes.

SUSAN: But I think that film stars only get married because the public expects it.

BEVERLY: Do you?

SUSAN: Yes. I do.

ANGELA: I think people take divorce for granted. I think if they stuck it out, they'd be all right, don't you?

BEVERLY: Yeah. But, mind you, there are times, Ang, let's face it, when you could hit them on the head with a rolling-pin, and clear out. D'you know what I mean?

ANGELA: Yeah, well that's like Tony and me. I mean we've only been married nearly three years, but we're always having rows, aren't we?

TONY: Yeah.

BEVERLY: She give you a bad time, Tone?

TONY *(taking drink)*: Ta. Shocking.

ANGELA: And I think it spoils things, doesn't it?

SUSAN: Yes, it does.

BEVERLY: Mind you, I reckon a little row sometimes adds a sparkle to a relationship. You know.

ANGELA: Did you have a lot of rows with your husband?

SUSAN: No, we didn't, actually.

ANGELA: Oh.

BEVERLY: Well, there you go, you see, it doesn't always follow. It's funny, isn't it? D'you think people should get married, Tone?

TONE: Sometimes.

ANGELA: Oh, he's not so sure, you see, since he's been married to me!

BEVERLY: Perhaps we should all live in sin, and forget the whole thing, I don't know.

ANGELA: Did you live with Laurence before you got married?

BEVERLY: No, I didn't, actually.

ANGELA: D'you think if you had have done, you'd still have married him?

BEVERLY: No, I don't honestly think I would have done. Don't get me wrong: I do love Laurence, in my own way. But, if we'd have lived together, say for a year, I don't honestly think it would have worked out.

(Pause.)

TONY: I think if you're going to have kids you ought to get married.

BEVERLY: Oh yeah, definitely, Tone, give them a name, yeah.

ANGELA: Yes.

BEVERLY: You'll be having all this soon, Sue. Do you think Abigail is the marrying type?

SUSAN: I hope so.

ANGELA: Oh, you'll probably be getting married again yourself soon!

SUSAN: Oh, I don't think that's very likely.

ANGELA: You never know. 'Cos I never thought anyone would marry me. And you see, I met

Tony and we were married within a year, weren't we?

TONY: Eight months.

ANGELA: Yes. So you see, it can happen.

SUSAN: Really?

ANGELA: Have you got a boyfriend?

SUSAN: No.

(Pause.)

BEVERLY: Would you like to have kids, Ang?

ANGELA: Yes. Yes, I would.

BEVERLY: Would you, Tone?

TONY: Not for a while.

ANGELA: Not till we get settled in.

BEVERLY: Yeah, get yourself sorted first, yeah. He'd make a nice dad, though, wouldn't he?

ANGELA: Yes.

BEVERLY: I could just see you, actually, with a little boy — you know: taking him out, and looking after him!

ANGELA: Be nice to have one of each.

BEVERLY: Yes, like Sue. It's funny, though, with Sue's kids, to me, Abigail and Jeremy aren't a bit alike. Are they, Sue?

SUSAN: No. They're not.

BEVERLY: They're like chalk and cheese, Ang.

ANGELA: Do they take after you or your husband?

SUSAN: Neither of us, really: Jeremy looks more like my brother. Abigail doesn't look like anyone in the family.

BEVERLY: The Black Sheep. Eh, Sue: how did Jeremy get on packing his little overnight bag?

SUSAN: Oh, he loved it!

BEVERLY: Did he? Yeah! You know what kids are like, Sue was telling me, he was so excited about packing all his little things.

SUSAN: He'd have taken the kitchen sink, if

I'd let him.
ANGELA: Where's he gone?
SUSAN: Round the corner.
TONY: How old is he?
SUSAN: Eleven-and-a-half.

(Pause.)

ANGELA: Would you like kids?
BEVERLY: No, I don't•think I would, actually.
Don't get me wrong, it's not that I don't like kids,
'cos I do, but, let me put it to you this way: I
wouldn't like to actually have to have them. I
mean — did you have your kids in hospital, Sue?
SUSAN: Yes.
ANGELA: Did you have an easy labour?
SUSAN: Well . . . Abigail was really very difficult.
But Jeremy was fine. He was born very quickly.
BEVERLY: Yes, you see, to me, having to go into
hospital would be like being ill, and I couldn't
stand that. And I know it sounds horrible, but all
that breast-feeding, and having to change nappies,
would make me heave. I don't honestly think I've
got that motherly instinct in me.
ANGELA: You see, it'd be different for me, 'cos
I'm used to looking after children.
BEVERLY: Yeah.
ANGELA: And if I can look after a wardful of sick
children, I can easily manage a couple of my own.
BEVERLY: Yeah.
ANGELA: Because the thing is, with children that
are ill, is, that you've got to watch them every
minute. Like, recently, we had this little girl, she
was only about two, and she kept picking at her
dressing. She picked it all off, and got right down
into the wound —
BEVERLY: I'm sorry, Ang, but would you stop?
It's just that if you carry on, I'll faint.

TONY: Leave it out, Ang!

ANGELA: No, it's all right, 'cos she wasn't in any pain, but she actually got the stitches —

TONY: Drop it!!

(Pause.)

ANGELA: Did you know my husband used to be a professional footballer?

BEVERLY: Really?

ANGELA: Yes, he used to play for Crystal Palace, didn't you?

TONY: Yeah.

BEVERLY: Oh, that is fantastic.

ANGELA: That was before I met him.

BEVERLY: What, d'you used to play for the reserves, Tone?

ANGELA: Oh, no; it was the first team.

BEVERLY: Honestly, is that true?

TONY: Yeah.

BEVERLY: You're not kidding me?

ANGELA: No.

BEVERLY: What, honestly, the first team?

TONY: For a bit, yeah.

BEVERLY: Oh, that is fantastic. Hey, Sue, we didn't know we had a celebrity moved into Richmond Road, did we?

SUSAN: No, we didn't.

BEVERLY: That is fantastic, Tone: that's really made my night, actually.

(Enter Laurence. He stops, registers suddenly remembering something, curses silently, spins round, and rushes out.)

BEVERLY: Laurence! *(She gets up.)* Would you excuse me a minute? *(Going.)* Laurence!

(Exit Beverly. Pause. We can still hear Abigail's music.)

ANGELA: Nice music. Isn't it, Tony?

(Pause. Tony gets up and picks up a plate of cheese-pineapple savouries.)

TONY: Would you like one of these?
SUSAN: Thank you.

(Angela gestures for one. He gives her one silently.)

ANGELA: Ta. I shouldn't be eating these. 'Cos we had a big tea. Did you eat earlier?
SUSAN: Er . . . no. No, I didn't!
ANGELA: Oh, you must be hungry. Here, have some peanuts.
SUSAN *(taking some)*: Thank you.
ANGELA: Are they having a barbecue?
SUSAN: No.
ANGELA: Oh, 'cos it's a nice idea, that, if you've got a big garden.
SUSAN: Yes, it is.
ANGELA: I'd love to have a barbecue — you know, do baked jacket potatoes . . .
SUSAN: Lovely . . .
ANGELA: Have sausages and chops. And you can do chestnuts. And have an ox — you know, on a spit!

(Enter Beverly.)

BEVERLY: Hey, it's all happening at your place, Sue. Oh, it's so funny, Ang. You know your bay window, Sue, at the front? — Well it's wide open and there's this bloke, Ang, he's gotta be twenty stone, and he's wedged in your bay window; he's

got one of those purple vests on, you know? —
and a great big fat belly. And there's a girl, Sue,
standing in your front garden, she's as thin as he's
fat, and she's draped round him like this, Ang,
and they're snogging away — you've never seen
anything so funny in all your life!

SUSAN: Oh, dear.

BEVERLY: Now — don't worry, Sue: 'cos they're
only having a bit of fun, I mean, they're only
teenagers, aren't they?

SUSAN: I wonder if I dare just pop down there for
a minute.

TONY: Would you like me to go and have a look
for you now?

SUSAN: Er, no.

ANGELA } .Tony doesn't mind.
TONY   } 'It's no problem.

SUSAN: No . . . ; thank you; but I think perhaps
it's better not.

BEVERLY: No, Sue's right: it's best not to pop
down there. They're only having a bit of fun. And
let's face it, when Laurence gets back we can
discuss it then. Okay? Now, who's for another
drink? Come on, Ang!

(Angela joins Beverly at the bar.)

How about you, Sue?

SUSAN: No, thank you.

BEVERLY: Yeah, come on, Sue, give you a little
top-up, just to settle your nerves. That's it. How
about you, Tone? Another drink?

TONY: Ta. Where is Laurence, anyway?

BEVERLY: I don't know, actually, Tony. I wish I
did know.

(Angela is wandering round the room.)

ANGELA: Oh, what a lovely table. This is just what we need. It's the next thing we're going to get. 'Cos at the moment we're eating off our knees. It's unusual, isn't it? — with the wooden top and the modern legs.

BEVERLY: Yeah; it was expensive, that one, actually.

ANGELA: Yes. Ah! — and this is what I'd really love!

BEVERLY: What, the candelabra? Yeah, it's brilliant, isn't it?

ANGELA: Yes. Is it real silver?

BEVERLY: Yeah, silver plate, yeah.

ANGELA: Yes. And it looks so lovely, and with the light.

(Angela wanders into the kitchen. Beverly gives Susan her drink.)

BEVERLY: Sue.

SUSAN: Thank you.

BEVERLY: You all right, Sue?

SUSAN: Yes, fine, thank you.

BEVERLY: Yeah. *(Pause.)* Sue, you must think I'm dreadful! I do apologise: I haven't offered you anything to eat. I'm sorry! Have some nuts.

SUSAN: Thank you.

BEVERLY: Take some crisps, as well.

SUSAN: Thank you.

BEVERLY: Now then, Sue, let's see . . . would you like a little cheesy-pineapple one?

SUSAN: Thank you.

BEVERLY: Tone? A little cheesy-pineapple one?

TONY: Ta.

BEVERLY: Take another one, Sue — save me coming back.

SUSAN: Thank you.

BEVERLY: Now then, Sue — a little cigarette?

SUSAN: No, thank you, not just at the moment.
BEVERLY: Sorry, Sue — I'll tell you what I'll do: I'll pop it on here for you, Sue, and then you can light it when you've finished those. Okay? Lovely.
ANGELA *(from kitchen)*: Tony, come and have a look at this beautiful kitchen!
BEVERLY: It's lovely, isn't it?
ANGELA: Oh, these tiles are gorgeous. Were they here when you came?
BEVERLY: Yeah, we were lucky, actually.
ANGELA: You were. 'Cos our kitchen's nothing like this. Tony, come and have a look.
BEVERLY: Yeah, go and have a look, Tone, they're beautiful, actually; go on — go and have a look.
ANGELA: Tony!
BEVERLY: Go on.

(Tony goes.)

ANGELA: Is this a freezer part with your fridge?
BEVERLY: Yes, it's a freezer at the top, yeah. *(To Sue.)* He's nice, isn't he?
SUSAN: Yes.
BEVERLY: Yeah, he's fantastic. Yeah . . . they're a very nice couple, actually; aren't they?
SUSAN: Yes.
ANGELA: Oh, the sink's got its own light.
TONY: Leave it!
ANGELA: And you've got one of these!
BEVERLY: What, the rotisserie? Yeah.
ANGELA: D'you cook chickens and things on it?
BEVERLY *(joining Angela and Tony)*: Well, you can do, but to be honest I'm not much of a cook, so I haven't actually used it yet, but you can do. And you can also do kebabs, they're very nice.
ANGELA: Oh, lovely.

(Laurence has entered, with a carrier bag.)

BEVERLY: Would you excuse me, Tony?
LAURENCE: Oh, hullo Sue. You all right?
SUSAN: Yes, fine, thank you.
BEVERLY: Laurence, where have you been, please?
LAURENCE: To the off-licence.
BEVERLY: Those want to go in the fridge, Laurence, to chill. Sorry, Ang, sorry, Tone — come through!
ANGELA: Thanks.
BEVERLY: Like to sit down?
TONY: Ta.

(Laurence has taken the lagers to the kitchen. Angela and Tony sit down.)

BEVERLY: Now then, Sue, let's see . . . that little cigarette . . .
SUSAN: Oh, thank you.
BEVERLY *(lighting Sue's cigarette)*: There we are, Sue.
SUSAN: Thank you.
BEVERLY: Now; everybody all right?
ANGELA ⎫ Yes thanks.
TONY ⎬ :Yes, thank you.
SUSAN ⎭ Yes . . . thank you.
BEVERLY: Great.

(Beverly collects her drink and sits. Laurence returns from the kitchen. Pause.)

LAURENCE: Right now: who's for a drink? Tony, light ale?
TONY: Not just yet, thank you.
BEVERLY: Go on, Tone, have a light ale, 'cos he got them specially for you.
LAURENCE: If he doesn't want one, he doesn't have to have one, Beverly. Sue?
SUSAN: No, thank you.

LAURENCE: Angela?

ANGELA: No, I'm all right thanks.

LAURENCE: Beverly?

BEVERLY: No, I'm fine thank you.

LAURENCE: Laurence? Yes, please. *(He gets his glass.)* Thanks very much.

(Only Angela laughs. Laurence pours his drink.)

LAURENCE: Well, the party certainly seems to be hotting up at your place, Sue.

SUSAN: Yes . . . so Beverly said.

BEVERLY: Yeah, we were just saying, actually, Laurence, it might be a good idea if a little bit later on, if you and Tony would pop down there.

LAURENCE: What for?

BEVERLY: Just to check that everything's all right, for Sue — put Sue's mind at rest. Because I know she's a little bit worried.

SUSAN: I think it'll be all right.

LAURENCE: Yes, Sue, I don't think there'll be any problems.

SUSAN: No.

BEVERLY: Laurence, I'm not saying there'll be any problems — all I'm saying is, would you please pop down for Sue?

ANGELA: You don't mind do you, Tony?

BEVERLY: No, of course he doesn't mind.

TONY: No, I don't mind.

LAURENCE: Well, I've just been past, and everything seems to be all right.

ANGELA: Didn't you see what was happening in the garden?

LAURENCE: Well — yes . . .

ANGELA: The couple, snogging through the window?

LAURENCE: Through the window?

ANGELA: With the dirty vest?

LAURENCE: No. No, I saw a couple down the side of the house, and there were a few in the porch. But I didn't see anybody in the window.
TONY: Would you like to sit down here, Laurence?
LAURENCE: No, no — you stay where you are.
ANGELA: No, sit here — there's plenty of room.
LAURENCE: Thank you.

(Laurence sits on the sofa between Angela and Susan.)

LAURENCE: Anyway, Sue: these sort of things, they happen at parties.
SUSAN: Yes, of course.
LAURENCE: I'm sure it's nothing to worry about.
SUSAN: No.
BEVERLY: Actually, Laurence, I think you're being very unfair to Sue.
SUSAN: Oh, not at all.
BEVERLY: Now, Sue, don't make excuses for him. And apart from anything else, Tony has already agreed to go actually.
LAURENCE: Oh, have you?
TONY: Yeah.
LAURENCE: Yes, well, I didn't say I wouldn't go. If she wants us to go down there, surely, of course we'll go.
SUSAN: Well, I don't know that I do, really.
LAURENCE: Fine.
ANGELA: Tony doesn't mind going on his own, do you?
TONY: No, I don't.
LAURENCE: I didn't say I wouldn't go.
BEVERLY: Fine, then, Laurence, are you going, please?
LAURENCE: Yes.
BEVERLY: Thank you.
LAURENCE: That's quite all right.

(Pause.)

BEVERLY: I'm not saying there'll be any trouble, but, with teenagers, they have a drink, and they get over-excited —
ANGELA: Yes, well it starts with one kiss . . .
BEVERLY — then they find their way to the bedrooms.

(Pause.

Sue flicks ash from her cigarette.)

LAURENCE: Sue: do you like olives?
SUSAN: Yes.
LAURENCE *(getting up)*: Fine: I'll get you some!
SUSAN: Thank you.

(Laurence goes to the kitchen.)

BEVERLY: You've got a friend for life there, Sue.
SUSAN: Oh?
BEVERLY: None of us like olives, you see.
SUSAN: Ah, I see.
BEVERLY: I can't stand them. It's those stuffed olives — you know that little red bit that sticks out? Well, it reminds me of — well, I'm not going to say what it reminds me of, but I can't eat them, it puts me off.

(Laurence has returned.)

LAURENCE: Sue?
SUSAN: Thank you.

(During following Laurence sits between Susan and Angela, and eats a couple of olives. After a while he starts looking for something in his

pockets.)

ANGELA: Well, not everyone can like everything, can they? It's like Tony, he doesn't like curry, and I love it. So we never go in Indian Restaurants now, do we?
TONY: No.
ANGELA: And you can get English food in Indian Restaurants — I mean you can have chips with your meal instead of rice. But you see Tony had a bad experience in an Indian Restaurant — this was before I knew him —
BEVERLY: Yes?
ANGELA: He had a nasty dose of gastro-enteritis after he'd had a curry, and you see that put him off.
BEVERLY: Yes.
ANGELA: And he won't even eat curry at home, now. Which is a shame, because I enjoy making it; it's a good way of using up leftovers. Have you ever tried pilchard curry?
BEVERLY: No.
ANGELA: That's a very economical dish. And it's easy: just get one of those big tins of pilchards in tomato sauce, and mix it with curry powder and onions, and it's really tasty.
BEVERLY: Oh?
ANGELA: I used to share this flat with these girls, and we often used to do that. But you see, Tony won't touch it. But then, I don't like Turkish Delight, and you see, Tony loves that.

(Laurence is looking in his pockets for something.)

BEVERLY: Darling, have you got heartburn?
LAURENCE: No.
BEVERLY: Have you got heartburn?
LAURENCE: No, I haven't got heartburn. *(Laurence*

gets up and goes to his case.) Just a slight case of indigestion, that's all.

(During following, Laurence gets out an antacid tablet and eats it. Then he gets out a small cigar.)

BEVERLY: I thought so. This is it, you see, Ang. He came in late, and he was all upset; 'cos he's very highly strung, Sue, and this gives him heartburn.

ANGELA: He must be careful, then; because when I was working in intensive care, the people who'd had a cardiac arrest, they were nearly all business men, and those who were worrying about their work.

BEVERLY: I hope you're listening to this, Laurence.

LAURENCE: Yes, I'm listening! Cigar?

TONY: No, thank you. I've just given up.

LAURENCE: Are you sure?

BEVERLY: Yeah, go on, Tone, take a little cigar, enjoy yourself go on, take one!

LAURENCE: Yes, go on, take one.

TONY: Thank you. *(He takes one.)*

ANGELA: Tony! Oh, well, that counts, doesn't it? I mean, if he's having a cigar . . .

BEVERLY: Yeah, come on, Ang!

(Angela taking a cigarette.)

LAURENCE: Sue —

ANGELA: Thanks!

LAURENCE: Would you like one?

SUSAN: Er — no, thank you.

LAURENCE: Some women do like them, you know, Sue?

SUSAN: Yes, so I understand, but I've got a cigarette.

LAURENCE: Oh. *(To Tony.)* Light?

TONY: Ta.

ANGELA: 'Course, smoking's one of the chief causes of heart disease.

SUSAN: But it's just contributory, isn't it?

ANGELA: Well, yes, but if somebody's got a tendency towards that condition, they really shouldn't smoke.

LAURENCE: No, no, no. I don't believe that smoking, in moderation, can do any harm at all.

BEVERLY: Laurence, would you like to put a record on for us, please?

LAURENCE: Yes, surely; what would you like to hear?

BEVERLY: Feliciano.

LAURENCE: Oh, no, Beverly. *(going to records)* We don't want to listen to that blind Spaniard caterwauling all night.

BEVERLY: Darling, not classical.

LAURENCE: Light classical — just as background *(producing a record)* Sue, d'you know James Galway?

SUSAN: Yes, I've heard him.

LAURENCE: He's a very up-and-coming young flautist. Do you like him?

SUSAN: Yes, he's very good.

LAURENCE: Fine, I'll put it on for you.

BEVERLY: Laurence, I'm sorry, but we don't want to listen to classical music at the present moment.

LAURENCE: Well, what do you want to listen to, then, Beverly?

BEVERLY: Feliciano.

LAURENCE: Well, if everybody wants to listen to Feliciano, we'll put it on.

BEVERLY: Tone, d'you like Feliciano?

TONY: Yeah, I do.

BEVERLY: Yeah, he's fantastic, isn't he? Sue?

SUSAN: I don't know him, I'm afraid.

ANGELA: Oh, you'll like him. He's lovely.

BEVERLY: Yeah, Sue, he's really great. Sue: would you like to hear him?

SUSAN: Yes . . .

BEVERLY: Yeah? Laurence, Angela likes Feliciano. Tony likes Feliciano, I like Feliciano, and Sue would like to hear Feliciano: so please: d'you think we could have Feliciano on?

LAURENCE: Yes.

BEVERLY: Thank you.

(During following, Laurence puts on the record José Feliciano: Feliciano, *Track One, California Dreamin'.)*

ANGELA: Oh, it changes colour, doesn't it?

BEVERLY: What, the fibre-light? Yeah! Isn't it beautiful, Ang?

ANGELA: Oh, it's lovely!

BEVERLY: Yeah . . . D'you know what I do, Ang? I put a record on, and I sit in that chair, and I just gaze at it for hours.

ANGELA: Do you?

BEVERLY: Yeah. It's funny, it always reminds me of America. I don't know why, but it does.

(Pause.)

ANGELA: Oh yes, it's New York, isn't it?

BEVERLY: Yes, I suppose it is, really . . .

ANGELA: How are you enjoying your cigar?

TONY: Very nice, thank you: how's your cigarette?

ANGELA: Oh, it's lovely. Mind you don't choke on it! You see, he's not used to smoking a cigar: he doesn't know what to do with it.

BEVERLY: He'll be all right. Tone: would you like another drink?

TONY: Ta.

BEVERLY: Yeah? How about you, Ang?
ANGELA: Please.
BEVERLY *(taking glass)*: Thanks. Sue?
SUSAN: Oh, no, thank you.
BEVERLY *(taking Sue's glass)*: Yeah, come on, Sue
— I'll give you a little top-up. That's it.

(Beverly is joined at the bar by Tony. The music is just starting. During following, Laurence returns to sit between Angela and Susan.)

BEVERLY: Like to help yourself, Tone?
TONY: Ta.
BEVERLY: It's a fantastic drink, Bacardi, isn't it?
TONY: Yeah.
BEVERLY: Yeah.
TONY: I first started drinking it when I went to Majorca.
BEVERLY: You've been to Majorca?
TONY: Yeah.
BEVERLY: Ah, great. Where d'you go?
TONY: Palma.
BEVERLY: Not Palma Nova?
TONY: That's right, yeah?
BEVERLY: Oh, fantastic — isn't it beautiful there?
TONY: Yeah.
BEVERLY: They drink it very long there, don't they, with lots of ice and coke and all that, yeah. It's my dream, actually, just lying on the beach, sipping Bacardi-and-Coke.
ANGELA: Have you always had a moustache?
LAURENCE: What d'you mean?
ANGELA: Have you had it for a few years?
SUSAN *(given drink)*: Thank you.
LAURENCE: Yes.
ANGELA: Never thought of having a beard to go with it?
LAURENCE: No.

BEVERLY: No, Laurence wouldn't suit a beard, Ang, his face is too small.

LAURENCE: Actually, I think a beard can look very scruffy.

ANGELA: Yes, but I think a man with a moustache and a beard, they look more masculine.

BEVERLY: Sexier, isn't it?

ANGELA: Mmm. Has your husband got a beard?

SUSAN: No, no. He used to have . . . a long time ago . . . when I first knew him.

ANGELA: Why did he shave it off?

SUSAN: Well, he grew out of it.

(Pause.)

LAURENCE: Do you play any instruments yourself, Sue?

SUSAN: No. No, I used to play the piano when I was a child.

LAURENCE: Oh, the piano?

SUSAN: Just a little.

LAURENCE: I once went for guitar lessons . . . but I never kept them up.

SUSAN: That's a pity.

LAURENCE: Yes, I've often regretted it.

(Pause.)

LAURENCE: You know, I think that musicians and artists, they're very lucky people; they're born with one great advantage in life. And d'you know what that is? Their talent. They've got something to cling to. *(Pause.)* I often wish I'd been born with that sort of talent. *(Pause.)* Most people, they just drift through life, without any real aims. They're weak. It's no good just sitting there, whining. You've got to get up, and do something about it. Not that it isn't a fight. Of course it is.

Life is a fight — people always seem to be against
you. Not that I've done badly — oh, no: I've done
all right! But it's certainly an uphill battle.

ANGELA: I once went to a party, and they said,
"Can anyone play the piano?" And I said, "Oh,
yes, I can." And you see, I can't play the piano —
I'd just learned this one tune from a friend. It was.

> "Buy a broom
> Buy a broom
> Buy a broom,
> And sweep the room!"

— And that's all I knew. And you see, they
wanted me to play for musical chairs. So I started:

> "Buy a broom
> Buy a broom . . . "

— And I played it a few times.

BEVERLY: Yeah?

ANGELA: And then I thought, well I'll have to do
something a little bit different. So I started,
y'know, just —

BEVERLY: What, vamping?

ANGELA: Yeah.

BEVERLY: Yes.

ANGELA: But as I can't play, it sounded terrible.
And I felt such a fool. I thought, why did I say,
y'know, I'd play?

BEVERLY: When was this, Ang?

ANGELA: Oh, it was only when I was eight.

BEVERLY: Oh, I see!

ANGELA: Oh, yes. I still felt a fool, though.

BEVERLY: Would anybody mind if I turned this
next track up? Because it's my favourite, it's
"Light My Fire", and I'd like us all to hear it.
Anybody mind?

ANGELA ⎫
TONY   ⎬ :No.
SUSAN ⎭

BEVERLY: No? Great. *(She turns record up.)*

Fantastic, isn't he?

ANGELA: Yeah. I know this one.

BEVERLY: Yeah? D'you think he's sexy, Ang?

ANGELA: Yes. But it's a pity he's blind.

BEVERLY: Yeah. Mind you, I reckon that makes him more sensitive. D'you know what I mean?

ANGELA: Mmm. Yes.

(Beverly proceeds to dance solo in front of the others, and across the room.)

BEVERLY: D'you like him, Tone?

TONY: Yeah.

BEVERLY: Knockout, isn't he?

(Beverly continues dancing, helping herself to a crisp as she passes by the coffee table.)

BEVERLY: This used to turn me on at parties, Tone, eight years ago — that's how long I've liked him. *(More dancing.)* Ang, imagine making love to this? D'you know what I mean?

ANGELA: *(laughs)*

BEVERLY *(squeezing Laurence's shoulder)*: Are you all right, Laurence?

(Beverly dances away from the others with her back to them. Laurence suddenly jumps up, rushes to the stereo and turns it off.

LAURENCE: Are you ready, Tony?

BEVERLY: Thank you, Laurence!

LAURENCE: Don't mention it. Are you ready?

TONY: What for?

LAURENCE: Well, Sue wants us to go and inspect the party; I think we should go and inspect it.

BEVERLY: Fine, Laurence: would you like to go now, please?

LAURENCE ⎱ I am going.
SUSAN ⎰ Oh but, I really think it would be
better —
BEVERLY: It's all right, Sue.
LAURENCE: Are you coming, Tony?
TONY: I think so.
LAURENCE: Well, come on, then!

(Laurence goes. Tony gets up to follow . . .)

SUSAN: I really think it would be better if you
didn't.
TONY: It's all right. Just take a walk past your
house: put your mind at rest.
BEVERLY: Don't worry, Sue; Tony'll handle it.
TONY: Won't be long.
BEVERLY: Take care.

(Exit Tony. Pause.)

BEVERLY: I'm sorry about that.
ANGELA: Oh, that's all right. Shall I put the record
on again?
BEVERLY: No, don't bother, Ang, because he's
spoiled it now.
ANGELA: Oh, and you were enjoying yourself!
BEVERLY: Yeah, well we were all enjoying our-
selves, weren't we? *(Pause.)* To be quite honest,
he's a boring little bugger at times, actually.
(Pause.) Anyway, sod him. Come on, let's all have
a drink!
ANGELA: Yeah.
BEVERLY: Come on, Sue!
SUSAN: Oh, no, really —
BEVERLY *(taking Susan's glass)*: Yeah, come on,
Sue, that's it!

(Angela has joined Beverly at the bar.)

BEVERLY: I'll tell you what: let's all get pissed. Yeah!

ANGELA: Yeah. We can enjoy ourselves.

BEVERLY: Yeah. Cheers, Ang!

ANGELA: Cheers!

BEVERLY: Cheers, Sue.

SUSAN: Thank you.

ANGELA: Cheers!

SUSAN: Cheers.

BEVERLY: Come on, Ang: have a little cigarette while he's gone, sod him.

ANGELA: Oh, yeah, while he's out.

BEVERLY: Yeah, come on. That's it.

(Beverly and Angela light their cigarettes.)

SUSAN: I think I'm going to be sick.

ANGELA: Are you? Come along, then.

BEVERLY: Come on, Sue.

ANGELA: Where's the toilet?

(Angela and Susan are on the way out of the room.)

BEVERLY: Under the stairs, Ang, in the hall. Take deep breaths, Sue.

ANGELA: Hold on a minute.

BEVERLY: Take deep breaths: you'll be all right.

(Pause. The following from offstage . . .)

ANGELA: That's the way. Bring it all up. That's it. Better out than in.

(Beverly reacts.)

BLACKOUT.

ACT TWO

(Same as Act One. A bit later. Beverly has put the lights on, and is pouring drinks. Enter Angela.)

ANGELA: She'll be all right now.
BEVERLY: Yeah, she'll be all right, Ang.
ANGELA: I've just left her on her own for a minute, to sort herself out.
BEVERLY: Yes. She's been sick, hasn't she?
ANGELA: Yes.
BEVERLY: Yeah. And I'm making her a little black coffee, Ang, so that'll help to revive her a little bit, you know?
ANGELA: Mmm.
BEVERLY: Cheers, Ang.
ANGELA: Cheers!
BEVERLY: Cheers!

(They drink. We can still hear Abigail's music.)

ANGELA: I think she's had a few too many gin-and-tonics.
BEVERLY: So do I.
ANGELA: And on an empty stomach.
BEVERLY: Really?
ANGELA: Oh, yes — she's not had anything to eat tonight.
BEVERLY: Now, she's silly, isn't she? She should have had a meal.
ANGELA: Yeah, well we had a big meal earlier on.
BEVERLY: Yeah, well, I had a meal.
ANGELA: We had lamb chops.
BEVERLY: Did you? Yeah, I had a little frozen pizza.
ANGELA: And she's trying to keep up with us.
BEVERLY: Yeah, yeah; and another thing, Ang, I think she's the type, her nerves, give her a

nervous stomach. She has a few drinks, and that makes her sick.

ANGELA: I knew that, and I thought, that's what brought this on.

BEVERLY: Yeah. And it's a shame, 'cos she's ever so nice, isn't she?

ANGELA: Yes.

BEVERLY: Yeah.

ANGELA: I feel a little bit sorry for her.

BEVERLY: So do I, Ang.

(Enter Susan.)

ANGELA: All right?

SUSAN: Er — yes . . . thank you.

BEVERLY: All right, Sue? — ah, come through. That's it. She still looks a little bit pale, doesn't she, Ang?

ANGELA: Yes. *(taking Susan's glass)* I'll take that.

SUSAN: Thank you. Sorry.

BEVERLY: Don't worry, Sue. That's all right.

ANGELA: Come and sit down. That's it. You sit down here and your soda-water's there. Now, lean forward a minute, lean forward.

(She props an extra cushion behind Susan's back.)

That's it. Lovely. All right.

BEVERLY *(coming from kitchen)*: Now look, Sue, I've made you a little black coffee, now I've made it nice and strong, and I haven't put any milk in it, case that makes you sick again. All right?

SUSAN: Actually, I think it would be better if I didn't.

BEVERLY: Are you sure, Sue?

SUSAN: Yes.

BEVERLY: Oh, all right, then, I'll tell you what I'll do: I'll pop it on here for you. Now, will you try

and sip that for me, Sue? — because it will help to
revive you. All right?

ANGELA: Have you got a headache?

SUSAN: Yes, just a bit.

BEVERLY: Would you like a little Aspro, Sue?

SUSAN: Oh, no, thank you.

BEVERLY: Are you sure?

SUSAN: Yes.

ANGELA: No, she's better just with soda-water,
'cos she'll only bring it up.

BEVERLY: I've got it! Just a minute; let's see . . .
(looking in her handbag) yeah, here we are. Now
look, Sue, this is only a very light perfume . . .

SUSAN: I'm all right, actually!

BEVERLY *(applying perfume to Susan's face)*:
Now, Sue, it will just help to freshen you up a little
bit. Because when you've been vomiting, Ang, you
feel horrible, don't you?

ANGELA: Yeah.

BEVERLY: Yes. That's it. *(applying some to her
own hand)* It's lovely, actually. It's Estee Lauder,
"Youth Dew".

ANGELA: Mmm.

BEVERLY: Would you like to try some, Ang?

ANGELA: Oh, yes!

BEVERLY: Yeah.

(Angela helps herself to a liberal dose.)

BEVERLY: You only need a little drop, Ang!

ANGELA: Oh.

BEVERLY: 'Cos it's quite strong, actually, yeah.
That's it.

ANGELA: Mmm, it's nice.

BEVERLY: Yes, it's beautiful, isn't it? Now does
that feel a little bit fresher, Sue?

SUSAN: . . . Thank you.

BEVERLY: Yeah?

(Pause.)

SUSAN: Sorry about that.

ANGELA: Oh, there's no need to be sorry, is there?

BEVERLY: Sue — Don't worry. Let's face it, it could happen to any of us, couldn't it?

ANGELA: Yes, and it's better for it to happen while those two are away.

BEVERLY: Definitely, yeah.

SUSAN: I wonder — could you pass me my handbag, please?

ANGELA: Yes, where is it?

SUSAN: It's um, on the floor.

(While Angela gets the handbag, Susan removes the cushion from behind her.)

ANGELA: Here we are.

SUSAN: Thank you.

BEVERLY: No, 'cos when you're vomiting in front of blokes, Ang, it's embarrassing, isn't it?

ANGELA: Yes. And they're not usually that sympathetic.

BEVERLY: No.

ANGELA: Well, I know Tony isn't. 'Cos if I've got a headache, or my period pains, he doesn't want to know.

BEVERLY: Really?

ANGELA: In fact, it annoys him.

BEVERLY: Now, this is it, you see; I reckon a woman, she needs a bit of love and affection from a bloke. Okay, sex is important. But, Ang, it's not everything.

ANGELA: No. You see, if Tony comes home, and he's in a bad mood, I can't do anything right. 'Cos they pick on you, don't they?

BEVERLY: Is he like that?

ANGELA: Oh, yes, he's very quick-tempered.

BEVERLY: Is he?

ANGELA: I think it's because of his red hair.

BEVERLY: Yeah. It's funny, isn't it, Sue? To see him, sitting there, he looks ever so quiet and gentle, doesn't he?

SUSAN: Yes.

BEVERLY: Is he very violent?

ANGELA: No, he's not violent. He's just a bit nasty. Like, the other day, he said to me, he'd like to sellotape my mouth. And that's not very nice, is it?

BEVERLY: It certainly isn't, Ang!

ANGELA: Was your husband violent?

SUSAN: No, not at all. He was a bit irritable sometimes, a little difficult. But — I think we all are.

ANGELA: Ah! She's one of the lucky ones, isn't she?

BEVERLY: Definitely, Sue, definitely.

ANGELA: Mind you, if Tony wasn't around, I'd miss him.

BEVERLY: Would you?

ANGELA: Yes.

BEVERLY: Yeah. It's funny, isn't it? I suppose I would miss Laurence inasmuch as I need a bloke — well, let's face it, we all need a bloke, don't we? And, okay, credit where it's due: he's very good with money. I mean, if I want a new dress, make-up, have my hair done, whatever it is, the money is there. But, apart from that, it's just boring, know what I mean?

ANGELA: Yes. Well, I think that comes from being married, doesn't it?

BEVERLY: Do you?

ANGELA: The fun wears off.

BEVERLY: Yeah.

ANGELA: Oh, your cushion's slipped.

SUSAN: I'm all right, actually.

ANGELA: Come on, lean forward.

BEVERLY: Yeah, come on, Sue.

ANGELA: Make you comfy.

BEVERLY: 'Cos Angela knows.

(Enter Laurence.)

ANGELA: Everything all right down there?

LAURENCE: Yes, I think so.

BEVERLY: How many's at the party, then?

LAURENCE: Well, I don't know — I didn't stop to count them. *(to himself)* This is my glass. *(He goes to the bar.)*

SUSAN: It's all right, is it?

LAURENCE: Yes!! — Oh, I'm sorry, Sue: Yes, yes, I went in, and I had a few words with them, and everything seems to be all right.

ANGELA: Where's Tony got to?

LAURENCE: Perhaps you'd better ask him that, when he gets back.

SUSAN: Did you see Abigail?

LAURENCE: I certainly did.

SUSAN: Is she all right?

LAURENCE: I think so.

ANGELA: Where is he?

LAURENCE: Well, I don't know. I'm not his keeper.

SUSAN: Did you talk to her?

LAURENCE: Well, I asked her to turn the music down, yes.

ANGELA *(to Beverly)*: He's stayed at the party!

SUSAN: Was she upset?

LAURENCE: I don't think so.

BEVERLY *(to Angela)*: He's probably being raped by a load of fifteen-year-old schoolgirls!

ANGELA: Oh, lucky them!

BEVERLY: I'll tell you something: at least they had a bit of taste — they didn't pick him! *(Indicating Laurence.)*

ANGELA: I hope he's feeling a bit more enthusiastic than when I leap on him!

BEVERLY: Is he one of those?

ANGELA: Yes, he turns over.

BEVERLY: I've met those before, actually.

LAURENCE *(going to case for antacid tablet)*: Beverly!

BEVERLY: Ang, I can just see it, right, the music's thumping away, and your Tone's lying on the floor, and there's all these girls, right, you know, piling on top of him, and your Tone just turns over, and goes to sleep.

LAURENCE: That's enough, Beverly!!

BEVERLY: Oh, Christ, Laurence! Every time I'm enjoying myself . . . !

LAURENCE: Can't you see you're embarrassing Sue?

BEVERLY: Oh, now I'm sorry, Sue. Now, listen, I didn't mean to embarrass you, Sue; it was only a little joke; all right?

ANGELA: You see, Sue's not been feeling too good, anyway.

BEVERLY: No.

LAURENCE: Oh, really? What's been the problem, Sue?

SUSAN   : Oh, it was nothing.

BEVERLY : She's been vomiting, actually.

LAURENCE: That's all right, thank you, Beverly! Sue can speak for herself!

ANGELA: You see, she's had a few too many gin-and-tonics, and you've not had any tea, have you?

SUSAN: No.

BEVERLY: No.

LAURENCE *(offering her a cheese-pineapple savoury)*: Well, would you like one of these, Sue?

SUSAN: Er, no thank you.

BEVERLY: Laurence, she doesn't want one of those on an empty stomach, now does she?

LAURENCE: A sandwich, then. Would you like a
sandwich, Sue?
SUSAN: No, thank you.
BEVERLY: Laurence, she doesn't want a sandwich!
LAURENCE: Well, I want a sandwich! Now do you
want a sandwich, Sue, yes or no?!
SUSAN: No. Thank you.
LAURENCE: Okay. Fine!

*(Laurence rushes to the kitchen, and starts to
make a sandwich.)*

BEVERLY: I hope it chokes you!

*(Laurence rushes back from the kitchen, with a
kitchen-knife in one hand, and a tub of margarine
in the other.)*

LAURENCE *(pointing the knife at Beverly)*: What
did you say, Beverly?
BEVERLY *(shrieking)*: Oh, Christ, Ang, I'm going
to get stabbed.
LAURENCE: Don't tempt me.
BEVERLY: Well, go on, then: do it!

(Pause. Then Beverly pushes away the knife.)

BEVERLY: Laurence, would you please go back in
the kitchen and finish making your little
sandwich, all right?

(Pause.)

LAURENCE: Are you sure you don't want a sand-
wich, Sue?
SUSAN: Yes. Thank you.
LAURENCE: Fine.

(Laurence goes back to the kitchen. Pause. Then the front door bell chimes. Angela and Beverly shriek with renewed mirth.)

ANGELA: Oh, he's here at last. They must've let him out!
BEVERLY: They've obviously had their fill!

(The following from offstage:)

TONY: Everything all right?
LAURENCE: What d'you mean?
TONY: I wondered where you'd got to.
LAURENCE: Yes, well I wondered where you'd got to. Come in.
TONY: What's that for?
LAURENCE: I'm making a sandwich! Go in.

(Laurence returns to kitchen. Enter Tony. He looks slightly flushed and dishevelled.)

ANGELA: Where've you been?
TONY: Southend.
ANGELA: Did you enjoy yourself there?
TONY: Wonderful!
ANGELA: Where've you been? — Laurence has been back for ages.
TONY *(to Susan)*: Everything's all right — nothing to worry about!
SUSAN: Good. Not too rowdy?
TONY: No.
SUSAN: Thank you.
TONY: 't's all right.

(Beverly has joined Tony near the bar.)

BEVERLY: Would you like a drink?
TONY: Yes, please.

BEVERLY: What would you like?
TONY: Light ale, please.
BEVERLY: Like a little Bacardi to go with it?
TONY: No, thank you.
BEVERLY: Are you sure?
TONY: Yeah.
BEVERLY: Are you all right?
TONY: Yeah.
BEVERLY: Great!

(She fixes the drink, whilst:)

SUSAN: Was Abigail all right?
TONY: I think so.
SUSAN: You saw her?
TONY: I didn't actually see her, but I think she's all right.
BEVERLY *(giving drink)*: Tone.
TONY: Ta.
BEVERLY: Your shirt's all wet.
ANGELA: What is it?
TONY: Nothing.
BEVERLY *(feeling his chest)*: But you're soaking wet!
ANGELA *(getting up)*: What've you been doing?
TONY: Nothing.

(Angela feels his chest.)

Get off! *(to Susan)* I just bumped into somebody accidentally — minor incident: nothing to worry about.
BEVERLY: D'you want to sit down, Tone?
TONY: Ta.
ANGELA: Laurence didn't come back with his shirt all wet, did he?
BEVERLY: Dead right he didn't. Laurence comes back looking like he's spent a day at the office.

ANGELA: I don't think you two have been to the same party, have you?

TONY: 'Course we've been to the same party. What are you talking about?

BEVERLY: Ah, lay off her, Tone — she's only having a little joke.

ANGELA: See what I mean?

TONY: What?

(Susan gets up.)

BEVERLY: Are you all right, Sue?

SUSAN: Yes. But I think I'd better go and see Abigail myself.

BEVERLY: No, Sue, please. Don't go down there. Now, listen to me, Sue: you know what Abigail is like, now, she's only going to shout at you, and then you'll be upset. Now please, Sue, come on, sit down. Now look, Tony's only just come back — now, it was all right, wasn't it, Tone?

TONY: Oh, yeah.

BEVERLY: Yeah?

TONY: There's nothing to worry about.

SUSAN: Are you sure?

TONY: Yep.

BEVERLY: Yeah — now come on, Sue, sit down. Now I'll tell you what I'll do, I'll put a little record on for us, ey? Yeah! Then we can all have a little listen to that, yeah. Now, let's see what we've got . . . Tell you what now, look, Sue: d'you like Elvis?

SUSAN: Yes, he's all right.

BEVERLY: Yeah, he was great wasn't 'ee? D'you like him, Ang?

ANGELA: Mmm.

BEVERLY: Yeah. Now we'll put this on for Sue . . .

Beverly puts on the record (Elvis Presley: Elvis's

40 greatest, *Track One, "Don't"). Whilst she is
doing so:)*

ANGELA: Is Abigail always having parties?
SUSAN: No.

(Pause.)

BEVERLY: Ready, Ang?
ANGELA: Mmm.

(The music starts.)

BEVERLY: Oh, isn't he great?
ANGELA: Yeah!
BEVERLY: Yeah. *(Pause.)* I won't be a sec, I'm just
going to the toilet, all right?

(Exit Beverly.

*Laurence, having finished making his sandwich,
has been sitting with it for some time at the dining
table. As she passes him on her way out, Beverly
gives him a squeeze.*

Long pause.

*Laurence gets up, adjusts his dress, and goes to
the stereo. He turns down the volume.)*

LAURENCE: That's better. Now at least we can
hear ourselves think.
ANGELA: D'you want to sit here.
LAURENCE: No, thank you.
ANGELA: Come on . . .
LAURENCE: No, thanks!!
TONY: Steady!

(Pause.)

LAURENCE: I expect you've seen a few changes since you've been here, eh, Sue?

SUSAN: Not really, no.

ANGELA: When did you move here?

SUSAN: In 1968.

ANGELA: Oh, you've been here a long time, then, haven't you?

SUSAN: Yes.

ANGELA: D'you think you'll stay here?

SUSAN: Till the children are older.

ANGELA: Oh, yes, then I suppose when you're on your own, you'll get somewhere a little bit smaller?

SUSAN: Yes, I expect so.

LAURENCE: Oh, come on, Sue — surely you must have seen some changes?

SUSAN: Well . . . there are the new houses on the other side of Ravensway.

LAURENCE: Ah, yes, the houses! But what about the people?

SUSAN: What about them?

LAURENCE: The class of people, now don't you think that's changed?

SUSAN: Not really, no.

LAURENCE: The tone of the area — don't you feel it's altered?

SUSAN: Not particularly.

LAURENCE: You don't think it's gone down?

SUSAN: No.

(Pause.)

LAURENCE: And you, Tony, yes, come on, what do you think, eh?

TONY: I wouldn't know, would I?

LAURENCE: Oh, no — of course! You've only

just moved in yourselves, haven't you?
ANGELA: Yes.
TONY: Yes.
LAURENCE: Yes! Drink?
TONY: No, thank you.
LAURENCE: Angela?
ANGELA: Please.

(Laurence takes Angela's glass, and proceeds to fix her drink.)

SUSAN: It's more mixed, that's all.
LAURENCE: Mixed? Yes, I suppose you could say it was mixed! — More cosmopolitan.
SUSAN: There's nothing wrong with that.
LAURENCE: Oh, you don't think there's anything wrong with that?
SUSAN: No, I don't.
LAURENCE: Well, that's a matter of opinion. Would you like another drink, Sue?
SUSAN: I'm just drinking soda-water, thank you.
LAURENCE: Fine: would you like some more soda-water?
SUSAN: Thank you.
LAURENCE *(getting Susan's glass)*: We like to keep our guests happy. *(fixing Susan's drink)* Do you read, Tony?
TONY: Sometimes.
LAURENCE *(giving drink)*: Sue.
SUSAN: Thank you.
LAURENCE: Have you read any Dickens?
ANGELA: Oh, yes. I've read "David Copperfield".
LAURENCE: "David Copperfield"? Well, I have the Complete Works here.

(He takes one book out, and displays it.)

ANGELA: Oh, they're a lovely set, aren't they?

LAURENCE *(demonstrating book)*: Yes, they are very well-bound. They're embossed in gold.
ANGELA: Mmm . . . really nice.

(Laurence displays it briefly to Tony; then goes over to Sue for a demonstration.)

LAURENCE: Sue.
SUSAN: Very nice.

(He shows her the pages, then offers it to her.)

LAURENCE: Please!
SUSAN *(taking book)*: Thank you!
LAURENCE: And just what do you read, eh, Tony?
TONY: All sorts.
LAURENCE: All sorts! — well, for instance?
ANGELA: What was that one you were reading?
TONY: "Computer Crime".
LAURENCE: "Computer Crime"!! — ooh, that sounds interesting. D'you know Shakespeare?
TONY: Not personally. I read it at school, yeah.
LAURENCE: Oh, at school!

(Laurence has gone to his set of Shakespeares.

Enter Beverly and sits down.

Laurence takes out one volume, demonstrates it, then selects a page.)

"Macbeth". *(Pause.)* Part of our heritage. *(Pause, he puts it back.)* Of course, it's not something you can actually read. Sue?
SUSAN *(returning Dickens)*: Thank you.

(Laurence replaces Dickens.)

ANGELA: Your house is a lot older than ours, isn't it?

SUSAN: Yes.

LAURENCE: Sue: 1936. Yes?

SUSAN: I'm not sure. But it was built before the war.

LAURENCE: I thought so.

ANGELA: Oh, there's nothing wrong with an old house. I mean, there's some quite nice ones. I like old and I like new. I like those old Tudor houses round here.

LAURENCE: No, Angela: Mock-Tudor.

ANGELA: Are they?

LAURENCE: Oh, yes. There are some real Tudor properties in Hadley Village itself. But the ones you're thinking of are Mock-Tudor.

ANGELA: The trouble with old houses is they haven't got any central heating.

LAURENCE: Ah, yes, but of course central heating can be installed into older properties. It may cause some shrinkage of the beams, etcetera, but, if it's done by an expert, there shouldn't be any problems. D'you know the Belvedere Hotel?

ANGELA: Yes. Yes, I do.

LAURENCE: Yes, well, originally, on that site stood a Tudor mansion.

ANGELA: Oh, it doesn't look very old.

LAURENCE: No, no, the present property is late Victorian — neo-Gothic. No, no, the original building, the mansion house, was Tudor. They owned all the land round here.

BEVERLY: D'you want another, Ang?

LAURENCE: I've seen to the drinks, thank you, Beverly!

(The following dialogue runs simultaneously with the preceding passage, and starts after Laurence's line, "It may cause some shrinkage of the beams".)

BEVERLY: You all right, Sue?
SUSAN: Yes, thank you.
BEVERLY: You don't feel sick again, do you?
SUSAN: No.
BEVERLY: No.
SUSAN: No. It seems to be settling.
BEVERLY: Good. You all right, Tone?
TONY: Yes, thank you.
BEVERLY: Great.

(Beverly gets up and goes over to Tony.)

D'you want a drink?
TONY: Ta.
BEVERLY: D'you want another, Ang?
LAURENCE: I've seen to the drinks, thank you, Beverly!
BEVERLY: Oh, I'm sorry, Laurence: it's just that I can't hear through two brick walls.

(Beverly goes to the bar.)

LAURENCE: Yes, er . . . it was all part of the Belvedere Estate.
BEVERLY: Laurence, would you like to turn that record up, please?
LAURENCE: How can we hold a conversation with that racket blaring out?
BEVERLY: Laurence, we're not here to hold conversations, we are here to enjoy ourselves. And for your information, that racket happens to be the King of Rock'n'Roll.
LAURENCE: Oh, really? Well I always thought that Bill Haley was the King of Rock'n'Roll!

(Beverly turns the volume up. Laurence turns it off. Beverly goes to turn it on; Laurence grabs her arm. Pause: they are locked together.)

BEVERLY: All right, Laurence.

(Pause. He lets go. Pause.)

LAURENCE: Sorry about that.
ANGELA: Oh, that's all right. We're all getting a
little bit merry, aren't we? And it's nice for us to
have a chance to enjoy ourselves, 'cos since the
move, we've hardly been out.

(Susan gets up.)

BEVERLY: Where are you going, Sue?!
SUSAN: Er . . . I'm just going to the toilet.
BEVERLY: You don't feel sick again, do you?
SUSAN: No, I'm fine, thank you.
ANGELA: D'you want me to come with you?
SUSAN *(going)* No, thank you.

(Exit Susan.)

BEVERLY: Give us your glass, Ang. I'll give you a
little top-up.
ANGELA: You see, Sue's been vomiting up her gin,
and while you were away, I had to take her to the
lavatory.
BEVERLY *(giving drink)*: Ang.
ANGELA: Thanks.
BEVERLY: Cheers, everyone. Cheers!
ANGELA: Cheers!
LAURENCE: Cheers.
TONY *(miming his glass)*: Cheers!
BEVERLY: Oh, I'm sorry, Tone, I forgot your light
ale, didn't I? I do apologise.
LAURENCE: I'll get it.
BEVERLY: Thank you, Laurence! *(Beverly sits.
Pause.)* Ang: shall we have a little dance?
ANGELA: Yeah. Be nice.

BEVERLY: Tone: d'you fancy a little dance?
TONY: Yeah, I don't mind.
BEVERLY: Yeah?
LAURENCE: There's no room to dance in here, Beverly.
BEVERLY: Laurence, if I'd wanted somebody to put a damper on the idea, I would have asked you first okay? Come on, Ang: give us a hand moving the couch. Come on.

(Laurence gives Tony his drink.)

TONY: Ta.

(Beverly and Angela prepare to move the couch.)

BEVERLY: Got it?
TONY ⎱ It's all right, Beverly, I'll do that.
LAURENCE ⎰ I'll do it, Angela.

(The men take over.)

ANGELA: I'll take this end.
LAURENCE: No, you just sit down.
BEVERLY: Cheers, Tone.
TONY: You got it, Laurence?
LAURENCE: Yes.

(Tony and Laurence pick it up. Laurence drops his end.)

BEVERLY: Oh, for Christ's sake, Laurence!
LAURENCE: Don't interfere, Beverly. You ready?
TONY: Where d'you want to put it?
LAURENCE *(to Beverly)*: Well, where d'you want it?
BEVERLY: Oh, for God's sake: just put it back there!
LAURENCE: Just back.

(Tony and Laurence move the couch.)

BEVERLY: Ang, I've got this fantastic record I'm gonna play for us, right? Just hang on a sec. Now, this record, Ang, it turns my husband on, and when he hears it, he cannot resist my charms.

(Beverly proceeds to put on the record (Sam - The Man - Taylor & His Orchestra, or any similar 'smoochy' music. During this:)

ANGELA: They're still enjoying themselves down there, aren't they?
TONY: Yes.
ANGELA: What were they getting up to?
TONY: Nothing much.
BEVERLY: Ready, Ang?
ANGELA: Mmm.

(The music starts.)

BEVERLY: Fantastic, isn't it? Oh, I'm sorry, Laurence, is it too loud for you, my darling? I do apologise. I'll turn it down. Because we don't want to upset him, do we, Ang? *(She turns down the volume.)* Is that better? Fancy a little dance, Tone?
ANGELA: Dance with Beverly.
TONY: Perhaps Laurence'd like to dance?
BEVERLY: No, I don't think he would, actually. Come on, Tone: have a little dance, go on. *(Tony gets up and dances with Beverly. Angela and Laurence remain seated. After a short while, enter Susan.)* You all right, Sue?
SUSAN: Yes. Fine, thank you.

(Susan sits. Pause. Beverly and Tony continue to dance.)

BEVERLY: You don't mind me mauling your husband, do you, Ang?
ANGELA: No, you go ahead.

(Pause.)

TONY: Go on — dance with Laurence.
ANGELA: No, I can't.
TONY: 'Course you can: get up and dance!
BEVERLY: Don't worry, Ang — you'll be quite safe with Laurence. He won't rape you.

(Angela gets up.)

ANGELA: Would you like to dance?

LAURENCE *(getting up)*: Surely, if you'd like to.

(Laurence places his glass on the coffee table, and joins Angela; just as he reaches her, she starts 'bopping', which is inappropriate, as the music is 'smoochy', and Beverly and Tony are 'smooching'.

Laurence musters the vague gesture of a 'bop'.)

ANGELA *(whilst dancing)*: I'm not very good at these slow dances.
LAURENCE: No.
ANGELA: I'm better at this sort. *(Demonstrates a quick 'bop'.)* Would you like to dance with us?
SUSAN: Oh. No, thank you.
ANGELA: Come on — we can all three dance together!
SUSAN: No, really, I'm fine, thank you.

(The dancing continues until the track ends.)

LAURENCE *(shaking Angela's hand)*: Thank you.
ANGELA: Laurence was shaking my hand!
BEVERLY: Was he? Christ, he'll be shaking mine next. Now who'd like a drink? Ang?
ANGELA: Oh — please!
BEVERLY: Never say no! Tone, would you like a drink?
TONY: No thanks, I'm all right.
BEVERLY: How about you, Sue?
SUSAN: No, thank you.
BEVERLY: Are you sure?
SUSAN: Yes.
BEVERLY: Yeah!
ANGELA: He's a good dancer, isn't he?
BEVERLY: He's fantastic.
ANGELA: I never knew you could dance so well. We don't usually dance like that, do we?
TONY: No.
BEVERLY *(giving drink)*: Ang!
ANGELA: Thanks.
BEVERLY: Cheers, everyone, cheers!
TONY
ANGELA } : Cheers!
SUSAN *(getting soda-water)*: Cheers.
BEVERLY: Darling, why don't you dance with Sue?
LAURENCE: I really don't think Sue wants to dance, thanks very much. Darling.
BEVERLY: Then why don't you ask her, Laurence?

(Pause. Then Laurence gets up and crosses to Sue.)

LAURENCE: Sue, would you like to dance?
SUSAN: Er, no thank you.
LAURENCE: There you are — Sue doesn't want to dance!
BEVERLY: Of course she wants to dance! Go on, Sue, have a little dance with Laurence. Enjoy

yourself, go on — have a little dance.
LAURENCE: Would you like to, Sue?
SUSAN: All right.
LAURENCE: I'll take your glass for you.

(Laurence and Susan embrace formally. Beverly rejoins Tony.)

BEVERLY: Come on, Tone.

(Beverly and Tony go into a more intimate embrace than previously.)

BEVERLY: Ang — d'you wanna dance with Tone?
ANGELA: No: you're all right.

(Pause: the dancing continues.)

LAURENCE: Are you going on holiday this year, Sue?
SUSAN: I hope so.
LAURENCE: Expensive business, holidays.
SUSAN: Yes.
LAURENCE: D'you know Paris?
SUSAN: A little.
LAURENCE: Oh. You've been there?
SUSAN: Yes. A long time ago. Have you?
LAURENCE: No. We're hoping to get there.

(Pause.)

SUSAN: I like Paris.
LAURENCE: Oh, yes . . . Montmartre by night, the Champs Elysées, boulevard cafes . . .

(When the track ends, they stop dancing. Laurence shakes Susan's hand briskly and formally.)

Thank you.
BEVERLY *(to Tony)*: Thanks very much.
TONY: Ta.

(They all drift to seats except Tony. The empty seat is now between Susan and Beverly on the sofa.)

BEVERLY: D'you wanna sit down, Tone?
TONY: Ta.
BEVERLY: Ang, do us a favour, throw us me fags. Would you, please? *(Angela throws the cigarettes. Tony picks them up and gives them to Beverly.)* Cheers, Tone. *(Tony leans back. The bar-flap now protrudes over the back of the sofa.)*

SUSAN: Mind your head.
ANGELA: It's too big.
TONY: What?
ANGELA: It's too big.
TONY: What is?
ANGELA: Your head.
TONY: Give it a rest!

(Pause.)

TONY: Feeling better now, are you?
SUSAN: Oh — much. Thank you.
TONY: Good.

(Pause.)

BEVERLY: Ang, d'you want a cigarette?
ANGELA: Oh, I would. Can I have a cigarette?
TONY: D'you want one?
ANGELA: I'd love one.
TONY: Why don't you have one, then?

(Beverly throws a cigarette across to Angela. She lights it.)

BEVERLY: Ang, do us a favour — give us a light, would you, please?

(Angela goes over to light Beverly's cigarette. She returns.)

ANGELA: You see, once you've had one cigarette, you want to keep on smoking, don't you?

BEVERLY: This is it, yeah.

SUSAN: What sort of work d'you do?

TONY: I'm in computers.

ANGELA: He's an operator.

BEVERLY: Still play football, Tone?

TONY ⎤. No —
ANGELA ⎦ No, he gave it up when he was twenty.
He plays for the firm's team, though; and he's so much better than all the others.

TONY: It's not the firm's team, and I've only played twice!

ANGELA: He looks so funny in his shorts!

BEVERLY: Why d'you give it up?

TONY: Things didn't work out.

ANGELA: You've got footballer's legs, though, haven't you?

BEVERLY: Has he? Have you? Let's have a little look. Oh yeah, so he has. I like footballer's legs, actually — they're nice and muscly, aren't they? Can't stand blokes with skinny legs, Ang, can you? Puts you off — d'you know what I mean?

LAURENCE: Talking of Paris, Sue, do you like Art?

SUSAN: Er — yes.

LAURENCE: So do I. Beverly doesn't. Of course, Paris is the centre of the Art World. D'you like Van Gogh?

SUSAN: Yes.

LAURENCE *(crossing the room)*: This is a Van Gogh.
SUSAN: Yes.
LAURENCE: They called him a Post-Impressionist,
but to my mind he was more of a symbolist. D'you
like the Impressionists?
SUSAN: Yes.
LAURENCE: Oh, you do? That's good. Fine. Fine.

(He crosses back to his seat. Sits.)

BEVERLY: You all right, Tone?
TONY: Yeah!
BEVERLY: Great.
LAURENCE: Of course, you know, Van Gogh was a
very unstable man. Not only did he cut his ear off
and leave it in a brothel, he also ate paint, and he
shot himself.
BEVERLY: Thank you, Laurence! We don't want
all the gory details.
LAURENCE: I'm talking to Sue, and Sue is interested
in these things.

*(He rushes across the room, and takes the Van
Gogh off the wall.)*

LAURENCE: This is a picture of his chair in the
corner of his room at Arles. It wasn't actually
yellow, no, no, no: he painted it yellow because
yellow symbolised so much for him.
BEVERLY *(turning record off)*: Shall we liven
things up a bit?
TONY ⎫
ANGELA ⎭ Yeah.
BEVERLY: Yeah?
LAURENCE: Do you like Art?
ANGELA: Yes!
LAURENCE: Good. This is a Lowry! Now, did you
know, his father was an Estate Agent?

ANGELA: Oh.

BEVERLY: For Christ's sake, Laurence, give it a rest!

LAURENCE: Give what a rest?

BEVERLY: Nobody is interested.

LAURENCE: Oh yes, they are!

BEVERLY: Oh no, they're not!

LAURENCE: D'you know something, Beverly? You're ignorant!

BEVERLY: Oh, so I'm ignorant, now, am I?

LAURENCE: Now? You always have been!

BEVERLY: It's not a question of ignorance, Laurence, it's a question of taste!

LAURENCE: Taste! And what would you know about taste?

BEVERLY: The trouble with you, Laurence, is if somebody doesn't happen to like what you like, then you say that they've got no taste!

LAURENCE: That's rubbish!

BEVERLY: Oh, is it rubbish?

LAURENCE: Yes!

BEVERLY: Then what about that picture I've got upstairs in the bedroom, then?

LAURENCE: That is cheap, pornographic trash!

BEVERLY: Laurence, just because a picture happens to be erotic, it doesn't mean it's pornographic.

LAURENCE: Oh, shut up, Beverly!!

(Laurence rushes to the kitchen. During the following he is pouring and drinking a glass of water.)

BEVERLY *(continuing immediately)*: I've got this fabulous picture, right, it's really beautiful; I brought it home, and he wouldn't let me put it up in here, oh, no: I had to hang it in the bedroom!

LAURENCE *(from kitchen)*: If I had my way it

would be in the dustbin!

BEVERLY: Yeah, well you're dead from the waist down anyway, let's face it!

ANGELA: Can I see it?

BEVERLY: D'you wanna see it, Ang?

ANGELA: Oh, yes.

TONY *(rising)*: Actually, Angela's got to be getting up early in the morning for work, so I think we ought to be going now.

SUSAN *(rising)*: Yes, I think I ought to be getting along . . .

TONY: You can see the picture another time.

ANGELA: We don't have to go early just 'cos of me.

BEVERLY: You sure, Ang?

ANGELA: Yeah, I'll be all right!

LAURENCE *(having joined the others)*: She's got to get up in the morning!

BEVERLY: Oh, shut up, Laurence!

LAURENCE: Don't tell me to shut up!

TONY: Angela: COAT!!

ANGELA: No, it's all right.

SUSAN: I really think I ought to be going.

BEVERLY: Now don't be silly, Sue, because we haven't had a cup of coffee yet — now sit down.

(Exit Beverly.)

LAURENCE *(following her)*: Beverly!

ANGELA *(to Susan)*: We're going soon, anyway.

(The following offstage:)

LAURENCE: Beverly, don't bring that picture downstairs!

BEVERLY: Oh, sod off, Laurence!

LAURENCE: Beverly!

BEVERLY: Drop dead!!

TONY *(to Angela)*: You just can't keep your big mouth shut, can you? GET UP!!

(Angela gets up. Enter Laurence quickly. Goes to the stereo, looks for and finds a record, which he puts on the turntable. Then he turns on the machine. During the pause before the music actually starts:)

LAURENCE: Sit down — please!

(He sits. Angela sits. Susan sits. Tony does not sit. Laurence jumps up, goes to look at the record, walks towards the door, stops, looks at Tony, sits, waits. The music starts: Beethoven's Fifth Symphony, *the first movement.*

Laurence now suffers a heart attack. He tries to suppress it for a time, as it approaches, whilst the others look on, confused. Then, a spasm, and he passes out. Angela, Susan and Tony go over to him during following.)

ANGELA: Laurence? Laurence!
SUSAN: What's the matter?
TONY: What's wrong with him, Ang?
ANGELA: Just a minute.

(Angela is examining Laurence: she loosens his tie.)

TONY: Ang, what's wrong with him?
ANGELA: I don't know yet!

(Angela examines Laurence's eyes.)

Tony, can you help me get him on the floor? *(Angela and Tony move Laurence, helped by*

Susan. Enter Beverly, displaying picture 'The Wings of Love' by Stephen Pearson. Throughout the following, Angela monitors Laurence's pulse.) Get me something for his head. And get his feet up higher. No, that's too big.

BEVERLY: What's going on? What's the matter with him? Mind, Sue. Laurence! What's happened, Ang, has he passed out? Laurence!

SUSAN: Tony, can you lift his feet?

BEVERLY: Tony!

(Tony and Susan see to Laurence's feet.)

Sue, go and get him a glass of water, quickly, please. Now, Laurence, come on, you're all right, come on, Laurence, Laurence!

ANGELA: No, leave him.

TONY: Leave him.

BEVERLY: Actually, Angela, he happens to be my husband, all right?

ANGELA: Yeah, but we've got to let him breathe.

BEVERLY: Yeah, well he is breathing, for Christ's sake.

BEVERLY: *(shaking him)* Laurence, come on, come on!!

ANGELA: Can you get an ambulance, instead of sitting there?

TONY: Ambulance?

ANGELA: Yes!

SUSAN: Beverly, leave him alone!

BEVERLY: All right then, Angela, what is the matter with him?

ANGELA: I think he's had a heart attack.

TONY: Where's your 'phone?

BEVERLY: A heart attack, Ang?

TONY: Where's your 'phone?

BEVERLY: Under the bar. Ang, are you sure?

ANGELA: He hasn't got false teeth, has he?

BEVERLY: No, of course he hasn't got false teeth!
Ang, look his lips are going all blue, look.
ANGELA: Don't worry.
BEVERLY: Ang, his hands are going freezing.
ANGELA *(to Susan)*: Can you get him a blanket or
something to keep him warm?

(Exit Susan.)

BEVERLY: Laurence . . . Now Laurence. Can he
hear me, d'you think, Ang?
ANGELA: Yes.
BEVERLY: Yeah. Laurence, Laurence.
ANGELA: No, leave him, he's got to lie still!
BEVERLY: Oh Christ, Ang!

*(Beverly gets up, goes to the bar, and pours herself
a brandy.)*

ANGELA: Have you got through yet?
TONY: I'm trying to get a bloody line.

*(Susan has come back, with a duvet. She covers
Laurence with it.)*

BEVERLY: Ang, his face is going all blue, look!
TONY: Ambulance.
ANGELA: Tell them it's urgent.
TONY: What? Someone turn that fucking record
off! Er — 503-9041.

(Susan turns off the record.)

BEVERLY: Ang, Ang. Listen to that noise he's
making.
TONY: Hullo, er, could we have an ambulance
please? *(Pause.)* What's the number of your
house? What's the number of your HOUSE?!

SUSAN: Er — thirteen!
BEVERLY: Thirteen, thirteen.
TONY: 13, Richmond Road.

(For the rest of the telephone conversation that follows, Tony and Beverly can overlap slightly.)

BEVERLY: Angela, I told him this would happen.
TONY: Er, he's had a heart attack.
BEVERLY: I said to him, Laurence you're going to have a heart attack.
TONY: 503-9041.
BEVERLY: But he wouldn't listen to me, Ang.
TONY: That's right, yeah.
BEVERLY: But I never thought it would happen at this age; I thought it'll be more when he was 50 or 60.
TONY: Thank you.

(Tony hangs up.)

BEVERLY: Oh, Christ. Christ, Sue, listen to that noise he's making, Sue!!
SUSAN: Angela, is there anything we can do?
ANGELA: No, we must just wait for the ambulance.

(Beverly lights a cigarette.)

BEVERLY: Ang, what happens when they get him to the hospital? Will they give him oxygen to revive him?
ANGELA: They've got everything he needs in the ambulance.
BEVERLY: Yeah?

(Susan is putting away the Beethoven.)

Oh, Christ! *(She goes back to the bar for more*

brandy.) Sue, d'you want a little drop of brandy?

SUSAN: No, thank you.

BEVERLY: Tone?

TONY: No, thank you!

BEVERLY ⎱ .Ang, d'you want a little drop of brandy?
ANGELA ⎰ 'No, no.

BEVERLY: Now, Ang, listen to me . . . d'you think it would be a good idea if I put a little dab of brandy on his lips?

ANGELA: No!

BEVERLY: Now I don't mean for him to drink it — no? Well, how about a little dab of water, then, eh?

ANGELA: No, he must just lie still.

BEVERLY: Well, shall I get a cold flannel and lay it across his forehead?

ANGELA: He'll be all right if he lies still.

BEVERLY *(kneeling)*: 'Cos I am very fond of him, you know, Ang.

TONY: Keep that cigarette out of his face!

BEVERLY: All right, Tony, lay off me if you don't mind, please!

SUSAN: Beverly, you're flicking ash all over him!

BEVERLY: All right, Sue, that'll do from you as well!

SUSAN: Calm down!

BEVERLY: Look, Sue: it's all right for you, your husband isn't lying here with a heart attack, is he?

SUSAN: Angela, is there nothing we can do?

ANGELA: No! Just sit down.

(Susan sits.)

BEVERLY: It's my fault, isn't it? I know it is, Ang. But, I didn't mean to upset him tonight, I didn't, Sue, I wouldn't do that. But, Sue, he is argumentative with me. And when he shouts, I can't help but shout back; but I didn't mean to upset him

tonight. You see, and when he started talking
about his pictures, I should have kept quiet, but I
couldn't. And I shouldn't have brought that
picture down, Sue, 'cos he hates that picture.
(Pause.) Oh, Christ, this is ridiculous! Tony,
where's that ambulance? Ang, shall we give them
a ring again?

SUSAN: Beverly, we've only just 'phoned them!

BEVERLY: I know we've only just 'phoned them,
Sue, but you don't know what's going on at these
places, they could have taken the address down
wrong, or anything — they might go to the wrong
road for all we know! Tony, do me a favour, get
on the 'phone, and just check what's going on,
please!

TONY: Shall I ring them again, Ang?

BEVERLY: Look, never mind her, I know she's a
nurse, but I happen to be his bloody wife!

TONY: All right!

BEVERLY: Now get on the 'phone!

(Tony dials 999. Beverly sits.)

SUSAN: How is he?

ANGELA: He's all right.

BEVERLY: Mind you, Sue: he's brought this on
himself. I'm sorry, but he has. If you knew, Sue,
the number of times I have pleaded with him to
take a day off and relax, and he wouldn't — he
wouldn't listen to me, Sue. He wouldn't take any
notice of me, Sue! And d'you know why? Because
basically he's stubborn, and he's pig-headed!!!

TONY: Ambulance. 503-9041. Yes.

BEVERLY: 13 Richmond Road, tell 'em, Tony, and
it's off Ravensway. Make sure they've got it right.

TONY: Hallo — er, we 'phoned for an ambulance
earlier, and it doesn't seem to have arrived.

BEVERLY: Listen, Tony, tell them we've been

waiting for ten minutes actually and there's a man
lying here with a heart attack.

TONY: Shut up!!!

SUSAN: Beverly. BE QUIET!!!

BEVERLY: I beg your pardon, Sue?

SUSAN: Will you just shut up for a minute?

BEVERLY: Look, Sue, I'm telling you now: this is
my house, and if you don't like it, piss off!

ANGELA: Oh, shut up, please.

TONY: 13, Richmond Road. 503-9041. Ta. Thank
you.

(Tony hangs up.)

BEVERLY: What did they say, Tone?

TONY: It's on its way.

BEVERLY: Great.

*(Pause. The shrieking voices of a few teenage girls
are heard in the street. Then the Rock music from
the party starts again.)*

Oh, for God's sake, Sue; would you go down and
tell Abigail?

SUSAN: It's not my fault they're making such a
row.

BEVERLY: I know, Sue, but she's your daughter,
isn't she?

SUSAN: Well, I can't help that! Can I use the
'phone?

BEVERLY: Yeah, go on.

ANGELA: Now it's all right — just lie still.

(Laurence has started to come round.)

BEVERLY: What is it, Ang? Is he coming round a
little bit, is he?

ANGELA: Yeah. You're gonna be fine — keep still.

BEVERLY: Now Laurence. Laurence, it's Beverly
speaking! Now, listen to me, Laurence. I'm just
putting me cigarette down, 'cos we don't want to
blow smoke in your face, do we? Now, listen to
me, Laurence. Now Laurence, you're not well.
You're gonna be all right, we're gonna take you to
the hospital — now listen to me . . . I'm gonna
stay with you all the time, Laurence, and I'm not
gonna leave you, all right? Now Ang is looking
after you, see?

*(Angela is now pounding Laurence's chest,
Laurence having died at about the point where
Beverly was saying, "I'm just putting me cigarette
down".)*

Ang! Ang, what're you doing?
SUSAN: Could I speak to Abigail, please?
Abigail!
Abigail Lawson!

*(Angela listens to Laurence's chest. Then she
starts to administer the kiss-of-life. Then she
stops.)*

ANGELA: Tony, can you hold my hair out of my
face?
TONY: Eh?
ANGELA: Tony!

*(Tony crosses, and holds Angela's hair out of the
way, while she does the kiss-of-life. This goes on
for some time. Eventually, she gives up. Tony lets
go of her hair. She sinks back against an armchair.*

Pause.

Beverly throws her arms round Tony with a

gasp, holding the embrace.

Pause.

Angela leaps up suddenly, grasping one leg.)

Ur, shit! Ur, Tony, Tony. Tony!

(Angela flies across the room. Tony disengages himself from Beverly.)

TONY: What's the matter? You haven't got cramp again, have you? Come here — give us your leg! Stretch it. Stretch it!

(Angela is relieved, and lies still on the floor. Tony kneels in exhaustion. Beverly sobs.)

SUSAN: Abigail, it's Mummy here.
Abigail?
ABIGAIL!!

Blackout.

The Rock music surges.

CURTAIN

ONCE A
CATHOLIC

by
Mary O'Malley

ONCE A CATHOLIC

The English Stage Company presented *Once a Catholic* at the Royal Court Theatre, London on 10 August 1977, with the following cast:

MOTHER PETER	*Pat Heywood*
MOTHER BASIL	*Jeanne Watts*
MOTHER THOMAS AQUINAS	*Doreen Keogh*
MR EMANUELLI	*John Boswall*
FATHER MULLARKEY	*John Rogan*
MARY MOONEY	*Jane Carr*
MARY McGINTY	*June Page*
MARY GALLAGHER	*Anna Keaveney*
MARY O'GRADY	*Kim Clifford*
MARY HENNESSY	*Lilian Rostkowska*
MARY MURPHY	*Sally Watkins*
MARY FLANAGAN	*Rowena Roberts*
DEREK	*Daniel Gerroll*
CUTHBERT	*Mike Grady*

Directed by Mike Ockrent
Designed by Poppy Mitchell
Lighting by Jack Raby

From the Royal Court *Once a Catholic* was transferred on 4 October 1977 for a West End run at Wyndham's Theatre.

CHARACTERS

MOTHER THOMAS AQUINAS, a tall, thin, fairly young and very refined Irish nun with spectacles. Headmistress of the Convent of Our Lady of Fatima.

MOTHER PETER, a tall, fat, middle aged Irish teaching nun.

MOTHER BASIL, a short, fat, elderly Irish teaching nun.

MARY MOONEY, a 5th former. She is plain and scruffy and has ginger hair, freckles and a very good singing voice, soprano.

MARY McGINTY, a well developed, blonde and pretty 5th former.

MARY GALLAGHER, a sensible, attractive, dark haired 5th former.

FATHER MULLARKEY, an Irish Priest.

MR EMANUELLI, a very old Music Master, non specifically foreign. He has white hair down to his shoulders, a bandage on one leg, two walking sticks and a baritone voice.

DEREK, a tall, thin Teddy boy in his late teens.

CUTHBERT a Catholic 6th former with a fairly bad case of acne.

Pupils of Form 5A
  MARY O'GRADY
  MARY HENNESSY
  MARY MURPHY
  MARY FLANAGAN

The play is set in the Convent of Our Lady of Fatima, a Grammar School for Girls, and in and around the streets of Willesden and Harlesden, London NW10, from September 1956 to July 1957.

The school uniform for winter is a gymslip, blouse, cardigan and tie with a mackintosh and felt hat for outdoors. For summer the uniform is a shapeless dress with a blazer and a panama hat. Sensible shoes and ankle socks are worn throughout the year.

Music could be played between some of the scene changes. Hits of the fifties and excerpts from the old Latin Mass, as appropriate.

ACT ONE

SCENE 1. *The Chapel*
SCENE 2. *The Classroom*
SCENE 3. *The Canteen*
SCENE 4. *The Music Room*
SCENE 5. *A Street in Harlesden*
SCENE 6. *The Biology Lab.*
SCENE 7. *Mother Thomas Aquinas' Office*
SCENE 8. *The Schoolroom*
SCENE 9. *The Classroom*
SCENE 10. *Mother Thomas Aquinas' Office*
SCENE 11. *A Street Corner*
SCENE 12. *Cuthbert's House*
SCENE 13. *A Lavatory*
SCENE 14. *The Classroom*
SCENE 15. *The Street*
SCENE 16. *Derek's House*

ACT TWO

SCENE 1. *Derek's House*
SCENE 2. *The Presbytery*
SCENE 3. *The Garden*
SCENE 4. *The Garden*
SCENE 5. *The Garden*
SCENE 6. *Derek's House*
SCENE 7. *Cuthbert's House*
SCENE 8. *A Side Room*
SCENE 9. *Mother Thomas Aquinas' Office*
SCENE 10. *The Classroom*
SCENE 11. *The Back of the Chapel*

ACT ONE

Scene 1

The Chapel.

Father Mullarkey is officiating at Morning Mass assisted by Cuthbert dressed as an altar boy. Mr Emanuelli is on the organ and the congregation consists of Mother Thomas Aquinas, Mother Peter, Mother Basil, Mary Mooney, Mary McGinty, Mary Gallagher and the members of Form 5A.

EVERYBODY IS SINGING: Qui cum Patre et Filio simul adoratur, et conglorificatur: qui locutus est per Prophetas. Et unam sanctam catholicam et apostolicam Ecclesiam Confiteor unum baptisma in remissionem peccatorum et expecto resurrectionen mortuorum. Et vitam venturi saeculi. Amen.

(Father Mullarkey kisses the altar and turns to the congregation.)

FATHER MULLARKEY: Dominus vobiscum.
CONGREGATION: Et cum spiritu tuo.
FATHER MULLARKEY *(turning back to the altar)*: Oremus.

Scene 2

The Classroom.

The girls of Form 5A are at their desks.
Mother Peter walks on carrying some books and a brown paper parcel.

GIRLS: Good morning, Mother Peter.
MOTHER PETER: Good morning, 5A.

(Mother Peter makes the Sign of the Cross.)

MOTHER PETER AND GIRLS: In the name of the
Father and of the Son and of the Holy Ghost
Amen. Oh Jesus through the most pure heart of
Mary I offer thee all the prayers, works and
sufferings of this day for all the intentions of thy
divine heart. *(She makes the sign of the Cross
again.)* In the name of the Father and of the Son
and of the Holy Ghost Amen.

(Mother Peter sits down and opens the register.)

MOTHER PETER *(reading the names rapidly)*:
Mary Brennan
Mary Clancy
Mary Delaney
Mary Fahy
Mary Flanagan
Mary Gallagher
Mary Hennessy
Mary Hogan
Mary Kelly
Mary Keogh
Mary Looney
Mary Mooney
Mary McGettigan
Mary McGinty
Mary McGuinness
Mary McHugh
Mary McLoughlin
Mary McManahon
Mary Murphy
Mary Nolan
Mary O'Connor

Mary O'Driscoll
Mary O'Grady
Mary O'Malley
Mary O'Rourke
Mary O'Shea
Mary O'Toole
Mary Walsh
Mary Whelan
Maria Zajaczkowski

(Mother Peter gets up from her desk.)

MOTHER PETER: Now. Who's going to tell me what day it is today? Mary Mooney?

MARY MOONEY: It's Tuesday, the 8th September, Mother Peter, 1956.

MOTHER PETER: Oh, sit down, you little simpleton and think before you speak. Will somebody with a bit of sense please tell me what day it is today? *(Long pause.)* Well? Doesn't the eighth of September ring a bell? A very important bell indeed? *(Pause.)* Evidently it does not I'm sorry to see. Oh, aren't you the fine pack of heathens! It's Our Blessed Lady's birthday, that's what day it is. I hope you're all ashamed of yourselves. Just imagine how insulted Our Lady must be feeling. Go into the chapel every one of you at dinner time and beg for her forgiveness. Is this an example of the standard I can expect from 5A this year? I hope you realise that this is the most crucial year of your academic life. In January you'll be sitting the mock O level exams. And in June the O levels proper. And I don't intend to have any failures in my form. Any girl showing signs of imbecility will be sent straight down to 5B. And see will that get you to Oxford or Cambridge. Of course nobody ever passed any exam of their own accord. Only prayer will get results. The best thing each one of you can do is to pick out a particular saint and pray to him or her to get you through. Your Confirmation saint, perhaps, or any saint you fancy. But not St Peter the Apostle, if you wouldn't mind. He's my saint, so he is, and don't any of you go annoying him now. We've had a great understanding myself and Peter. He's never let me down in all the years I've been beseeching him for favours. Oh, he's a wonderful man and a glorious martyr. I'm mad about him. There are plenty of other saints. Indeed you've a choice of five thousand and more. From St Aaron the Hermit to St Zoticus the Roman Martyr. And, you know, there are lots of other St Peters apart from the real St Peter. A hundred and thirty-three of them altogether. St Peter of Nicodemia, St Peter Gonzalez, St Peter the Venerable, St Peter Pappacarbone. And a big batch of Chinese and Japanese St Peters. So take your pick of them. Now you must be prepared for a heavy burden of homework. At least three hours every evening. Plus revision. And double that amount at the weekend. If any girl has ideas about serving behind the counter of a Woolworth on a Saturday she can put such ideas right out of her head. Under no circumstances will Mother Thomas Aquinas give permission for a girl from Our Lady of Fatima to take on a job of work. And anyway, your parents have a duty to provide you with sufficient pocket money. They also have a duty to supply you with the correct school uniform which must be obtained from Messrs Houlihan and Hegarty and only Messrs Houlihan and Hegarty. There's no greater insult to this school than to see a girl dressed up in a shoddy imitation of the uniform. Mary Mooney, step up here to me and face the class.

(Mary Mooney comes forward and stands next to Mother Peter's desk. She is wearing a large, shapeless hand knitted cardigan and a thick pair of striped, knitted knee length socks.)

Will you look at this girl's cardigan! Who knitted you that monstrosity, Mary Mooney?

MARY MOONEY: My mother, Mother Peter.

MOTHER PETER: Did she now? Have you no school cardigan to wear?

MARY MOONEY: No, Mother Peter.

MOTHER PETER: Will you please inform your mother that she must order you two school cardigans from Houlihan and Hegarty immediately. And don't dare come into school wearing that thing again.

MARY MOONEY: No, Mother. Sorry, Mother. *(Goes off.)*

MOTHER PETER: Come back here a minute.

(Mary Mooney comes back.)

Mary Mooney, have you joined a football team?

MARY MOONEY: No, Mother.

MOTHER PETER: Well what are those horrible socks doing on your feet? Is this another example of your mother's handiwork?

MARY MOONEY: Yes, Mother.

MOTHER PETER: God help the girl. Isn't her mother a martyr for the knitting. Go back to your place now and don't ever let me see you wearing socks like that again.

MARY MOONEY: No, Mother. Sorry, Mother.

(Mary Mooney goes off. Mother Peter opens the brown paper parcel and holds up a thick pair of long legged bloomers.)

MOTHER PETER: Now you all know what this is, don't you? It's the Our Lady of Fatima knicker and it's the only type of knicker we want to see worn at this school. It seems that an increasing number of girls have been leaving off this knicker and coming to school in . . . in scanty bits of things that wouldn't cover the head of a leprechaun. And showing them off under their PE shorts. Hands up every girl who has on a knicker like this. Is that all? Hands up every girl who has a knicker like this at home. And why haven't you got them on you that's what I'd like to know. Oh, aren't you the brazen little madams! You know well there's a man out in the garden. A man who has to walk up and down with his wheelbarrow right past the tennis courts. Mary Gallagher come up here and give out two knickers to every girl who hasn't any. I'll collect the cash first thing tomorrow morning.

(Mary Gallagher gives out the knickers.)

Well now. Let us think about Our Lady on the occasion of her birthday. No woman on this earth was ever worthy of the holy name of Mary. Our Blessed Lady is elevated high above all other human creatures. Because of the special privileges given to her by God. Mary Mooney, who were our Lady's parents?

MARY MOONEY: I'm sorry, Mother Peter. I can't remember.

MOTHER PETER: You can't remember the names of Our Lady's parents. Why can't you?

MARY MOONEY: I don't know, Mother Peter.

MOTHER PETER: Mary Gallagher, will you enlighten this irreligious girl.

MARY GALLAGHER: Our Lady's mother was St Anne, Mother. And Our Lady's father was

St Joachim.

MOTHER PETER: Quite correct. It's a very great pity we don't know more about the lives of St Anne and St Joachim. Indeed we know nothing at all about either one of them. But they must have been two of the holiest saints that ever walked the earth. Mary Mooney, tell your mother you'll be late home from school tomorrow evening. You'll be staying behind to write out the names of Our Lady's parents one hundred times. And I want to see the lines written out in a legible hand. The same applies to all work handed in to me. I hope you each have your very own fountain pen. If you haven't then you must go out and get one. And I'll tell you what you must do when you get the pen home. Take a clean sheet of paper and write on it the holy names of Jesus, Mary and Joseph. Then thrown the sheet of paper into the fire. That way the pen will never let you down. Mary O'Grady will you tell me one of our Lady's special privileges.

MARY O'GRADY: The Assumption, Mother Peter.

MOTHER PETER: Correct. At the end of her life on earth Our Lady did not die. Our Lady was assumed into Heaven. Taken straight up body and soul to reign as Queen in everlasting glory. The Mother of God could not be subjected to such an indignity as death. Death and corruption in the coffin are part of the penalty of original sin. The rest of us will have to wait until the end of the world when we'll all have a reunion with our bodies on the Day of Judgement. Mary Flanagan?

MARY FLANAGAN: Please Mother Peter, if somebody loses a leg on earth will he get it back on the Day of Judgement?

MOTHER PETER: Indeed he will. And he'll get a higher place in Heaven into the bargain. Mary McGinty?

MARY MCGINTY: Please Mother, will the souls in
Hell get their bodies back at the end of the world?
MOTHER PETER: Oho, they most certainly will.
They'll be brought up for the Day of Judgement
along with the rest of us. And when their
wickedness has been revealed they'll go back down
to Hell taking their bodies with them into the everlasting fire. And remember, no sin ever goes
unrecorded. Every little lapse will be brought to
judgement. And not only your actual deeds. But
every iniquitous thought that was ever carried
inside your head will be revealed. And the sinner
will stand alone and be shamed in front of family,
friends, neighbours, teachers and every member
of the human race. *(Pause.)* Well now, 5A, we've
a hard year's work ahead of us. But there are,
nevertheless, a number of treats in store. And the
most exciting event of all will be during the Easter
holidays. When we'll be taking a party of girls
away on a pilgrimage. A very special pilgrimage to
Fatima. What do you think of that, now? Isn't it
wonderful news? We'll be sending the full
information out to your parents. I'm sure they'll
be happy to make a financial sacrifice in order to
give you the benefit of this splendid opportunity.
And now we'd better have some nominations for
the election of a captain of the form.

Scene 3

The Canteen

*Mary McGinty and Mary Gallagher are sitting at a
table. Mother Basil is pacing up and down. Mary
Gallagher is laboriously eating a plate of rice
pudding. She has an empty dinner plate in front of
her. Mary McGinty is still struggling through her
dinner.*

MOTHER BASIL: Mary McGinty, will you stop playing about with that stew and eat it up.

MARY MCGINTY: I can't swallow the meat, Mother Basil.

MOTHER BASIL: Oh, isn't it a pity for you? Why don't you try opening your mouth and see will that help you at all.

MARY MCGINTY: There's great big lumps of gristle in this meat, Mother Basil.

MOTHER BASIL: There's no gristle in that meat, is there Mary Gallagher? You don't realise how lucky you are. Think of all the poor blackfellows dropping down dead in the heart of Africa for want of a bit of stewing steak. Look at Mary Gallagher. She's finished all hers and is eating her pudding up nicely.

MARY GALLAGHER: Please may I leave this last little bit, Mother Basil?

MOTHER BASIL: You may not! Eat every single bit and offer it up for all the souls in Purgatory. Come on now. Just imagine all the souls you're getting a bit of remission for. Oh, damn the two of yeez with your fussing and finicking. D'you think I have all day to be standing here? Well I haven't. I've a lot of things to do. A lot of very important things. D'you hear me?

MARY GALLAGHER: I've finished it, Mother.

MOTHER BASIL: All right. Go on and get out of it.

(Mary Gallagher goes off.)

Come on now, Mary McGinty. Eat it up or I . . . I . . . I . . . I . . . I'm not going to stand for any more of this old nonsense.

MARY MCGINTY: Please Mother, I think I'm going to be sick.

MOTHER BASIL: Ah! Puke away then. Go on and be as sick as you like. But you'll stay behind and clear it all up after you.

MARY MCGINTY: I just can't eat it, Mother. I can't I honestly can't.

MOTHER BASIL: You can't? You mean you won't. Well you will! Give me that knife and fork!

MARY MCGINTY: I'm eating it, Mother. I'm eating it.

MOTHER BASIL: That's the idea. Keep it up now. I'll tell you what we'll do. Let's see if you can polish it all off in the time it takes me to say a Hail Holy Queen. Are you ready now? In the name of the Father and of the Son and of the Holy Ghost Amen. Hail Holy Queen Mother of Mercy, Hail Our Life, Our Sweetness and Our Hope. To thee do we cry, poor banished children of Eve. To thee do we send up our sighs, mourning and weeping in this vale of tears. Turn then, most gracious advocate, thine eyes of mercy towards us and after this our exile, show unto us the blessed fruit of thy womb, Jesus. *(She beats her breast three times.)* O clement! O loving! O sweet Virgin Mary! Pray for us O holy Mother of God . . .

MARY MCGINTY *(nearly choking)*: That we may be made worthy of the promises of Christ.

MOTHER BASIL: Good girl.

(Mary McGinty retches.)

Scene 4

The Music Room.

Mr Emanuelli comes hobbling in with two walking sticks. He sits down on a chair and grunts.

GIRLS: Good afternoon, Mr Emanuelli.

MR EMANUELLI: What good afternoon? My leg is

giving me gip. I am crucified with pain and you
tell me good afternoon. It's a rotten afternoon.
(He points with one stick.) Look at me! Don't
look to the left or the right, look straight up here
at me, please! Now. *(He sings.)*

> When Jesus Christ was four years old
> The angels brought him toys of gold

(He stops singing and points with his stick.) You!
The girl with the frizzly hair. Sing for me! Come
on, come on. Stand up and sing it if you please.
When Jesus Christ . . . *(He gets ready to conduct
with his walking stick.)*

MARY FLANAGAN *(extremely off key)*:

> When Jesus Christ was four years old
> The angels brought him toys of . . .

MR EMANUELLI: No, no! No, no, no, no, no, no,
no, no, no. That is not singing. That is ruddy
awful caterwauling. In future you will sit at the
back of my class and mime the words without the
use of the voice. Can you hold in your hand a
broom? Well? Can you?

MARY FLANAGAN: Yes, Sir.

MR EMANUELLI: Good. Then you will sweep the
stage for my production of The Mikado. Look at
me! *(He sings.)*

> And yet with these he would not play
> He made him small fow ow owl out of clay.

(He points with his stick.) You! The girl with the
glasses. Whatdoyoucall. National Health. Sing it.

MARY HENNESSY *(croaking in a very low octave)*:

> And yet with these he would not play
> He made him small fow ow owl . . .

MR EMANUELLI: Enough! Enough! Where am I? I
can't be in the Convent of Our Lady of Fatima. I
must be in the zoological gardens. At Regents
Park. This voice is bad. Bad, bad, bad. I will not
have such a honking in my Gilbert and Sullivan
chorus. A Nanki-Poo will be needed for The

Mikado. And one little maid from the school. I will not have second raters in my productions. You have seen my Iolanthe, my Pinafore, my Pirates. You know what a professional standard I demand. I was once a professional myself, you know, but because I am one no longer it doesn't mean that I have turned into an amateur. Oh no. You have heard all the rumours about my reputation in the past, eh? Psst, psst, psst, psst, psst. He's supposed to have been a famous opera singer before the nineteen fourteen-eighteen war. You have heard that, eh? You! *(He points with his stick.)* The little tiny girl. Have you heard such a rumour about me?

MARY O'GRADY: Yes, Sir.

MR EMANUELLI: It's a fact. I was certainly one of the best. Famous the world over. But what happened to me, eh? You think you know what happened? Something to do with my leg? Eh? You have heard all about my leg, of course. I wonder what is wrong with Mr Emanuelli's leg. Is it gangrene? Is it gout? Is it a war wound? Psst, psst, psst, psst, psst. Whatever it is it certainly stinks out the music room. Can anyone smell this leg? Well? Speak out! Yes or no?

GIRLS: No, Sir.

MR EMANUELLI: You are all a load of liars because I can ruddy well smell it myself. Look at me! *(He sings.)*

> Jesus Christ thou child so wise
> Bless my hands and fill my eyes

(He points with his stick.) You! The girl there, lurking low. Sing it!

MARY MOONEY:

> Jesus Christ thou child so wise
> Bless my hands and fill my eyes

MR EMANUELLI:

> And bring my soul to Par ar adise

To Par ar adise

MARY MOONEY:
    And bring my soul to Par ar adise
    To Par ar adise

MR EMANUELLI: Yes. Yes, yes, yes, yes. This one is good. Quite good. But I don't believe it. Such a plain, young missy. Come here. Come on, come on. Come right up here and let me look at you.

(Mary Mooney comes forward.)

Yes, yes. You will be Nanki-Poo. He is a young man. And you are a boyish looking girl. Come to see me later. Now go away.

(Mary Mooney goes off.)

We will all sing Jesus Christ together. *(He gets up.)* I am coming to find a pretty little Peep-Bo. My ear is coming close to every mouth. So warble away and don't let me hear any cacophony. One, two, *(they sing)*
    When Jesus Christ was four years old
    The angels brought him toys of gold
    Which no man ever bought or sold . . .
(Mr Emanuelli goes hobbling off.)

Scene 5

A Street in Harlesden.

Mary McGinty, Mary Gallagher and Mary Mooney are walking along carrying heavy satchels and eating Mars Bars. Mary McGinty has her hat in her hand.

MARY GALLAGHER: Put your hat back on, McGinty.

MARY MCGINTY: No. I refuse to walk the streets with a pisspot on my head. It's bad enough having to wear a gymslip and stupid looking socks.

MARY GALLAGHER: What if a prefect sees you. You'll only get reported.

MARY MCGINTY: It wouldn't worry me if I got expelled. I wonder what you have to do to get expelled from that old dump.

MARY GALLAGHER: You could tell them you'd become a member of the pudding club.

MARY MCGINTY: Yeah. Or you could make a big, long willy out of plasticine and stick it on the crucifix in the chapel.

MARY MOONEY: You mustn't say things like that.

MARY MCGINTY: Why not? D'you reckon a thunderbolt is gonna come hurtling down from Heaven?

MARY MOONEY: It doesn't happen straight away. It happens when you're least expecting it. You'd better make an Act of Contrition.

MARY MCGINTY *(looking up)*: Beg your pardon, Jesus.

MARY MOONEY: My Dad knows this man who used to be a monk. But he couldn't keep his vows so he asked if he could leave. On the day he came out of the monastery he went skipping down the path with his dog collar in his hand. When he opened the monastery gate he saw an alsatian sitting outside. So he hung his collar round the alsatian's neck. After that he started going into pubs every night and boasting to all the people about what he'd done with his collar. Then one day he went and got married. And while he was on his honeymoon he started to get a really bad pain in his back. He was in such a terrible agony he could only walk about with a stoop. And soon he was completely bent up double. Then he started to lose his voice. He went to loads of different doctors but none of them could do anything to help him. And now he can only get about on all fours. And when he opens his mouth to say anything he barks just like a dog.

MARY GALLAGHER: Is that true?

MARY MOONEY: Yes. He lives in Shepherds Bush.

MARY MCGINTY: Why can't you keep your stupid old stories to yourself. You're as bad as Mother Peter, you are.

MARY MOONEY: No I am not. Huh. I bet if you were knocked down by a trolley bus this evening you'd be yelling your head off for a priest.

MARY MCGINTY: Oh, no I wouldn't.

MARY GALLAGHER: Well I certainly would.

MARY MCGINTY: Oh shit! I was only having a joke about trying to get expelled. I don't even have to get expelled, come to think of it. I'm old enough to go out to work.

MARY GALLAGHER: You wouldn't get much of a job without any qualifications.

MARY MCGINTY: Huh. I couldn't care less about exams.

MARY GALLAGHER: Well that's the main difference between you and me, McGinty, because I do happen to care.

MARY MOONEY: Yes, and so do I.

MARY MCGINTY: Huh. There's millions of jobs I could do. *(She sees Derek.)* Oh blimey!

DEREK: Afternoon, girls. I must say you're looking very smart.

MARY MCGINTY: Leave off. What you doing round here, anyway?

DEREK: Just having a bit of a promenade. You don't mind, do you? Or is this a private road?

MARY MCGINTY: Aren't you supposed to be at work?

DEREK: Had to take the day off, didn't I. Touch of the old neuralgia.

MARY MCGINTY: Don't give me that.

DEREK: Are you calling me a liar, darling?

MARY MCGINTY: No . . .

DEREK: Well just make sure you don't, cos nobody accuses me of telling lies. All right? *(He looks over at the other two girls.)* How you doing, girls? *(to Mary McGinty)* Ain't you gonna introduce me to your two lovely mates?

MARY MCGINTY: Yeah, well that's Mary Gallagher. And that's Mary Mooney. His name's Derek.

(Derek winks and clicks his tongue at them. Then he turns back to Mary McGinty.)

DEREK: You gonna be down the White Hart tonight, by any chance?

MARY MCGINTY: I might be.

DEREK: Oh, well, I'll see you inside, then, shall I?

MARY MCGINTY: You've got to be joking. You don't think I'm gonna go wandering in there and have everybody staring at me all on me tod.

DEREK: All right, all right. I'll see you outside then. Half past seven. And you be there, darling. Right. *(He clicks his tongue and winks at the other two then he goes swaggering off.)*

MARY GALLAGHER: Is that your bloke?

MARY MCGINTY: Sort of.

MARY GALLAGHER: How long have you been going out with him?

MARY MCGINTY: About two and a half weeks. D'you think he's nice looking?

MARY GALLAGHER: Well . . . he's not exactly my sort of bloke.

MARY MCGINTY: No, well, of course we all know your type, don't we. Smarmy little Catholic schoolboys, with short back and sides. And acne.

MARY GALLAGHER: Cuthbert has not got acne.

MARY MCGINTY: He did have the day I saw him.

He had a beautiful crop of blackheads on his boat-race. And he had a load of pimples, all about ready to pop. Ugh!

MARY GALLAGHER: Well at least he's not bow legged like that long streak of paralysed piss that's just gone by. I wonder where he left his horse.

MARY MCGINTY: Oh shut your face.

MARY MOONEY: I'd like to know how you're going to get your homework done if you're going to be gadding about all night.

MARY MCGINTY: I was thinking of copying your History on the trolley tomorrow morning. And having a lend of Gallagher's Latin after lunch.

MARY GALLAGHER: You've got some nerve.

MARY MCGINTY: I'll do the same for you some time.

MARY GALLAGHER: Oh yes, and pigs might fly.

MARY MCGINTY *(to Mary Mooney)*: You'd better be waiting for me tomorrow morning at Willesden Green.

MARY MOONEY: All right.

MARY GALLAGHER: And don't forget your knicker money, will you.

MARY MOONEY: I didn't have to have any knickers off Mother Peter.

MARY MCGINTY: Oh, no, you wouldn't of course. You always wear passion killers, don't you.

MARY MOONEY: You'll be wearing them yourself from tomorrow.

(Mary McGinty takes a pair of bloomers out of her satchel and puts them over her head.)

MARY MCGINTY: How's that? She didn't actually say you had to put them on your bum.

(They go off.)

Scene 6

The Biology Lab.

Mother Basil, wearing a bloodstained apron, is dissecting a female rabbit.

MOTHER BASIL: Now this is the abdomen, which contains the remainder of the alimentary canal together with the organs of excretion and reproduction. The female ova are produced in the two ovaries which you can see here lying behind the kidneys. Close to each ovary there's a fallopian tube. Each fallopian tube widens out into an oviduct leading to a uterus which in turn opens out together with the second uterus, here, into a much larger tube, the vagina. *(The Angelus bell tolls loudly several times. Mother Basil wipes her hands and makes the Sign of the Cross. The 'Hail Mary' part of the following prayer is recited very rapidly indeed.)* In the name of the Father and of the Son and of the Holy Ghost Amen. The Angel of the Lord declared unto Mary.

GIRLS: And she conceived of the Holy Ghost.

MOTHER BASIL: Hail Mary full of grace the Lord is with thee. Blessed art thou amongst women and blessed is the fruit of thy womb Jesus.

GIRLS: Holy Mary Mother of God pray for us sinners now and at the hour of our death Amen.

MOTHER BASIL: Behold the handmaid of the Lord.

GIRLS: Be it done unto me according to thy word.

MOTHER BASIL: Hail Mary full of grace the Lord is with thee. Blessed art thou amongst women and blessed is the fruit of thy womb Jesus.

GIRLS: Holy Mary Mother of God pray for us sinners now and at the hour of our death Amen.

MOTHER BASIL: And the word was made flesh.

GIRLS: And dwelt amongs us.

MOTHER BASIL: Hail Mary full of grace the Lord is with thee. Blessed art thou amongst women and blessed is the fruit of thy womb Jesus.

GIRLS: Holy Mary Mother of God pray for us sinners now and at the hour of our death Amen.

MOTHER BASIL: Pray for us O holy Mother of God.

GIRLS: That we may be made worthy of the promises of Christ.

MOTHER BASIL: Pour forth we beseech thee O Lord thy grace into our hearts that we to whom the Incarnation of Christ thy Son was made known by the message of an Angel, may by his Passion and Cross be brought to the glory of his resurrection through the same Christ Our Lord Amen. *(Sign of the Cross.)* In the name of the Father and of the Son and of the Holy Ghost Amen. Now, this organ here, the vagina, at its anal end leads to a much smaller tube, and urethra which opens to the exterior. As the breeding season approaches the ova will pass down the fallopian tube through the oviduct and into the uterus. For the purposes of reproduction an enormous number of sperm from the male will be introduced into the vagina. The sperm will swim along the uterus and through the oviduct into the fallopian tube. Yes, Mary Mooney?

MARY MOONEY: Please Mother Basil, could you tell us how the sperm from the male gets introduced into the vagina?

MOTHER BASIL: What?

MARY MOONEY: Could you tell us how . . .

MOTHER BASIL: I heard what you said, you little madam. Get out of here this minute and stand outside till the lesson is over.

(Mary Mooney gets up and goes off.)

God bless us and save us! I'm going to send that girl upstairs to see Mother Thomas Aquinas. Now. When an ovum has been fertilised it'll be implanted in the uterus where the protective membranes and the placenta will be formed. The dirty little devil! Trying to make a laughing stock out of me! The placenta is the organ by which the embryo is attached to the uterus of the mother. Oh, the cheek of it! Mother Thomas Aquinas will deal with her. This uterus here, by the way, is known as a duplex uterus. I never heard the like of it before. The little trollop! All rabbits and rodents have this type of uterus. There is also the simplex uterus which is found in the higher primates including man, or rather woman, but we don't want to be going into that. A detention is no good to that one. What she wants is a good, hard kick up the behind.

Scene 7

Mother Thomas Aquinas' Office.

Mary Mooney is standing in front of Mother Thomas Aquinas' desk.

MOTHER THOMAS AQUINAS: How dare you ask Mother Basil such a precocious question? How dare you?
MARY MOONEY: I'm sorry, Mother Thomas Aquinas, but I didn't know I was asking anything wrong.
MOTHER THOMAS AQUINAS: You didn't know? Are you sure you didn't know?
MARY MOONEY: No Mother. I mean yes Mother.
MOTHER THOMAS AQUINAS: In that case you must be an extremely ignorant girl. Is that what you are,

Mary Mooney? Ignorant?

MARY MOONEY: I don't know, Mother Thomas
Aquinas.

MOTHER THOMAS AQUINAS: Don't you? Hasn't
your mother ever had a little chat with you?

MARY MOONEY: Yes Mother. But she doesn't ever
chat about rabbits.

MOTHER THOMAS AQUINAS: Never mind the
rabbits. Hasn't she ever warned you about boys?

MARY MOONEY: No, Mother Thomas Aquinas.

MOTHER THOMAS AQUINAS: The woman is
evidently guilty of neglecting her duties. Such
ignorance is inexcusable in a girl of fifteen. I must
write to your mother this afternoon and tell her to
start instructing you immediately on certain
matters. Go along now. And try to be a bit more
mature.

MARY MOONEY: Yes Mother Thomas. Thank you
Mother Thomas. Sorry, Mother Thomas.

Scene 8

The Schoolroom.

MARY MCGINTY: Fancy her not knowing the facts
of life. You know when you get married you have
to go to bed with your husband.

MARY MOONEY: No. My Mum and Dad don't.

MARY GALLAGHER: Don't they?

MARY MOONEY: No. My Dad always goes to bed at
nine o'clock. Me and my Mum go at ten. After
she's finished her packing.

MARY GALLAGHER: Her what?

MARY MOONEY: Well she gets out all our best
dresses and packs them in a suitcase with her real
fox fur and her jewellery. Then she gets out her
canteen of cutlery and her best bone china tea set

and she puts them in with a tin of corned beef and a crucifix.

MARY MCGINTY: What for?

MARY MOONEY: In case we have an air raid in the night.

MARY GALLAGHER: I heard the war ended eleven years ago.

MARY MOONEY: Yes, but we have to be ready for the next one. The devil works in threes, don't forget. And this country's got a lot more coming to it for the things it did to Ireland.

MARY GALLAGHER: What things?

MARY MOONEY: Things that'd make your hair stand up on end if only you knew.

MARY GALLAGHER: Such as what?

MARY MOONEY: I don't know. I wasn't there. My Mum was, though.

MARY MCGINTY: D'you share a bedroom with your Mum?

MARY MOONEY: Yes. And my Dad.

MARY MCGINTY: Bloody hell.

MARY MOONEY: Well we've only got one bedroom. Me and my Mum have the double bed. And he's got one on his own.

MARY GALLAGHER: Does she ever get in his bed?

MARY MOONEY: No!

MARY MCGINTY: She must have done once.

MARY GALLAGHER: You have to get in bed with your husband to have a baby.

MARY MCGINTY: And they both have to take their pyjamas off.

MARY MOONEY: Oh no! How could they. I'd never do anything so rude.

MARY GALLAGHER: You'll have to if you ever get married. Our Lady was the only one who never had to do it.

MARY MOONEY: Wasn't she lucky.

MARY MCGINTY: It wasn't so lucky for poor old

Joseph, though. I reckon he must have used it to
stir his tea.

MARY MOONEY: Used what?

MARY MCGINTY: His cock.

MARY GALLAGHER: Prick.

MARY MCGINTY: Dick.

MARY GALLAGHER: Tool.

(Mary McGinty and Mary Gallagher laugh.)

MARY MCGINTY: Sssh!

(The Nuns walk past.)

MARY GALLAGHER: When you're expecting a baby
you stop having the curse. That's how they can
tell.

MARY MOONEY: Are you sure?

MARY GALLAGHER: Yes of course.

MARY MCGINTY: You don't always have to have a
baby, though. Not if the man uses a French letter.

MARY GALLAGHER: You often see a used one lying
about in the park.

MARY MCGINTY: Yeah. Don't ever sit on the seat in
a public toilet.

MARY GALLAGHER: No. Just hover over it. In case
you get VD.

MARY MCGINTY: Your body breaks out in big
sores. And after a while it all starts to rot.

MARY GALLAGHER: I know someone who's had
VD. She stands outside Dollis Hill station selling
papers. All her nose has been eaten away. She's
just got a hole in the middle of her face.

MARY MCGINTY: Cor, I wouldn't buy a paper off
her.

(Mother Basil comes creeping along.)

MARY MOONEY: My Mum must be having a baby. I
know for a fact she's stopped having the curse. I
thought it was a bit funny.
MARY GALLAGHER: She must have got in his bed
while you were fast asleep.
MARY MOONEY: There isn't enough room for the
two of them.
MARY MCGINTY: They don't need all that much
room. The man lies on top of the woman.
MOTHER BASIL: Get up out of there this minute
and go and take some healthy exercise. Sitting
nattering like a bunch of old fishwives.

(The girls get up.)

I'd like to know what all that whispering was
about. That's what I'd like to know.

Scene 9

The Classroom.

*Mother Peter is at her desk. Two extra chairs have
been placed nearby.*

MOTHER PETER: Now sit up straight and clear the
tops of your desks. Give your answers loud and
clear and God help any girl who lets me down.

*(Father Mullarkey enters with Mother Thomas
Aquinas.)*

GIRLS: Good morning, Father Mullarkey. Good
morning, Mother Thomas Aquinas.
FATHER MULLARKEY: Good morning, Mother
Peter. Good morning, girls.

(Mother Peter goes to sit on one of the side chairs with Mother Thomas Aquinas.)

Have they been working hard, Mother Peter.
MOTHER PETER: Indeed they have, Father.

(Father Mullarkey takes a little red booklet out of his pocket. 'A Catechism of Christian Doctrine'. Throughout the following scene he flicks through this booklet.)

FATHER MULLARKEY: And do they know their Catechism?
MOTHER PETER: There's no excuse for any girl who doesn't.
FATHER MULLARKEY: Which girl is the Captain of the form, Mother Peter?
MOTHER PETER: Mary Hennessy is the Captain, Father.
FATHER MULLARKEY: Well now, Mary Hennessy. Stand up and tell me who is the head of the Catholic Church.
MARY HENNESSY: The Pope.
FATHER MULLARKEY: Is that a fact? Are you sure this girl is fit to be the Captain Mother Peter? Are the duties of leadership so exacting that she hasn't time to study her religion? Sit down, Captain Hennessy, and let the blondie girl over there tell us the answer to the question. Who is the Head of the Catholic Church?
MARY FLANAGAN: The Head of the Catholic Church is Jesus Christ Our Lord.
FATHER MULLARKEY: And has the church a visible head on earth?
MARY FLANAGAN: The church has a visible head on earth. The Bishop of Rome, who is the Vicar of Christ.
FATHER MULLARKEY: What is the Bishop of Rome

called?

MARY FLANAGAN: The Bishop of Rome is called the Pope, which word signifies Father.

FATHER MULLARKEY: Make a note of that, Mary Hennessy. And now stand up and tell me is the Pope infallible?

MARY HENNESSY: The Pope is infallible.

FATHER MULLARKEY: Correct. Now, that girl there. Which are the four sins crying to Heaven for vengeance?

MARY MOONEY: The four sins crying to Heaven for vengeance are Wilful Murder, The Sin of Sodom, Oppression of the Poor and Defrauding Labourers of their Wages.

FATHER MULLARKEY: Is it a great evil to fall into mortal sin?

MARY MOONEY: It is the greatest of all evils to fall into mortal sin.

FATHER MULLARKEY: Why is it called mortal sin?

MARY MOONEY: It is called mortal sin because it kills the soul and deserves Hell.

FATHER MULLARKEY: Now you there with the horse's tail. Is it a mortal sin to neglect to hear Mass on Sundays and Holydays of Obligation?

MARY O'GRADY: It is a mortal sin to neglect to hear Mass on Sundays and Holydays of Obligation.

FATHER MULLARKEY: Make no mistake about it, there's no greater sin on all this earth than the deliberate missing of Mass. *(He bangs on the desk.)* A person who lies in bed and refuses to get up for Mass is committing a far more serious sin than a person who lashes out and murders his wife in a fit of fury. God would surely be merciful to the man who lost control. But you can't expect God to condone a premeditated decision to stay away from Holy Mass. The blondie girl again. Where is God?

MARY FLANAGAN: God is everywhere.

FATHER MULLARKEY: Had God any beginning?

MARY FLANAGAN: God had no beginning. He always was. He is and He always will be.

FATHER MULLARKEY: Has God any body?

MARY FLANAGAN: God has no body. He is a spirit.

FATHER MULLARKEY: Is there only one God?

MARY FLANAGAN: There is only one God.

FATHER MULLARKEY: Are there three persons in God?

MARY FLANAGAN: There are three persons in God; God the Father, God the Son and God the Holy Ghost.

FATHER MULLARKEY: Are these three persons three Gods?

MARY FLANAGAN: These three persons are not three Gods. The Father, the Son and the Holy Ghost are all one and the same God.

FATHER MULLARKEY: Does God know and see all things?

MARY FLANAGAN: God knows and sees all things, even our most secret thoughts.

FATHER MULLARKEY: How are you to know what God has revealed?

MARY FLANAGAN: I am to know what God has revealed by the testimony, teaching and authority of the Catholic Church.

FATHER MULLARKEY: Now then Captain Hennessy. What is the Sixth Commandment?

MARY HENNESSY: The Sixth Commandment is thou shalt not commit adultery.

FATHER MULLARKEY: Good. Now I want to say a little word to you about the vital importance of purity. You're all getting to be big girls now. Indeed some of you are bigger than others. Isn't it a great joy to be young and healthy with all your life before you. Sooner or later you might want to share your life with a member of the opposite sex.

The best way to find a boyfriend is to join a Catholic Society where you'll have scope for all sorts of social activities. Now when you've met your good Catholic boy and you're getting to know each other he might suggest a bit of a kiss and a cuddle. Well let him wait. And if he doesn't want to wait let him go. Any cuddling and kissing is bound to arouse bad feelings and desires for the intimate union allowed only in Matrimony. *(He bangs on the desk.)* The intimate union of the sexes is a sacred act. A duty to be done in a state of grace by a man and his wife and nobody else. So until the day you kneel at the altar with a bridal veil on your head you must never be left alone in a room with your boyfriend. Or in a field for that matter. Let the two of you go out and about with other young couples to dances and to parties and the like. But a particular word of warning about the latter. There's no doubt at all that alcoholic drinks make a party go with a swing. The danger is that after a couple of drinks a boy and a girl are more inclined to take liberties with each other. To indulge in such liberties is sinful. The girl has the special responsibility in the matter because a boy's passions are more readily aroused, God help him. Show your affection by all means. But keep to holding hands with an occasional kiss on the cheek. A Catholic boy, in his heart of hearts, will be impressed by such insistence on perfect chastity. Ask Our Blessed Lady to keep you free from the temptations of the flesh. And make no mistake about it a passionate kiss on the lips between a boy and a girl is a serious mortal sin. *(He bangs on the desk.)* When you've the wedding ring on your finger you can fire away to your heart's content. Now has anyone any question she'd like to ask? Yes? That girl there.

MARY MOONEY: Please, Father, could you tell

me what is the Sin of Sodom?

FATHER MULLARKEY: The what? Whatever put that.into your head?

MARY MOONEY: It's one of the four sins crying to Heaven for vengeance, Father.

FATHER MULLARKEY: Oh yes. So it is. That's right. Well it's a very bad sin indeed. But it's nothing you need bother your head about. Sit down now. Are there any more questions? No? That'll be all then. Thank you, Mother Peter. Mother Thomas Aquinas. *(He blesses the class.)* In nomine Patris et Filii et Spiritus Sancti Amen.

VOICES OFF: Good morning, Father. Thank you Father.

Scene 10

Mother Thomas Aquinas' Office.

Mary Mooney is standing in front of Mother Thomas Aquinas' desk.

MOTHER THOMAS AQUINAS: What a foul, despicable creature you are. I'm thoroughly disgusted with you. Was it your own idea to ask that question, or did somebody put you up to it?

MARY MOONEY: No, Mother Thomas.

MOTHER THOMAS AQUINAS: No what? It wasn't your own idea?

MARY MOONEY: Yes, Mother Thomas. But . . .

MOTHER THOMAS AQUINAS: It was your own idea. To embarrass the poor priest in front of the entire class. May I ask why?

MARY MOONEY: I don't know, Mother Thomas.

MOTHER THOMAS AQUINAS: I'm sorry but I don't believe you. I suggest you know full well why you chose such a question. To make yourself the centre of attraction and procure a cheap laugh at Father Mullarkey's expense. The last time you were in this office you tried to hoodwink me into believing you to be an innocent girl, immature for your years. You might like to know that I wasn't entirely convinced. And I'm now quite certain that you're not in the least bit innocent. You're an exceedingly sophisticated girl, full of knowing far beyond your years. As to the question of punishment, I hardly think a detention would serve any useful purpose. Instead I am going to send you into the chapel after lunch today and every day for nine consecutive days to recite a Novena to Our Lady of Perpetual Succour. On the Saturday and Sunday you will visit your parish church. Take this. *(She opens a drawer and takes out a small booklet.)* And recite the prayer on page five. O Mother of Perpetual Succour behold me a miserable sinner at thy feet and so on. Followed by nine Hail Marys. The intention of this Novena is to ask Our Lady to alleviate your apparent obsession with carnal knowledge and to restore your mind and heart to childlike innocence.

MARY MOONEY: Thank you Mother Thomas.

MOTHER THOMAS AQUINAS: Now get out!

Scene 11

A Street Corner.

Mary McGinty, wearing a slightly tarty fifties outfit, is leaning up against a wall with Derek who has one arm around her. He puts his other arm around her and tries to kiss her. She turns her face away.

DEREK: Here. What's up with you?

MARY MCGINTY: Nothing.

(Derek tries to kiss her again. She turns her face away again.)

DEREK: What you playing at?

MARY MCGINTY: Nothing. It's dead late, Derek. I'd better be getting indoors.

DEREK: What about my goodnight?

MARY MCGINTY: Yeah. Well goodnight then. *(She pulls away from him and gives him a peck on the cheek.)*

DEREK: Oh yeah? You trying to drop me a hint by any chance? Trying to tell me something without saying nothing? Look here, darling, if I've done anything wrong I've got a right to know what it is.

MARY MCGINTY: If you must know it's to do with mortal sins.

DEREK: How's that?

MARY MCGINTY: Mortal sins. They're sins what you go to Hell for if you die with one on your soul. You know, like murder. Or eating meat on a Friday.

DEREK: Oh yes? I had pork-pie for me tea on Friday, you're not holding that against me, I hope?

MARY MCGINTY: Look, the priest came to school today to give us this big long lecture. And one of the things he said was that snogging is a mortal sin.

DEREK: Pull the other leg.

MARY MCGINTY: That's what he told us. Honestly.

DEREK: Never. You must have got it wrong. How can you go to Hell for having a snog? I mean, it's only your bloomin' cakehole after all. Wrapping it round somebody else's. Where's the harm in that for Christ's sake? You sure he wasn't talking about something a bit more on the sexy side?

I mean, I know for a fact that Catholics are not allowed to . . . er . . . you know . . . until they're married. Everyone's aware of that. And myself, I wouldn't er . . . whatsname with a girl if I respected her. And I wouldn't respect a girl if she let me . . . er . . . you know. Have a bit.

MARY MCGINTY: He definitely meant snogging, Derek. I swear to you. A passionate kiss on the lips between a boy and a girl is a serious mortal sin. That's what he said. And he must know if he's the priest. D'you realise I've gone and committed hundreds of mortal sins, thanks to you.

DEREK: Oh that's right. Put the blame on me. Ain't it marvellous, eh? I never even heard of a mortal bleedin' sin until five fucking minutes ago. Er . . . sorry about using that word in front of you.

MARY MCGINTY: That's all right.

DEREK: Well I mean, it's no sin for me, is it, darling.

MARY MCGINTY: No. And it's not bloomin' fair. Protestants don't have sins, the lucky sods. I wonder where they go when they die, though.

DEREK: They stop in the cemetery like everybody else.

MARY MCGINTY: What are you supposed to be? Church of England?

DEREK: Yeah, well that's what I stick down if I have to fill up a form for something or other. C of E. It don't mean nothing, do it, except you're an ordinary English person. It's hard luck for you, ain't it, having an Irish Mum and Dad. You know, you don't strike me as being one bit Irish yourself. I mean, you could easily pass yourself off as a normal person. It's more the fellers really, ain't it. Funny how you can spot a Mick a mile off. No offence to your old man or nothing. I mean, I've got nothing against them apart from the fact that

they drink too much and they're always picking
fights among themselves. It makes me die
laughing the way their hair stands all up on end.
Half of them have got that diabolical ginger hair,
ain't they. And all of 'em have got them big red
faces. And them bleedin' great flapping trousers.
You see 'em wearing them down the Kilburn High
Road; you could fit half a dozen navvies into one
leg alone. Myself, I reckon they all take religion a
bit too serious. I mean, you can understand it
more with the Italians, having the Pope stuck in
the Vatican there, keeping his eye on them. But
the Irish are bleedin' miles away. Why should they
have to take orders from the Pope? If I was you
I'd be a bit suspicious of that Heaven you're so
keen to get up to. It's gonna be packed out with
some of the worst types of foreigners. The Irish'll
be the only ones up there speaking English.
The rest of them'll all be Italians, Spaniards,
Portuguese . . .

MARY MCGINTY: Mexicans.

DEREK: Yeah. Bolivians. Peruvians. All that mob.
I can't see you fitting in somehow. No. If I was
you I'd start taking it all with a pinch of salt. You
don't really believe in it, do you?

MARY MCGINTY: I don't know. One minute I do.
The next minute I don't.

DEREK: I know you have to make out you believe it
in front of all them nuns and priests and your
Mum and Dad. Fair enough. You don't wanna
cause them no trouble. You can play along with it
for a few more years. Then you can go your own
sweet way.

MARY MCGINTY: I can't, you know. Once a
Catholic always a Catholic. That's the rule.

DEREK: Yeah? Tough. Oh well, might see you
around sometime.

MARY MCGINTY: Couldn't we just be mates?

DEREK: What? I've got more mates than I know what to do with. I can't have you dragging round with us up the billiard hall and down the football field. Leave off.

MARY MCGINTY: It's not that I don't wanna go out with you any more, Derek. It's just . . .

(He puts his arms around her.)

DEREK: Come here. You can always go up to Confession on Saturday and get your soul dry cleaned. Where is your soul anyway?

MARY MCGINTY: It's inside your heart.

DEREK: Don't talk rubbish.

MARY MCGINTY: I always imagine it in the heart. It could be inside your head, I suppose.

DEREK: It's not in your heart or your head. It's not in your bum neither.

MARY MCGINTY: There's definitely something mysterious about Confession though; when you come out you feel all good and holy and all sort of excited in your head. A bit like when you've had a couple of gin and limes.

DEREK: Oooh. Touch of the old voodoo if you ask me.

MARY MCGINTY: It only lasts for about ten minutes. Then you come down to earth again and realise that just about everything you do or say or even think is a sin according to them and you just can't help committing the buggers if you're a normal human being.

DEREK: Oh well. You're just gonna have to choose between me and Jesus. *(He kisses her.)*

MARY MCGINTY: Oh Christ. That's another fucking mortal sin.

DEREK: Oy. I don't wanna hear you using that sort of language.

Scene 12

Cuthbert's House.

Mary Gallagher and Cuthbert, both in school uniform, are sitting on chairs. Cuthbert is holding a school copy of 'Macbeth'.

MARY GALLAGHER: O, full of scorpions is my mind, dear wife! Thou know'st that Banquo and his Fleance lives.

CUTHBERT *(in a high voice)*: But in them nature's copy not eterne.

MARY GALLAGHER: There's comfort yet . . . er . . . er . . .

CUTHBERT: They are assailable.

MARY GALLAGHER: They are assailable. *(She looks blank.)*

CUTHBERT: Then be thou jocund.

MARY GALLAGHER: Oh yes. Then be thou jocund; ere the bat hath flown His cloistered flight; ere to black Hecate's summons, Er . . . the . . . er . . . the something beetle with his . . . er . . . Oh, bollocks! I don't know it.

CUTHBERT: Yes you do. More or less.

MARY GALLAGHER: It's got to be word perfect for Mother Peter, you realise. Just in case she picks on me. She's such a crafty old cow. She makes us all learn it but she'll only pounce on one of us to test it. Whoever she happens to pick on will have to get up and act it. In front of the whole form. With her. She always gives herself the part of Lady Macbeth. God it's so embarrassing. Especially when she starts putting on an English accent and doing all the fancy gestures. Every time she opens her mouth a spray of spit comes flying across the classroom. We've all got to go on an outing with her next Wednesday. To see Macbeth.

She's taking us up to the Old Vic.

CUTHBERT: Big deal.

MARY GALLAGHER: Yeah. Have you ever been there?

CUTHBERT: God, who hasn't been to the Old Vic.

MARY GALLAGHER: Lots of people haven't. My Mum and Dad for a start. Neither of them have ever set foot inside a theatre.

CUTHBERT: Peasants! *(He takes out a packet of Senior Service, sticks one in a holder and lights it up.)*

MARY GALLAGHER: They only ever go to the pictures if a film comes round the Coliseum with a Catholic in the starring role.

CUTHBERT: Typical.

MARY GALLAGHER: They think an awful lot of Spencer Tracy. And Bing Crosby. He can do no wrong. And they both reckon the sun shines right out of Grace Kelly's arse.

CUTHBERT: How about Mario Lanza?

MARY GALLAGHER: Is he a Catholic?

CUTHBERT: He's entitled to be with a name like that.

MARY GALLAGHER: My Dad refuses to see a film if he thinks the star in it has ever been divorced. And he gets in a flaming temper if he ever catches sight of a picture of Lana Turner in the paper. Just because she's been married a few times. He rips the picture out of the paper and screws it up and stamps on it. *(In an Irish accent.)* One husband wouldn't satisfy you, ah? Ye two legged animal! Aaah!

CUTHBERT: I could quite fancy a session with Lana Turner.

MARY GALLAGHER: She's a bit old for you, isn't she?

CUTHBERT: Not half. I've got a definite weakness

for the older woman.

MARY GALLAGHER: Oh, have you.

CUTHBERT: Yes. I have actually. *(He takes half a bottle of whisky out of his blazer pocket and has a swig.)*

MARY GALLAGHER: Can I have a drop of that?

(He hands her the bottle and she takes a long swig.)

CUTHBERT: Go easy with it. Bloody hell. That cost me eighteen and four pence, you know.

MARY GALLAGHER: You're just stingy, you are.

CUTHBERT: No I'm not. But I only get ten bob a week off my Dad.

MARY GALLAGHER: Yeah. And the rest.

CUTHBERT: Come over here a minute.

MARY GALLAGHER: No.

CUTHBERT: Don't then.

MARY GALLAGHER: Guess who came to school today.

CUTHBERT: Cardinal Godfrey.

MARY GALLAGHER: No. Father Mullarkey actually. He was shouting his mouth off about purity.

CUTHBERT: Oh was he. Huh. I only have to hear the word purity and immediately I conjure up a picture of a fanny. And that's just what they tell you not to think about. And it's never any ordinary fanny. It's always a withered, shrivelled up old thing like the one the Virgin Mary's supposed to have had that they're forever saluting.

MARY GALLAGHER: I think I'd better be going.

CUTHBERT *(offering her the whisky)*: Would you like another sip? There's no such sin as impurity, you know.

MARY GALLAGHER: There is.

CUTHBERT: There is not. A couple of thousand years ago it was taken for granted that people had uncontrollable urges. Monks used to be able to take loose women up to their monasteries and nobody thought anything about it.

MARY GALLAGHER: Well why haven't we been taught that at school?

CUTHBERT: They don't want you to know, do they. Or they might not know themselves. There's an awful lot of ignorance about. I once asked my Mum if she knew how many illegitimate children Pope Alexander the Sixth had.

MARY GALLAGHER: What!

CUTHBERT: Christ, you're as bad as her. She's under the impression that all the Popes were paragons of purity. Well they bloody well weren't. They got up to all sorts of spicy things.

MARY GALLAGHER: They didn't. Did they really?

CUTHBERT: Alexander the Sixth, he was a filthy old fucker. His real name was Rodrigo. Rodrigo Borgia. He used to knock about with various tarts. One of them owned a string of brothels. Some old bag called Vanozza. He probably picked up the syphilis off her. I'm not making it up, you know. It's all on record in the Vatican. They've got a load of lascivious documents in there all about the Popes and their concubines and bastard kids. I'm definitely going to take a trip to Rome as soon as I get the chance and have a read of them for myself.

MARY GALLAGHER: What makes you think they'd let you into the Vatican to read about stuff like that?

CUTHBERT: It happens to be open to the public. Of course they don't let just anybody in. They give out special permits. They have to, otherwise there'd be queues down there day and night.

MARY GALLAGHER: Do you think Pope Pius has

girlfriends?

CUTHBERT: No. They don't do it any more. They haven't been doing it for quite a few centuries. I think it was Gregory the Seventh who put a stop to it. The cunt. Well, the way I see it is if it wasn't a sin once then it's not a sin now. You wouldn't catch me discussing my sexual habits in the Confessional.

MARY GALLAGHER: I don't know why you bother to go to Confession.

CUTHBERT: I'm quite prepared to confess any genuine misdeeds. Any sins against the religion itself. I really believe in some of the mysteries and the majority of the doctrines. It's definitely the one true faith. And the Mass is the greatest ceremony on earth. Agnus Dei. Ecce qui tollit peccata mundi Ecce. I've seriously thought about becoming a priest. It's a bloody great life. Especially if you can get into a better class of parish where they all put ten bob notes in the collection plate. I wonder if I've got a vocation. Of course I'd have to make sure there was a bit of discreet crumpet in the background. Or I might go off my head.

MARY GALLAGHER: Cuthbert. Would you know if the Sin of Sodom is supposed to be something impure according to them?

CUTHBERT: Oh yes, well that definitely is impure. Not only according to them. According to everyone. It's illegal.

MARY GALLAGHER: What exactly is it, though?

CUTHBERT: Haven't you got the slightest idea?

MARY GALLAGHER: No. That's why I'm asking you.

CUTHBERT: Well it's two blokes in one bed having it off together up their bums.

MARY GALLAGHER: Really?

CUTHBERT: Yes. I could show you some pictures

if you like.

MARY GALLAGHER: Could you?

CUTHBERT: Yes. There's some going round the school at the moment. I'll let you have a look when it's my turn to borrow them. There's quite a few homosexuals at St Vincents. I keep well out of their way. You've probably got some lessies at your school. Lesbian. That's what you call a woman homosexual. It's easy to spot a lesbian, you know. They all have very short hair and big gruff voices. They go to bed with each other and get up to all sorts of capers with cucumbers and carrots and bananas. And candles. Most people think all nuns are rollicking lesbians. They probably are but I like to think of them keeping their vows of chastity if it kills them. There's something quite erotic about a completely celibate woman. Their natural lust gets all damned up inside them and comes exploding out in all sorts of unexpected directions. That's why your Lady of Fatima nuns are so bad tempered.

MARY GALLAGHER: You can say that again. They'd love to hit us if they were allowed to. But instead they find all sorts of spiteful ways to punish us. Saying sarcastic things and showing us up in front of other people. I'd sooner have corporal punishment any day.

CUTHBERT: You wouldn't say that if you'd ever had the cane off Canon O'Flynn. He's a bastard. The biggest bastard ever to come across the Irish Sea. You have to go up to his office to get it. He's always waiting for you, pacing up and down with the shillelagh in his hand and the saliva dribbling down his chin. *(In an Irish accent)* 'Are you sorry for what you've done, boy? Are you? Well you will be in a minute. Oho, you will.' Then he gets up on his chair like this. *(Cuthbert stands on his chair and holds the copy of 'Macbeth' above his head.)* 'Put out your posterior'. *(Mary Gallagher bends over. Cuthbert jumps off the chair with a roar and hits her on the bottom with the book. She yells. Cuthbert puts his arm around her.)* Oh, sorry. Did I hurt you? Sorry. I got a bit carried away. *(He pulls her on to his lap and puts his arms around her and kisses her.)*

MARY GALLAGHER: If I don't tell this in Confession are you sure it'll be all right to go to Holy Communion afterwards.

CUTHBERT: Of course. I've been doing that for years. Nothing's happened so it must be all right.

Scene 13

A Lavatory.

Mary Gallagher and Mary McGinty are sitting on the seat with a Bible between them. Mary Mooney is standing up.

MARY MOONEY: And if a woman have an issue, and her issue in her flesh be blood, she shall be put apart seven days: and whosoever toucheth her shall be unclean until the even.

MARY MCGINTY: Cor, fancy putting that in the Bible.

MARY MOONEY: There's some better bits in Chapter Eighteen. I've underlined them in pencil. Don't let me forget to rub it out, though. My Mum would do her nut if she ever found it.

(They turn the page.)

MARY GALLAGHER: Thou shalt not uncover the nakedness of a woman and her daughter, neither shall thou take her son's daughter or her daughter's

daughter to uncover her nakedness. Christ, those
Jews must have been sex mad.

MARY MCGINTY: Look at this. Thou shalt not lie
with mankind as with womankind. It is an
abomination.

MARY GALLAGHER: That's the Sin of Sodom.

MARY MCGINTY and MARY MOONEY: Is it?

MARY GALLAGHER: Yes. Listen to this. Neither
shalt thou lie with any beast to defile thyself
therewith.

MARY MCGINTY: A beast! Cor, blimey O'Riley.

MARY GALLAGHER: Neither shall any woman
stand before a beast to lie down thereto. It is
confusion.

MARY MCGINTY: I should say it is. Bloody hell.
What sort of animals did they do it with?

MARY GALLAGHER: Whatever happened to be
trotting about at the time.

MARY MCGINTY: Camels.

MARY GALLAGHER: I suppose so. Horses. Pigs.
Anything.

MARY MOONEY: What would it be like now if Jesus
hadn't come down to put a stop to all that.

MARY MCGINTY: I'd probably be going down the
White Hart tonight with a monkey.

MARY GALLAGHER: You are, anyway.

MARY MCGINTY: Oh, shut up.

MARY MOONEY: Have a look at Chapter Twenty.

(They turn the page.)

MARY MCGINTY: And if a man shall take his sister,
his father's daughter or his mother's daughter and
see her nakedness and she sees his nakedness . . .

(Mother Peter raps on the door.)

MOTHER PETER: Who's in this toilet?

(The Girls jump up and look alarmed. Mary Gallagher puts the Bible down and shushes them silently.)

MARY GALLAGHER *(calling out)*: Me, Mother.
MOTHER PETER: Who's me?
MARY GALLAGHER: Mary Gallagher, Mother.
MOTHER PETER: Come out of there this minute, Mary Gallagher.

(Mary Gallagher pulls the chain, opens the door, comes out and closes the door behind her. Mother Basil pushes open the door and sees the other two.)

MOTHER BASIL: Oho! We knew well there were three of you in here. Come on out of it! *(She drags them out.)*
MOTHER PETER: How dare you go into the toilet together. Big girls of your age. Were you doing anything immodest in there? Were you? Tell the truth now and shame the devil.
MARY GALLAGHER
MARY MCGINTY } : No, Mother.
MARY MOONEY
MOTHER BASIL: I think they were smoking. Hand over the cigarettes.
MARY GALLAGHER: We haven't been smoking, Mother.
MOTHER PETER: Well what have you been doing in there.
MARY MOONEY: We were reading the Bible, Mother.
MOTHER BASIL: You lying little toad.
MOTHER PETER: You impudent little madam, you.

(Mother Basil goes into the toilet.)

MOTHER BASIL: There's a Bible inside of this

toilet, Mother Peter, believe it or not.

MOTHER PETER: Why would anyone go into the toilet to read the Bible?

(Mother Basil comes out and hands the Bible to Mother Peter.)

MOTHER PETER: Whose Bible is this?

(Pause.)

MOTHER BASIL: Is it a Catholic Bible, Mother Peter?

MOTHER PETER: Indeed it is. But I've a very strong suspicion there's more to it than meets the eye. I'm going to hand it in to Mother Thomas Aquinas and ask her to give it a thorough inspection. If the owner of this Bible wants it back let her go up to Mother Thomas Aquinas' office and explain herself.

MOTHER BASIL: What are we going to do with them, Mother Peter?

MOTHER PETER: I'll deal with them later, Mother Basil. I can't imagine what kind of bad things have been going on inside that toilet. But I'll find out. I'll find out so I will.

Scene 14

The Classroom.

Mother Peter is at her desk.

MOTHER PETER: There will be no lessons this afternoon. And no lessons again on the afternoon of the twenty-first. On that day we'll be having our little Christmas celebrations so bring in your cakes and snacks and your bottles of lemonade. And bring your party dresses with you to change in to. You may have the use of the gramophone so bring along some records to dance to. Bring your hit parade records by all means. But do not attempt to bring any Elvis Presley records into this school.

VOICES OFF: Oh no!

MOTHER PETER: I might as well tell you now that Mother Thomas Aquinas is sending out a letter to all parents to warn them about the corruption caused to innocent young minds by such a lewd and bestial artiste. Your parents have every right to go through your records, to take out the Elvis Presleys and put them into the dustbin where he belongs. There are plenty of good wholesome singers to enjoy. Joseph Locke now. He's one of the finest singers in the land. And I've heard great reports about Donald Peers. So forget about that old devil of a Presley. Now, this afternoon we're going to have a film show. Mother Basil is going show us 'The Barretts of Wimpole Street'. When the bell goes after lunch I want you to go straight into the Assembly Hall and take your seats for the film. With the exception of Mary Gallagher, Mary McGinty and Mary Mooney. Mother Thomas Aquinas has asked me to make it clear that any girls seen going into the toilet together will be banned from taking their O levels.

In nineteen seventeen, in the thick of the first world war, a festering abscess broke out upon the face of the earth. Communism. The devil's own doctrine. Horrible, heathen Communism, which denies the existence of God and the immortal soul. When the wicked Red scoundrels took control of Russia in the nineteen-seventeen Revolution this was only the start of a Communist crusade to be spread throughout the whole wide world. But in the very same year, thanks be to God, Our Blessed

Lady revealed herself to three little children in Fatima. God had seen fit to intervene in the affairs of the world by sending his own Blessed Mother down to earth to start a counter revolution.

(Mary Mooney comes in and stands next to Mother Peter's desk.)

Fatima is a village in the very centre of Portugal, about seventy miles from Lisbon. The scenery in those parts is stark and severe. I've heard tell it would put you in mind of Connemara but without the green. Mary Mooney, what time of day do you call this?

MARY MOONEY: I'm sorry, Mother Peter. But the trolley bus came off the rails.

MOTHER PETER: Did it indeed? And why couldn't you hop off it and on to another like any normal person?

MARY MOONEY: We weren't anywhere near a bus stop, Mother Peter.

MOTHER PETER: Never mind your feeble excuses. You've missed your morning prayers. Go into the chapel and say a few for the souls in Purgatory.

MARY MOONEY: Yes, Mother Peter.

MOTHER PETER: Now, have you got your deposit for Fatima?

MARY MOONEY: No, Mother Peter. I . . .

MOTHER PETER: You haven't. Well isn't that just typical, Mary Mooney. You knew that money had to be in by today at the very latest. Isn't it just like you to be upsetting the whole schedule and making extra work for myself and Mother Thomas Aquinas. Oh, Mary Mooney, I've a good mind to exclude you from the pilgrimage altogether.

MARY MOONEY: I won't be going anyway, Mother Peter.

MOTHER PETER: Oh? And why won't you?

MARY MOONEY: My father says he can't afford it, Mother.

MOTHER PETER: Nonsense. We're getting greatly reduced rates both for the journey and the accommodation. Didn't you make that clear to your father? Of course we know it's not a compulsory pilgrimage. Nobody is being dragged out to Fatima by the scruff of the neck. It just happens that all the other girls in this form will be going of their own free will. No doubt they'll tell you all about it when they get back. Now go to the Chapel.

(Mary Mooney goes off.)

On the thirteenth of each month from May to October, nineteen seventeen, Our Lady appeared to ten-year-old Lucia dos Santos and her two little cousins Jacinta and Francisco while they were tending their sheep about a mile from their home near Fatima. There was a blinding flash and Our Lady appeared hovering over a little evergreen tree. She wore a snowy white dress and veil, the dress embroidered with stars of gold, a golden cord around her neck. She had on little gold earrings and held rosary beads of sparkling white in one hand, in the other hand she held her own immaculate heart bleeding and wreathed with thorns. 'I want you to do something special for me', she told Lucia. 'I want you to ask the Pope to consecrate my immaculate heart to Russia. If this is done I promise that Russia will be converted. But if Russia is not converted she will spread her dreadful Communism throughout the world arousing wars and persecutions against the Church.' Our lady promised the children that she would work a miracle on the 13th of October and indeed she did.

On the thirteenth of October seventy thousand people came from far and wide to wait for the promised miracle. It was pouring with rain and the crowd made a roof of umbrellas. At noon the rain stopped and the Queen of Heaven appeared to the children. 'I am the Lady of the Rosary' she said to Lucia. 'Let them say the rosary every day. Let them offend Our Lord no more. The war is going to end but if men do not repent then another and far more disastrous war will come.' And then she disappeared. 'Oh, look at the sun!' cried Lucia. The sun was trembling and dancing and turning like a wheel of fireworks, changing colour as it turned round and round. Then suddenly it seemed to fall towards the earth casting the colours of the rainbow on to the people and the land. The people fell into a panic thinking the world was coming to an end and they fell upon their knees making the most fervent Acts of Contrition. But Lucia, Jacinta and Francisco were gazing in rapture up at the sky as they saw Our Lady in all her brilliancy standing to the right of the sun. She was now dressed in the blue and white robes of Our Lady of the Rosary. To the left of the sun St Joseph emerged from the clouds. He held the child Jesus in his arms. Then Our Lord himself appeared in the red robes of the Divine Redeemer and made the sign of the cross three times over the world. Beside him stood our Lady now clad in the purple robes of Our Lady of Sorrows. And then finally Our Lady appeared again in the simple brown robes of Our Lady of Carmel. The sun stopped dancing and the crowd breathed a sign of relief. The world hadn't come to an end but the miracle promised by Our Lady had come to pass. Two years later Our Lady came to take the boy Francisco up to Heaven. And Jacinta went up to join him the following year. They knew well they were going to die and accepted their sufferings gladly for the love of Jesus and Mary. Both children made their exit from this world in perfect peace and ecstasy. Lucia entered a convent and is still alive and well, guarding an important secret entrusted to her by Our Lady. This secret will be told to all the world as soon as Lucia receives permission from Heaven. But until then we must all be kept in suspense. A great many cures and conversions have taken place at Fatima. If any of your families or friends are in need of a miracle get them to write out their petitions and we'll deliver them to Our Lady's shrine. And while we're there we'll say a prayer for Mary Mooney's unfortunate father. That his arms may grow long enough to reach into his pockets. And, by the way, even though we are going to Fatima during the Easter holidays, Mother Thomas Aquinas has given orders that school uniform only will be worn for the duration of the pilgrimage.

GIRLS: Oh no!

MOTHER PETER: Oh yes. Oh yes indeed.

Scene 15

The Street.

Mary Mooney, dowdily dressed, is walking along carrying a couple of library books. Derek comes swaggering along in the opposite direction. They pass each other.

MARY MOONEY: Hello, Derek.

DEREK: Eh? *(He stops and turns round.)* Er . . . do I know you, darling?

MARY MOONEY: Not really. But I was with Mary McGinty that day you met her along the street near our school.

DEREK: Oh yeah?

MARY MOONEY: You probably won't remember
me but I'm Mary Mooney. There was another
Mary with us as well that day. Mary Gallagher.

DEREK: Oh, really?

MARY MOONEY: Yes. You asked Mary McGinty if
she'd meet you outside the White Hart that night.
D'you remember?

DEREK: Er . . . vaguely. Bit of a long time ago,
wasn't it.

MARY MOONEY: Not last term but the term before.
But I've got a good memory for faces.

DEREK: Oh, have you?

MARY MOONEY: Yes.

DEREK: Well you'll have to excuse me not recog-
nising you, darling. I mean, in them uniforms you
all look like peas in a bleedin' pod. Seeing you all
dressed up the way you are today I wouldn't lump
you in with none of them Lady of Fatima girls,
now would I? Here, why ain't you in Fatima?

MARY MOONEY: I didn't want to go.

DEREK: Very wise, darling. Very wise. They're
having a diabolical time, you know. I had a post-
card Tuesday. She's got corns coming up on her
kneecaps from having to say so many prayers.
They have to be in bed by nine o'clock every night.
And they have to go marching about all over the
place in a crocodile. *(He laughs.)* I bet you're glad
you stopped in Willesden, ain't you?

MARY MOONEY: Yeah.

DEREK *(he laughs)*: I hear they carted a midget
along with 'em.

MARY MOONEY: Oh, you mean Mary Finnegan in
5B. She's only as big as this. *(She holds her hand
up about three feet in the air.)*

DEREK: Oh yeah. Gonna be coming back as big as
this, is she? *(He holds his hand up about six*

feet in the air.)

MARY MOONEY: They're hoping she'll grow a bit bigger.

DEREK: She won't, you know. She'll be coming back as little as what she went. You wait and see.

MARY MOONEY: They won't be back for nearly another week.

DEREK: Yeah, I know. Poor sods. Here, turn your face to the side a minute. D'you know who you remind me of?

MARY MOONEY: Who?

DEREK: Rhonda Fleming.

MARY MOONEY: I don't.

DEREK: Yes you do. I see her in a film last Saturday. Yeah, you're definitely her double, you are.

MARY MOONEY: Am I?

DEREK: I'm telling you. Er . . . d'you fancy coming for a bag of chips?

MARY MOONEY: I've just had my dinner.

DEREK: Oh. Well how about a cup of tea then?

MARY MOONEY: I don't drink tea.

DEREK: Well what do you drink?

MARY MOONEY: Milk. Or water, or . . .

DEREK: What, holy water?

MARY MOONEY: Oooh, no.

DEREK: Don't look so serious, darling. They can probably do you a glass of whatever you happen to fancy round the caff.

MARY MOONEY: Well actually I was just on my way to the library.

DEREK: Yeah? *(He takes one of the books from under her arm.)* What's this? 'The Keys of the Kingdom', eh? Do a lot of reading do you, darling?

MARY MOONEY: There's not much else to do during the holidays.

DEREK: What's this one all about then?

MARY MOONEY: It's about a Catholic priest.
Father Chisholm. He's a missionary and he goes
out to China and . . .
DEREK: Sounds highly intriguing I must say. Of
course I don't go in for reading much myself. No.
I'd sooner watch the old TV.
MARY MOONEY: So would I if we had one. But we
haven't.
DEREK: Ain't you? Oh well, you'll have to come
round my house sometime and have a watch of
mine. Come round this afternoon if you like.
MARY MOONEY: Oh, I don't know.
DEREK: You're more than welcome, darling. I'm
not doing nothing special this afternoon. I would
have gone in to work but I had such a diabolical
neuralgia this morning I couldn't lift me head off
the pillow. You gonna come then?
MARY MOONEY: D'you really want me to?
DEREK: I wouldn't ask you, would I?
MARY MOONEY: All right then. I suppose I can
always go to the library another day.
DEREK: Course you can. Come on then, Rhonda.
Let's go and get the bus.

Scene 16

Derek's House.

*Mary Mooney is sitting on the settee watching 'Bill
and Ben the Flowerpot Men' which is just ending.
Derek comes in carrying a glass of orange liquid
and a very large biscuit tin.*

DEREK: Here are, mate. Glass of Tizer gone flat.
That's all she had in the cupboard.
MARY MOONEY: Oh, thanks.

(Derek switches off the television.)

DEREK: Cor, bleedin' chronic, ain't it. I don't know why they can't put nothing decent on of a daytime. Still, we've got 'The Cisco Kid' coming on a bit later, if you fancy watching that.

MARY MOONEY: I don't know what it's all about. I've only ever seen 'Carroll Levis's Discoveries'.

DEREK: That's always good for a giggle if nothing else.

MARY MOONEY: Where's your Mum, Derek?

DEREK: Down the biscuit factory, ain't she. She does afternoons down there. *(He offers her the tin.)* Want one?

MARY MOONEY: Oh, thanks.

(Derek takes off his Edwardian jacket.)

DEREK: You can't move in this house for biscuits. She brings 'em home by the bleedin' sackful. The old man goes round flogging 'em to all the neighbours. *(He sits down very close to Mary Mooney and puts his arm around the back of the settee.)* You . . . er . . . you going out with a regular bloke at all?

MARY MOONEY: No.

DEREK: You must have been out with a feller or two in your time.

MARY MOONEY: Oh yes.

DEREK: Yeah, you would have done of course, a fair looking bird like yourself. I expect you've had quite a few blokes after you, eh?

(Mary Mooney goes all coy.)

DEREK *(putting his hands up to his eyes)*: Cor, that sunshine ain't half playing havoc with me neuralgia. I'm gonna have to draw them curtains.

(He gets up. BLACKOUT.)

MARY MOONEY: I can't see a thing.
DEREK: No, well, I'm supposed to lie down in a darkened room whenever I get one of me attacks.
MARY MOONEY: Have you taken any aspirin?
DEREK: No. They don't do no good. Where are you? M Mooney. Oh! Oh, there you are.

(Pause.)

What's the matter, darling?
MARY MOONEY: I thought you were supposed to be Mary McGinty's boyfriend.
DEREK: She's in Fatima, ain't she.
MARY MOONEY: She will be coming back though.
DEREK: Look, darling, I don't wanna talk about her when I'm with you. *(Pause. Derek tuts. Whispering.)* Cor, that's a choice little pair of bristol cities you got there.
MARY MOONEY: Oh no! No! No! *(Pause. Sounds of protest from Mary Mooney.)*
DEREK: Ssh! It's all right. We don't have to go the whole way. Not if you don't want to. Even if we did which I'm not saying we would, but just supposing we did, which we wouldn't of course, but if we did you wouldn't have to worry cos I have got something on me, know what I mean? Give us your hand. See what you're doing to me, darling. Cor, yeah. Now that's better than taking an aspirin. Cor.

INTERVAL

ACT TWO

Scene 1

Derek's House.

The curtains have been drawn back. Derek is combing his hair. Mary Mooney is sitting all hunched up on the settee. She avoids looking at Derek.

DEREK: Er . . . D'you reckon you can find your own way to the bus stop, darling?

MARY MOONEY: I don't know.

DEREK: Well, what you do is, you turn left outside the gate, then you go right at the bottom of the road. Then it's the first on the right, second on the left, second on the right. Go round by the garage and through the little alleyway. That brings you out to the butchers. Then you go left. No. I tell a lie. You go right. Walk down as far as the Coliseum, cross over the road and there's your bus stop. Right?

MARY MOONEY: I think so.

DEREK: You wouldn't mind hurrying up, would you, only I want to get the place straightened up before me Mum gets in.

(Mary Mooney puts her coat on.)

There's just one thing. Er . . . you wouldn't go saying nothing to Mary McGinty, would you?

MARY MOONEY: No.

DEREK: No, well just make sure you don't otherwise there could be a bit of bother and we don't want none of that. I have been known to get nasty before now, know what I mean? If you ever do bump into me anytime when I'm with her, just act a little bit casual like. All right?

(Mary Mooney nods.)

Right? You ready?

MARY MOONEY: I haven't got any money to get home with.

DEREK: Oh yeah. Here are. Here's a tanner. All right? Don't forget your library books. Ta ta, mate. *(He pats her on the bottom. She goes.)*

Scene 2

The Presbytery.

Father Mullarkey is sitting at his dinner table. He is eating a plate of sausage and mash. A plate of pudding is in front of him. Mary Mooney comes in.

FATHER MULLARKEY: Come in and sit down, Mary Mooney.

(She sits down at the table.)

Miss Gavigan tells me you want to see me on a very urgent matter. Is that right?

MARY MOONEY: Yes, Father.

FATHER MULLARKEY: D'you want a sausage? *(He holds one out on a fork.)*

MARY MOONEY: No thank you, Father.

FATHER MULLARKEY: Ah, go on and have one. She's given me too many, the way she always does. *(He puts the sausage on a side plate and pushes it towards her.)* Miss Gavigan is only used to feeding big hulks of men. She's eleven brothers back at home not one of them under eighteen stone. Help yourself to the Lot's wife.

MARY MOONEY: The what, Father?

FATHER MULLARKEY: The salt. And put a good dollop of ketchup on it. What did you want to see me about?

MARY MOONEY: I must go to Confession, Father. Urgently.

FATHER MULLARKEY: Well you can't go to Confession tonight. The church is all locked up and I have to get down to the Off Licence.

MARY MOONEY: But I've committed a mortal sin, Father.

FATHER MULLARKEY: Ah, well, make an Act of Contrition and come up to Confession on Saturday. Could you manage a half of this old steamed pudding at all?

MARY MOONEY: No thank you, Father.

FATHER MULLARKEY: Ah, come on and help me out. I keep telling that woman don't be giving me any more of them steamed puddings. But she doesn't take a blind bit of notice. *(He gives her half the pudding. Then he burps.)* Beg your pardon. *(He lights up a cigarette.)*

MARY MOONEY: Father, I've committed a very serious mortal sin.

FATHER MULLARKEY: Ah well, it'll surely keep till Saturday.

MARY MOONEY: I might die before then.

FATHER MULLARKEY: Not at all. A big strapping girl like yourself in the best of health.

MARY MOONEY: But I might have an accident, Father. And if I did and I died I'd be sent straight down to Hell. *(She bursts into tears.)*

FATHER MULLARKEY: Oh come on now. You can't have done anything that bad, surely.

MARY MOONEY: Oh I have, Father. I have.

FATHER MULLARKEY: Well, if it's that serious you'd better make a quick Confession now. Come over here and kneel down.

MARY MOONEY: In here, Father?

FATHER MULLARKEY: It's as good a place as any.
I'll turn me back on you.

*(She kneels down by the side of his chair. He turns
away from her.)*

MARY MOONEY: Bless me, Father, for I have
sinned. It is five days since my last Confession.

FATHER MULLARKEY: Never mind about the venial
sins. Save them up for the next time. Just
concentrate on the big mortal sin.

MARY MOONEY: I . . . er . . . I . . . er . . . *(Pause)* I
. . . er . . . I . . . er . . .

FATHER MULLARKEY: Was it a sin against holy
purity?

MARY MOONEY: Yes, Father.

FATHER MULLARKEY: I thought as much. With
another person?

MARY MOONEY: Yes, Father.

FATHER MULLARKEY: A male or a female?

MARY MOONEY: A male, Father.

FATHER MULLARKEY: A boyfriend?

MARY MOONEY: Somebody else's boyfriend.

FATHER MULLARKEY: Indeed. What did you do
with him? Did you have sexual intercourse?

MARY MOONEY: No, Father, I don't think so.

FATHER MULLARKEY: You must surely know if
you did or you didn't. Unless . . . Were you drunk
at all?

MARY MOONEY: No, Father. But it was dark.

FATHER MULLARKEY: Did he force you to do anything?

MARY MOONEY: No, Father. But I didn't know
what he was going to do until he was actually
doing it.

FATHER MULLARKEY: He handled you, did he?

MARY MOONEY: Yes, Father.

FATHER MULLARKEY: How many times?

MARY MOONEY: I wasn't counting, Father.

FATHER MULLARKEY: More than once?

MARY MOONEY: Yes, Father.

FATHER MULLARKEY: And you think that's all he did?

MARY MOONEY: Yes, Father. But . . . but I did something impure as well.

FATHER MULLARKEY: What?

MARY MOONEY: I don't know exactly, Father. But I think he said it was a Twentieth Century-Fox.

FATHER MULLARKEY: What the devil?

MARY MOONEY: Oh, no it wasn't. It was a J Arthur Rank.

FATHER MULLARKEY: Glory be to God. I hope you're not going to be seeing this scoundrel ever again.

MARY MOONEY: No, Father.

FATHER MULLARKEY: You know you shouldn't be left alone in a room with any man.

MARY MOONEY: Yes, Father.

FATHER MULLARKEY: You must put the whole episode right out of your mind. If it ever comes into your mind uninvited you mustn't entertain it at all.

MARY MOONEY: No, Father.

FATHER MULLARKEY: Unless, of course, you think of it with disgust instead of delight. Do you?

MARY MOONEY: Yes, Father.

FATHER MULLARKEY: That's the idea. For your penance say five Our Fathers and five Hail Marys. Now make a good Act of Contrition. Oh my God . . .

MARY MOONEY: Oh my God because thou art so good I am very sorry that I have sinned against thee and by thy grace I will not sin again.

FATHER MULLARKEY: Ego te absolvo a peccatis

tuis, in nomine Patris et filii et Spiritus Sancti Amen. *(He gets up and puts on a pair of bicycle clips.)* I must be going out now. You can stay behind and say the Penance. I'll tell Miss Gavigan not to disturb you. Are you coming to the social on Saturday week?

MARY MOONEY: Yes, Father. I'll be coming with my mother and father.

FATHER MULLARKEY: Give my best regards to the two of them. *(He puts his hand into his pocket and brings out a booklet)* I wonder would you take a book of raffle tickets and see how many you can sell. We've a first prize of ten pounds. And the second is a bottle of whisky.

MARY MOONEY: Yes, Father. Thank you, Father.

FATHER MULLARKEY: Good girl. I'll leave you to it, then. Good night.

MARY MOONEY: Good night, Father.

(He goes off.)

Scene 3

The Garden.

Mother Peter is standing in front of the Girls who are sitting on the grass.

MOTHER PETER: The entire day will be devoted to prayer and contemplation. Father Mullarkey will give us a little talk followed by a collection for black babies in Africa. So bring in your sixpences and shillings. You may walk up and down and say the rosary, perhaps. Or sit down and read a good book. And I don't mean any old novel. I mean the biography of a saint or some other devotional work.

(Mother Basil comes in.)

Yes, Mother?

MOTHER BASIL: Carry on, please, Mother. I'll wait until you've finished.

MOTHER PETER: Absolute silence must be the rule for the whole day. And please do not resort to any preposterous sign language except in a case of absolute necessity. You will find the day will pass very quickly and the spiritual rewards will be very great indeed. Now, Mother Basil, can I help you at all?

MOTHER BASIL: I'm afraid I have a rather unpleasant duty to perform, Mother Peter. *(She reaches into her pocket and brings out a box of Tampax which she holds up)* This box of . . . of . . . things was found lying about on the floor of the downstairs cloakroom. I've been into 5B and 5C but no girl there has come forward to claim them. Indeed they have given me their word of honour that they know nothing about them at all. And I'm inclined to believe them, which means, I'm sorry to say, Mother Peter, that they must belong to a girl in 5A.

MOTHER PETER: I can't believe any girl in my form would dream of using such an immodest method of . . .

MOTHER BASIL: No self-respecting girl would abuse her body with such a contraption and that's a fact.

MOTHER PETER: Will the owner of this container please step forward and claim it.

(Long pause.)

I see. If this is to be the case then you will come to see me individually for questioning. I'll find out whose they are. I'll find out, so I will. And who-

ever it is let her shame be her only punishment.
GIRLS: Good morning, Father Mullarkey. Good
morning, Mother Thomas Aquinas.

Scene 4

The Garden.

*Father Mullarkey is standing behind a table.
Mother Aquinas is sitting to one side of him.*

FATHER MULLARKEY: When Adam bit into the
apple and defied his creator he put a plague upon
mankind forever after. The plague of original sin.
All babies emerge from the womb infected with
Adam's original sin. And there's only one way to
remove this sin. By the Sacrament of Baptism.
What happens to babies who die without receiving
Baptism? They are prevented from entering
Heaven. They must therefore go down into Hell.
Not into the wretched furnace, no. But into that
part of Hell known as Limbo. And what is it like
in Limbo? Is it anything like Purgatory? Not a bit
of it. In Purgatory the souls are punished by being
heated to a degree of real discomfort. But this is
only a temporary punishment. Sooner or later all
the souls in Purgatory will have earned themselves
a place up in Heaven. But the souls in Limbo must
stay where they are for all eternity. It's a bleak old
prison of a place so it is. The majority of babies in
Limbo are black, yellow and brown, and if it
wasn't for the wonderful work carried on by the
missionaries throughout the pagan world there'd
be many more babies piled up in Limbo. I'm going
to send round the mission box *(he picks it up and
rattles it)* and I hope it'll be filled to the brim. Now
wouldn't it be a marvellous idea if you started

your very own mission box at home. Think of a
little black baby and give him a name. Every week
put in a percentage of your pocket money and say
to yourself this is for Patrick or Joseph or Eamon
so that he can be baptised and grow up to be a
good Catholic. I want you to remember that
Baptism is the one Sacrament that doesn't have to
be administered by a priest. Anyone may baptise
in a case of necessity when a priest cannot be had.
If you should ever find yourself in the house of a
non-Catholic friend where there's a baby who
hasn't been baptised you'd do well to sprinkle
water on that baby's head and say 'I baptise thee
in the name of the Father and of the Son and of
the Holy Ghost. Amen.' And when you meet that
child above in Heaven you can be sure he'll come
up and shake you by the hand. Is it only babies
that are sent to Limbo? Mostly it is. Babies and
little children under the age of seven. After the age
of seven a child has reached the age of reason and
must decide for himself whether he wants to be
good or bad. If he's wicked he'll end up in Hell
like all other wicked persons. And it's the sins of
the flesh that put people into Hell, make no
mistake about it. The sins of the flesh. *(He bangs
on the table)* Now you may wonder about the sort
of Baptism administered to our poor misguided
brethren, who, though following the teachings of
Christ, do so within the confines of a false
religion. Is the quality of their Baptism as good as
our own. Indeed it is, bearing in mind that anyone
can administer Baptism. We must never consider
non-Catholics to be in any way inferior to ourselves.
God knows it is through no fault of their own that
they were born into heretical households. We must
continue to pray hard for Christian unity. Pray
that the heresy be removed from their hearts and
that they may be guided back under the infallible

umbrella of Rome. There is no other church but
the Catholic Church. The Catholic Church is the
one true religion. *(He bangs on the table)* The one
and only Ark of Salvation for the whole of
Mankind. *(He bangs on the table again.)*

GIRLS: Good morning, Father Mullarkey. Good
morning, Mother Thomas Aquinas.

Scene 5

The Garden.

*The Girls are in summer uniform. Mary Gallagher,
Mother Peter and Mary Mooney are walking up
and down in silence with rosary beads in their
hands. Mother Peter's lips are moving. She makes
the Sign of the Cross and goes off. Mary
Gallagher does a 'V' sign after her.*

MARY GALLAGHER: Oh Jesus, I'm bored out of
my mind.

(Mary Mooney puts her finger to her lips.)

Don't tell me you're not bored.

(Mary Mooney shrugs her shoulders.)

I'm sure they're trying to drive us mad. It's a well
known fact that too much silence can drive a
person insane. It's all right for them. They're
already round the bend. Especially Mother Peter.
If she hadn't put herself into a convent somebody
would have locked her up in a looney bin.

MARY MOONEY: Sssh!

MARY GALLAGHER: It's all right. There's nobody
about. Although they've probably put a load of

microphones into the bushes. And they're sure to have stationed Reverend Mother down in the basement on a periscope. Why the hell can't they have their idiotic retreats in the holidays. D'you want a Smartie? *(She takes a tube out of her pocket.)*

(Mary Mooney shakes her head.)

Oh have one, will you, for Christ's sake. We're not supposed to be fasting, you know. Hold out your hand. *(She pours some Smarties into Mary Mooney's hand)* Are you keeping quiet just to annoy me, by any chance?

(Mary Mooney shakes her head.)

I suppose you're scared of getting caught.

MARY MOONEY: No I'm not.

MARY GALLAGHER: You are.

MARY MOONEY: No I'm not.

MARY GALLAGHER: You are.

MARY MOONEY: I'm not.

MARY GALLAGHER: Well, what are you being so holy for? Come to think of it, though, you always have been a bit that way inclined.

MARY MOONEY: I have not. I'm no more holy than you are.

MARY GALLAGHER: Not much. I doubt if you've ever committed a genuine mortal sin in all your life.

MARY MOONEY: Oh yes I have. I've definitely committed one.

MARY GALLAGHER: Oooh, one. That's a lot isn't it.

MARY MOONEY: Why, how many have you committed?

MARY GALLAGHER: Millions.

MARY MOONEY: Have you really?

MARY GALLAGHER: Yes. You know that box of Tampax?

MARY MOONEY: Yes.

MARY GALLAGHER: They were mine.

MARY MOONEY: They weren't!

MARY GALLAGHER: They were, you know.

MARY MOONEY: Why didn't you go up and claim them?

MARY GALLAGHER: You must be joking. She didn't suspect me for a minute.

MARY MOONEY: Who got the blame in the end?

MARY GALLAGHER: Maria Zajaczkowski.

MARY MOONEY: That wasn't very fair.

MARY GALLAGHER: She's not bothered. They could just as easily have been hers. She went red when Mother Peter cross-examined her. Did you know she's going out with a really old bloke?

MARY MOONEY: No.

MARY GALLAGHER: Yes. He must be at least twenty-five. He hangs about outside the gate with a little black bag. He must be a doctor. Nearly everybody in our form has got some sort of a bloke. It's time you got yourself one, isn't it.

MARY MOONEY: You think I've never been out with a bloke, don't you?

MARY GALLAGHER: Well you haven't, have you?

MARY MOONEY: Oh yes I have, if you want to know.

MARY GALLAGHER: Oh yes? Since when?

MARY MOONEY: Since just after Easter actually.

MARY GALLAGHER: How come you've kept so quiet about it, then?

MARY MOONEY: If I told you something really confidential would you promise to keep it a secret?

MARY GALLAGHER: Yes, of course.

MARY MOONEY: Would you swear to God never

to tell a soul?

MARY GALLAGHER: Yes. You can trust me.

MARY MOONEY: Cross your heart and hope to die.

MARY GALLAGHER: All right.

MARY MOONEY: You know when you were in Fatima?

MARY GALLAGHER: Yes.

MARY MOONEY: Well I met a bloke in the street and he asked me to go to his house with him, so I did.

MARY GALLAGHER: What, you let a bloke pick you up just like that. And you didn't even know who he was?

MARY MOONEY: No. I mean yes. I did know who he was. That's just the trouble. You know who he is too.

MARY GALLAGHER: Who?

MARY MOONEY: Promise you won't tell anyone in all the world. Especially not Mary McGinty.

MARY GALLAGHER: Why not her?

MARY MOONEY: Well, see, this bloke . . . It was her boyfriend Derek.

MARY GALLAGHER: Cor! No!

MARY MOONEY: Yes.

MARY GALLAGHER: Are you sure you're not making it up? I can't imagine you and him together.

MARY MOONEY: Well we were.

MARY GALLAGHER: Christ. She'd go berserk if she ever knew.

MARY MOONEY: You won't tell her will you? Please.

MARY GALLAGHER: I wouldn't dare. Did he ask to see you again?

MARY MOONEY: I wouldn't want to see him again not as long as I live. He's horrible.

MARY GALLAGHER: Is he? How come Mary McGinty's so mad about him then?

MARY MOONEY: He was nice at first. But then he turned nasty. Well not exactly nasty, but rude. Do all blokes try to do rude things to girls?

MARY GALLAGHER: The majority of them, yes, if they get the chance.

MARY MOONEY: Has Cuthbert ever tried to be impure?

MARY GALLAGHER: He never thinks about anything else.

MARY MOONEY: But he's a Catholic.

MARY GALLAGHER: Yes. Terrible, isn't it.

MARY MOONEY: You've been going out with Cuthbert for a long time, haven't you?

MARY GALLAGHER: What about it?

MARY MOONEY: Is that why you've committed so many mortal sins? Because he makes you?

MARY GALLAGHER: He doesn't make me. What a thing to say. It's the devil who makes you commit sins.

MARY MOONEY: That Derek must be possessed by the devil!

MARY GALLAGHER: Why? What did he do? Oh dear, you haven't lost your priceless virginity, have you?

MARY MOONEY: No. No . . . but . . .

MARY GALLAGHER: What?

MARY MOONEY: I couldn't possibly tell you.

MARY GALLAGHER: I've probably heard it all before.

MARY MOONEY: I couldn't possibly say what he did. But I've got it written down in my diary. *(She takes a book out of her pocket)* I have to keep it with me all the time in case anyone should ever find it. My Mum'd swing for me if she saw it. You can have a look at it if you like.

MARY GALLAGHER *(reading the diary)*: Cor, fancy letting a bloke do that to you the first time you ever go out with him.

MARY MOONEY: I didn't want him to. But he was a lot stronger than me. He's not like a boy, that Derek. He's a proper big man, you know.

MARY GALLAGHER: They will usually stop if you tell them to.

MARY MOONEY: I did. But he said we all know no means yes. That doesn't make any sense though, does it?

MARY GALLAGHER: It means you liked what he was doing but you didn't want to admit it.

MARY MOONEY: I did not like it.

MARY GALLAGHER: Didn't you? You must be abnormal then.

MARY MOONEY: I'm not.

MARY GALLAGHER: You must be. Everybody else likes it.

MARY MOONEY: Well it wasn't all that bad, I suppose.

MARY GALLAGHER: You want to find a bloke of your own. It's not the done thing to go round borrowing other people's.

MARY MOONEY: Oh, shut your rotten face. And give me back my diary. *(She snatches the diary and goes marching off.*

Mary McGinty is sitting on a bench with a book. Mary Gallagher goes up and sits next to her.)

MARY MCGINTY: How much longer have we got?

MARY GALLAGHER: Another couple of hours.

MARY FLANAGAN: Shhh.

MARY MCGINTY: Oh, Christ. I can't stand it. Have you finished your book?

MARY GALLAGHER: No. I haven't read a word of it. I've been talking to Mary Mooney.

MARY MCGINTY: I bet she was keeping her mouth well shut.

MARY GALLAGHER: Not exactly, no. Actually

there's more to that girl than you might think.

MARY MCGINTY: How d'you mean?

MARY GALLAGHER: She's a bit of a dark horse if you did but know.

MARY MCGINTY: Oh yes?

MARY GALLAGHER: I've found out she's got a dead sly streak in her.

MARY MCGINTY: Really?

MARY GALLAGHER: I know it for a fact. I can't very well tell you what I've found out about her, though. I would tell you only it's something to do with you and you wouldn't like it if you knew.

MARY MCGINTY: You might as well tell me. Go on.

MARY GALLAGHER: You'll only be furious. I warn you. It's something that happened while we were away in Fatima.

MARY MCGINTY: What? Come on?

MARY GALLAGHER: Well . . . she met a bloke in the street and went back to his house with him.

MARY MCGINTY: What's that got to do with me?

MARY GALLAGHER: It was your Derek. The bloke.

MARY MCGINTY: My Derek?

MARY GALLAGHER: Yes.

MARY MCGINTY: He wouldn't look at Mary Mooney.

MARY GALLAGHER: He might not look at her. But he definitely went and touched her.

MARY MCGINTY: Is that what she told you?

MARY GALLAGHER: She's got it all written down in her diary. All the sordid details.

MARY MCGINTY: What, you mean you've read it?

MARY GALLAGHER: Yes.

MARY MCGINTY *(jumping up)*: I'll bleedin' kill her. Little slag. And him. Filthy dirty sod. *(She goes marching off.*

Mother Basil and Mary Mooney are walking up and down saying the rosary silently. Mary McGinty is pacing up and down on her own. Mother Basil goes off. Mary McGinty goes over to Mary Mooney.)

MARY MCGINTY: I wanna talk to you.

MARY MOONEY: What about?

MARY MCGINTY: You know bleedin' well what about.

MARY MOONEY: I suppose you've been gossiping with your friend Mary Gallagher.

MARY MCGINTY: Haven't I just.

MARY MOONEY: She promised me she wouldn't tell you.

MARY MCGINTY: You should know better than to open your big fat mouth, shouldn't you, you little scrubber. Making out you're so frigging holy. Why can't you get a bloke of your own?

MARY MOONEY: Look, I'm sorry. I didn't mean . . . Oh, God, I wish I'd never.

MARY MCGINTY: You gonna let me have a look at that dirty little diary of yours?

MARY MOONEY: No.

MARY MCGINTY: Why not? You let Mary Gallagher see it. You can just let me see it and all. It's my bleedin' bloke you've been scribbling about. Where is it? *(She tries to take the diary out of Mary Mooney's pocket. Mary Mooney struggles but Mary McGinty gets hold of it.)*

MARY MOONEY: Give it back. You mustn't read it. Please give it back to me. Please.

(Mother Basil comes marching along. Mary McGinty drops the diary and goes off. Mother Basil comes up to Mary Mooney and shakes her fist at her. They both bend down to pick up the diary and their heads collide. Mother Basil gives Mary Mooney a punch. She falls down. Mother Basil starts kicking her. Mother Basil goes marching off in a temper with the diary but

turns round and comes back again to deliver one final kick.)

Scene 6

Derek's House.

Mary McGinty is sitting on the settee. Derek is pacing up and down, chain smoking.

DEREK: Look, I've told you a hundred times she didn't mean nothing. And I didn't do nothing neither. Nothing much anyway. I mean, be fair. She come up and spoke to me in the street. I never knew her from Old Mother Hubbard, did I? You know how it is when I get me attacks of neuralgia. Me eyesight gets affected, don't it? I couldn't make out what she looked like in the street. She could have been a really beautiful bird for all I knew. And I couldn't help feeling chuffed, what with you being miles away. When I got her inside the house and see what she really looked like I had to draw the curtains double quick. Well, I'm only human, know what I mean? Not like you. No. You're about as warm as a Lyons choc ice you are, darling. It's about bleedin' time you faced up to the fact that I've been impairing me capabilities for the sake of respecting you. It's a wonder I ain't done myself some sort of a permanent mischief. Not that I get any credit for it, oh no. It's all been a bleedin' waste of time. It's quite obvious you don't wanna go out with me no more.
MARY MCGINTY: I didn't say that.
DEREK: You don't have to say it. I'm going by the way you're acting towards me.
MARY MCGINTY: Did she sit on this?

DEREK: I don't remember.

MARY MCGINTY: Yes you do. Which side did she sit on.

DEREK: The other side.

MARY MCGINTY: You sure?

DEREK: What difference does it make? Me Mum's been over it with the Hoover tons of time since then. She's got one of them attachments that gets right into all the corners.

MARY MCGINTY: I'm just wondering how many other birds you've been out with behind my back while you're supposed to have been going out with me.

DEREK: None.

MARY MCGINTY: I don't believe you. Anyway, I've heard otherwise.

DEREK: Who from?

MARY MCGINTY: Somebody who's seen you about.

DEREK: Well . . . they was only a couple of little tarts. I mean, I don't go looking for it, darling. But if it happens to come my way . . . I can't very well help myself, can I? And who in this world would blame me the way you behave towards me. You know my old Nan was half Italian, don't you?

MARY MCGINTY: Never mind your Nan. How many girls did you say you'd been out with?

DEREK: I told you. A couple.

MARY MCGINTY: How many's a couple?

DEREK: I don't know. Five or six.

MARY MCGINTY: What were their names?

DEREK: Gloria, Joyce. I don't know. I wasn't bothered about their names. Here, what's all this interrogation in aid of? I don't ask you no questions, do I. For all I know you could have been running about with all sorts of greasy foreigners out in Fatima.

MARY MCGINTY: Oh yeah? Some chance of that

with the nuns breathing down our necks day and night.

DEREK: That's what you tell me.

MARY MCGINTY: I did not go out with anyone in Fatima or anywhere else. But I bleedin' well would in the future.

DEREK: Would you?

MARY MCGINTY: You bet your life I would.

DEREK: Oh well. Please yourself.

MARY MCGINTY: Don't worry. I will.

(Pause.)

DEREK: Er . . . you wouldn't . . . er . . . No. It's just a thought. No. I mean . . . You can laugh if you like but how about . . . no. How about . . . er . . . d'you . . . er . . . d'you . . . d'you . . . er . . . d'you fancy getting engaged?

MARY MCGINTY: What?

DEREK: You heard.

MARY MCGINTY: Are you in love with me?

DEREK: Eh? *(He takes out his comb and combs his hair)*

MARY MCGINTY: Yes or no.

DEREK *(doing a terrible impersonation of Elvis Presley singing and gyrating)*:

    Well bless my soul what's wrong with me?
      I'm itching like a man up a fuzzy tree.
  My friends say I'm acting just as wild as a bug.
      I'm in love, Ooh, I'm all shook up.
    Uh huh huh, uh huh, yeah, yeah, yeah.

MARY MCGINTY: You don't have to take the piss.

DEREK: I wasn't in actual fact. I meant what I was singing.

MARY MCGINTY: Oh. Are you offering to buy me a ring by any chance?

DEREK: Yeah. Don't expect nothing too flash, though. I ain't no millionaire.

MARY MCGINTY: Does that mean you'd actually

want to get married some time?

DEREK: I probably would in a couple of years.

MARY MCGINTY: Before or after you do your National Service?

DEREK: There won't be none of that, darling. No. Not with this neuralgia.

MARY MCGINTY: I hope you get away with it.

DEREK: I will.

MARY MCGINTY: Why d'you want to marry me, Derek?

DEREK: Be a bit of a laugh, wouldn't it.

MARY MCGINTY: Oh, thanks very much.

DEREK: Well . . . I just happen to think you're one of the best looking birds I've seen knocking about Willesden for a long time. And I wouldn't mind kipping down in the same bed as you every night. If it was all right with you.

MARY MCGINTY: I wouldn't mind getting engaged to you.

DEREK: Oh. I didn't think you'd want to somehow.

MARY MCGINTY: Don't you want me to, then?

DEREK: Course I do, darling. I wouldn't have asked you, would I?

MARY MCGINTY: Well I've said I would.

DEREK: Yeah, well that's all right then, ain't it.

MARY MCGINTY: How would you feel about changing your religion, though?

DEREK: Do what? Leave off, mate.

MARY MCGINTY: But if you really want to marry me, Derek, you'll have to marry me in a Catholic Church.

DEREK: Oh no! No chance. No. That's definitely out, darling. I was thinking more along the lines of a register office myself.

MARY MCGINTY: If I got married in a register office I'd be living in sin in the eyes of the Catholic Church.

DEREK: All right, so change over to the Church of England.

MARY MCGINTY: Look, Derek, I've told you before. It's once a Catholic always a Catholic and that's all there is to it. We're not even allowed to set foot inside the door of a Protestant church without getting permission off a Bishop.

DEREK: No, but you expect people to come crawling into your churches whenever it suits you, oh yes.

MARY MCGINTY: That's only because the Catholic Church is the real Christian Church. In fact it's the only proper religion in the world. The others are all phoney.

DEREK: Is that right? Who said so, eh? Who laid that one down?

MARY MCGINTY: Jesus.

DEREK: He's got some cheek, ain't he. The only religion, eh? That's a downright diabolical insult to all the people in this country who go toddling off to the Church of England of a Sunday morning. And that includes my Aunt Ada and my Uncle Ernie. And my cousin Freda. Yea, and the Queen. They're all in the wrong, are they? And the Irish are in the right? Yeah? Rhubarb. Fucking rhubarb, darling. And I don't intend to apologise for saying that word in front of you. And what about all the other people in the world, eh? The Hindus and Mohammedans and the Four by Twos. They don't count for nothing with Jesus, do they? Oh no, Jesus only cares about the Irish. Anybody else is just a load of bleedin' riff raff. He come all the way down to Earth, did he, all the way to Nazareth for the benefit of the bleedin' Irish. Yeah. Very likely. Why didn't he go straight to Dublin, eh? Why not? He could have had a great time changing all the water into Guinness and dancing about to ceilidh bands.

MARY MCGINTY: Oh, shut up, Derek. I can't help the way I was brought up. I've got to think of my Mum and Dad. How would they feel if I went and got married out of the Church.

DEREK: And what about my Mum and Dad? Of course, I realise they're only a pair of little old Protestants. It don't matter about them having to get stunk out with incense and having to listen to a load of hocus fucking pocus. No. Don't worry about them.

MARY MCGINTY: Oh, sod you, Derek.

DEREK: Sod you and all, mate.

(Mary McGinty gets up and grabs her coat.)

MARY MCGINTY: I hope they put you in the bleedin' army and shave off all your hair.

DEREK: Thanks.

(She moves off but he goes after her and gets hold of her.)

Come here you silly cow. Look, why can't we just leave it at getting engaged and save all the rest of the rubbish for later on.

MARY MCGINTY: No. It's something that has to be settled now.

DEREK: Well I ain't changing into no Catholic darling. I just ain't got it in me.

MARY MCGINTY: You don't have to change. But I have to get married in a Catholic church.

(He puts his arms around her. His hands go wandering and she moves them as fast as they wander.)

DEREK: What if I said I might. They wouldn't expect nothing of me, would they?

MARY MCGINTY: You'd have to sign a document to promise you'd bring all your children up as Catholics.

DEREK: All me what? Here, hang about. You're being a little bit previous, ain't you. It just so happens I ain't all that struck on little nippers with nappies full of squashed up turds.

MARY MCGINTY: But we'd have to have children if we got married.

DEREK: Yeah. One maybe. Or possibly two. But I draw the line at fucking football teams. Er . . . sorry about using that word. But I've seen enough of them Irish women in Kilburn. Two in the pram. Three more hanging on to the handle. And half a dozen more waiting outside the boozer for the Daddy to come rolling out. No. You have your Catholic wedding, mate, and I'll have me packet of three. All right?

Scene 7

Cuthbert's House.

Cuthbert is lying on the settee. He is wearing a silk dressing gown, school socks and carpet slippers. Mary Gallagher is sitting on the floor with a bottle of whisky by the side of her. They each have a glass of whisky and slightly slurred speech. Cuthbert is smoking a Senior Service cigarette in a holder.

CUTHBERT *(holding out his glass)*: Pass the bottle up, would you. It's time I had a refill.

MARY GALLAGHER: You'll be lucky. It's nearly all gone. *(She shows him the empty bottle.)*

CUTHBERT: We haven't drunk all that, have we? Fucking hell. I was hoping to top it up with water and put it back in the cupboard.

MARY GALLAGHER: You wouldn't have got away with that.

CUTHBERT: I've done it before enough times. He drinks so much himself he doesn't know what he's drinking half the time. And he'll be completely out of his mind by the time he comes rolling back from County Mayo.

MARY GALLAGHER: And your Mum'll still be crying.

CUTHBERT: Yeah. Christ knows what for. She's been waiting for the old faggot to snuff it for the past twenty years.

MARY GALLAGHER: Did you know your grannie very well?

CUTHBERT: I only met her a couple of times when I was a little kid. I remember she had a beard. And bunions. Two of the biggest bunions you ever saw in your life trying to force their way out of the side of each boot. Apparently she never used to wear any drawers. Whenever she wanted to go for a piddle she'd just walk out to the cowshed, stand with her legs apart and let it flow. I can well believe it. They never had any toilets when I was taken over there as a kid. You had to sit on a smelly old bucket and wipe your arse with a handful of shamrock. Or whatever it is that grows over there. I'm bloody glad I didn't have to go this time.

MARY GALLAGHER: My Mum and Dad would never have trusted me on my own for a whole week.

CUTHBERT: They didn't have much choice. I couldn't very well leave my exams.

MARY GALLAGHER: One of them would have stayed behind in our house. They're a hell of a lot more suspicious than yours.

CUTHBERT: That's because you're a girl.

MARY GALLAGHER: Yeah. You're probably right. I only hope they don't go checking up to see if I'm at Mary McGinty's tonight.

CUTHBERT: Oh, sod 'em. Could you do me a big favour? See if there's anything else to drink in the cupboard.

(Cuthbert hurriedly takes out a packet of contraceptives and studies the instructions while she is at the cupboard.)

MARY GALLAGHER: There's no more whisky.

CUTHBERT: I know, worse luck.

MARY GALLAGHER: There's one bottle of Guinness. And apart from that it's mostly just dregs.

CUTHBERT: You might as well get it all out and we'll finish it up.

MARY GALLAGHER: Are you sure you won't get into trouble?

CUTHBERT: I'll think about that when the time comes. We'll have half the Guinness each and we can top it up with the various dregs. *(Mary Gallagher pours out the drinks)* I'll have to go and buy another bottle of whisky though. She's left me forty-five bob for food and stuff. A bottle of whisky is what? Thirty-six bob. Christ, I won't have much left over, will I.

MARY GALLAGHER: You could always come round to our house for dinner one night.

CUTHBERT: I wouldn't mind. But your Mum doesn't like me very much, does she?

MARY GALLAGHER: It's not you she doesn't like as much as your language.

CUTHBERT: Eh?

MARY GALLAGHER: She says it's a bit too ripe for a boy of your age.

CUTHBERT: What does she mean, ripe?

MARY GALLAGHER: She said she heard you

swearing in our front room.

CUTHBERT: She shouldn't be fucking listening, should she.

MARY GALLAGHER: You might know they'd listen when you're in there with me. And they look through the keyhole. It's only to be expected.

CUTHBERT: Wait till she hears I'm going to be a priest.

MARY GALLAGHER: You're not going to be any priest.

CUTHBERT: Oh yes I am. I went into Canon O'Flynn the other day and told him I'd got a vocation.

MARY GALLAGHER: What did he say to that?

CUTHBERT: He said he wasn't at all surprised. He'd guessed it all along.

MARY GALLAGHER: I bet you didn't tell him your views on celibacy.

CUTHBERT: There's no reason why I should. He hasn't told me his.

MARY GALLAGHER: They're bound to be slightly more conventional than yours. How could you possibly be a priest.

CUTHBERT: I can. And I will. There's nothing else I want to do. *(He sings)* Credo in unum Deum, Patrem omnipotentem, factorem caeli et terrae, visibilium omnium, et invisibilium. Et in unum Dominum . . .

MARY GALLAGHER: Oh, shut up, will you. I hear enough of that every Sunday.

CUTHBERT: Well I don't. I never get tired of the Mass.

MARY GALAGHER: Mother Peter says they'll be saying it in English before another decade is out.

CUTHBERT: What? They'd better not or I'll be kicking up the most appalling stink. They wouldn't change it, would they? They couldn't. It'd be no better than the Church of England. I'd have to go over to the Russian Orthodox. Or the Greek. No, they couldn't possibly change it. It's only a ridiculous rumour.

MARY GALLAGHER: It might not be such a bad idea. At least ordinary people would be able to understand it.

CUTHBERT: Huh. They can understand the Stations of the Cross and look how boring they are.

MARY GALLAGHER: You'd have to say them if you became a priest.

CUTHBERT: Only during Lent. I could always speed them up a bit or miss a couple out. Nobody'd notice. I can't expect to enjoy every duty I'd have to perform.

MARY GALLAGHER: How do you feel about hearing Confessions?

CUTHBERT: I'd never ask anyone 'How many times?' *(He yawns.)* I think it's time for bed.

MARY GALLAGHER: It's not. It's only half past eight.

CUTHBERT: You'd better go out by the back door in the morning. Just to be on the safe side. In case one of the neighbours happens to see you.

MARY GALLAGHER: I'll go straight round to Mary McGinty's and go to Mass with her.

CUTHBERT: Are you any good at washing?

MARY GALLAGHER: What do you mean?

CUTHBERT: Well you know my bed's only a little one. It's the same one I've had since I was six. We could go in my Mum and Dad's only I'd have to put some clean sheets on afterwards. There's one or two shirts I'd like washing as well. And some socks.

MARY GALLAGHER: Oh. All right.

CUTHBERT: Shall we go?

MARY GALLAGHER: Not yet. You will still respect me tomorrow won't you, Cuthbert?

CUTHBERT: Yes, of course.

MARY GALLAGHER: D'you promise?
CUTHBERT: Yes. Come on. I've got to be serving on the altar at seven o'clock Mass tomorrow morning.

Scene 8

A Side Room.

Mr Emanuelli is sitting on a chair. Mary Mooney is standing in front of him, singing. He is conducting her with one of his walking sticks. She is wearing Nanki-Poo's Japanese costume with a false bald head and a pigtail.

MARY MOONEY *(singing)*:
  And if you call for a song of the sea
   We'll heave the capstan round
 With a yeo heave ho, for the wind is free
 Her anchor's a-trip and her helm's a-lee
  Hurrah for the homeward bound.
MR EMANUELLI *(singing)*: Yeo-ho, heave ho. Hurrah for the homeward bound.
MARY MOONEY: To lay aloft in a howling breeze
   May tickle a landsman's taste
  But the happiest hour a sailor sees
  Is when he's down at an inland town
  With his Nancy on his knees, yeo-ho
  And his arm around her waist.
MR EMANUELLI: Then man the capstan off we go
   As the fiddler swings us round
 With a yeo heave ho and a rum below
  Hurrah for the homeward bound
   With a yeo heave ho
   And a rum below
BOTH: Yeo ho, heave ho,
Yeo ho, heave ho, heave ho, heave ho, yeo ho.

(He hums) La, la, la, la . . .

MARY MOONEY: A wandering minstrel I
          A thing of shreds and patches
          Of ballads, songs and snatches
          And dreamy lullaby
          And dreamy lul la, lul la by
          Lul la by.

MR EMANUELLI: It will have to do. The vibrato is all up the creek but it's the best we can manage for the moment. But please, please do not let me see you slinking on to the stage and apologising to the audience for your presence.

MARY MOONEY: No, Sir.

MR EMANUELLI: Enjoy a little limelight for once in your life. You are such a down-trodden little missy, all the time in fear and trembling. What is it you are so frightened of?

MARY MOONEY: I don't know, Sir.

MR EMANUELLI: You must learn to stand up for yourself or you'll find yourself trampled right into the ruddy ground. It will be better for you when you go away from this dump of a sanctimonious institution. You will go and study music. Learn to control your respiration, sing in Italian and enlighten your ear. I will help you. Do you have a gramophone at home?

MARY MOONEY: Oh yes, Sir.

MR EMANUELLI: What do you listen to on it?

MARY MOONEY: Irish records mostly, Sir.

MR EMANUELLI: Huh. What ruddy use is that to you? Eh? No. You will come in the holidays to my house and you will hear Mozart and Puccini. Come the first Wednesday afternoon at three o'clock. Do you know how to get to Hendon Central?

MARY MOONEY: Yes, Sir. But . . .

MR EMANUELLI *(getting out pen and paper)*: Here is my address. Bang hard on the window and I will throw you out the key. It will be good to have a visitor. Nobody comes to see me any more. I can't say I blame them. I wouldn't come to see me myself. Why such a face? Eh? Do you think I am putting you into a catapult and firing you off into a career you don't want really?

MARY MOONEY: No, Sir.

MR EMANUELLI: Well I cannot guess what is in your mind. Does this leg of mine offend you?

MARY MOONEY: No, Sir.

MR EMANUELLI: I don't see why it shouldn't when it certainly offends me.

MARY MOONEY: I've got used to it, Sir.

MR EMANUELLI: Well I tell you something. I can't ever get used to it. Not ever. Every night when I go to bed I think yes in the morning it will suddenly be better. But no. It never is. What kind of God is he up there to send me such an affliction when I haven't done nothing to him?

MARY MOONEY: He often sends suffering to good people, Sir. It's really a privilege in disguise.

MR EMANUELLI: What kind of talk is that, eh? It's not the talk of a young girl. It's the talk of a blasted nun, I loathe and detest nuns. I despise every one of them in this building. They should be tied up with string, laid out in a line and raped by the local police. Take no notice. I am being cantankerous. Some days I feel so cantankerous I could take a machine-gun into the streets and shoot down the whole population of Hendon Central; I don't know why. I would never have come to this convent if I could have found a little work somewhere else.

MARY MOONEY: I'll pray for your leg to get better, Sir.

MR EMANUELLI: Thank you very much but don't bother. I've tried it myself. Candle after candle burning uselessly in front of a statue of St Francis

of Assisi. A million Hail Marys wafting up into
the empty atmosphere. Even a journey to
Lourdes, wouldn't you know. Never in all my life
did I experience such humiliation. Seeing myself
lumped in among so many wretched unfortunates.
I came hobbling home and decided it was time for
Maximilian Emanuelli to disappear from the face
of the earth. I was going to go by way of the gas
oven. With one hundred codein tablets inside my
belly. Every day I had a dress rehearsal, but there
never could be an actual performance. How could
there be? No matter how unbearable his precious
life on earth if a Catholic dares to put an end to it
himself there'll be a far worse existence waiting on
the other side. Huh. I don't believe a word of it
and yet I know it's true. I will be shouting for the
priest to come running with the Sacrament of
Extreme Unction as soon as I see the Angel of
Death approaching. I must be saved from the fires
of Hell even though I know I would find in Hell all
the people with whom I have anything in
common. Especially Rudolph who always said he
would happily burn in Hell, the swine. For
eighteen years he and I were together, all the time
laughing, mostly at other people. It's a good thing
he went on before me. He never would have stood
for this leg. You are too young and green to
comprehend such things but I hope in your life
one day there will be a Rudolph. But you won't
find him in Willesden or Harlesden or Neasden or
Acton or Dollis Hill. You must travel all over the
world and meet lots of fascinating people. And
you must learn to be fascinating yourself. You are
not a good-looking girl but you can cheat. With
the help of something colourful out of a bottle you
can soon enrich the miserliness of nature. *(He
sings.)* Paint the pretty face, dye the coral lip.
Emphasise the grace of her ladyship. *(He gets up.)*

Now I have to go and inspect the orchestra. You will show me a good performance, yes?

MARY MOONEY: Yes, Sir.

MR EMANUELLI *(taking a medal and chain out of his pocket)*: I have something nice for you. Here. It was given to me and now I give it to you with my very best wishes.

MARY MOONEY: Thank you, Sir. What is it?

MR EMANUELLI: The eye of Horus. *(He puts it round her neck)* Horus was an Egyptian god who roamed the earth a long, long time ago. He was highly esteemed by the pagans. Let him bring you a little bit of luck. *(He pats her on the shoulder and goes off. Mary Mooney wrenches the chain from her neck and hurls it across the room.)*

Scene 9

Mother Thomas Aquinas' Office.

Mother Thomas Aquinas is at her desk. Mary Gallagher is sitting in front of her.

MOTHER THOMAS AQUINAS: Well, congratulations, Mary Gallagher.

MARY GALLAGHER: Thank you, Mother Thomas.

MOTHER THOMAS AQUINAS: You've done extremely well and we're all very pleased with you indeed. You'll go into the academic sixth form next year and we'll work towards getting you a place at university. Have you any idea at all about what you might like to take up as a career?

MARY GALLAGHER: I've thought about working in a laboratory, Mother. And I've thought about teaching Physics and Chemistry.

MOTHER THOMAS AQUINAS: You could do a lot worse than teach, my dear. Do you know, I really miss the teaching myself, after so many years of it. I never imagined I'd be sitting behind a desk all day with so much responsibility on my shoulders. But God knows best of course. It isn't for me to question his methods. Ah well. You'll find things very different in the academic sixth. Would you like to be a prefect?

MARY GALLAGHER: I'm not sure, Mother.

MOTHER THOMAS AQUINAS: Well I'd like you to become a prefect and help me keep the younger girls on their toes. Do you know, I dread the new intake every September. At one time, before the war, we knew exactly the type of girl we'd be getting when parents had to pay fees to send their daughters here. But since a decision was taken for this school to be swallowed up in the state school system I have to take in any old pupil that passes the eleven plus. And I seem to get a more uncultivated crop every year. The children of African immigrants and God knows what else. I can't help wondering where it's all going to end. There's just one thing that worries me slightly about you, my dear, and that's your rather strange choice of companion. When you do go up to the sixth form you will be mixing with a different set of girls. You can look forward to a most satisfactory and perhaps even a brilliant future with the help of God. All the best to you now and have a very enjoyable holiday.

MARY GALLAGHER: Yes, Mother Thomas. Thank you, Mother Thomas. *(Exits)*

(Mary McGinty comes in and stands in front of Mother Thomas.)

MOTHER THOMAS AQUINAS: Well now, Mary McGinty, I'm sorry to have to say your examination results were very disappointing indeed. Do you get nervous during exams at all?

MARY MCGINTY: Yes, Mother. A bit.

MOTHER THOMAS AQUINAS: Your work has always been up to standard if not particularly original. It's a shame to see you ending up with such a poor record. Have you any thoughts on a career at all?

MARY MCGINTY: No, Mother.

MOTHER THOMAS AQUINAS: Well I'd like you to go into the Secretarial sixth form in September.

MARY MCGINTY: Er . . . No thank you, Mother. I'd rather not.

MOTHER THOMAS AQUINAS: I beg your pardon.

MARY MCGINTY: I'd rather leave school now, Mother Thomas.

MOTHER THOMAS AQUINAS: You can't possibly leave school now. You must get yourself qualified for some kind of job and maybe even acquire an A level into the bargain.

MARY MCGINTY: I don't want to be a Secretary, thank you, Mother.

MOTHER THOMAS AQUINAS: And what do you think you're going to be out in the world with no training of any kind and only the one solitary O level to your name.

MARY MCGINTY: I might go and work in a shop.

MOTHER THOMAS AQUINAS: You didn't come to Our Lady of Fatima for five years to learn how to stand behind the counter of a shop, my dear girl.

MARY MCGINTY: Well I wouldn't mind being a hairdresser.

MOTHER THOMAS AQUINAS: Jesus, Mary and Joseph, did you ever hear the like? A hairdresser.

MARY MCGINTY: Well the thing is, Mother, I'll probably be getting married quite soon.

MOTHER THOMAS AQUINAS: Indeed. Is this just wishful thinking? Or do you actually have a fiancé?

MARY MCGINTY: Yes, Mother.

MOTHER THOMAS AQUINAS: I take it he's a Catholic boy.

MARY MCGINTY: Er . . . not exactly, Mother. He might be changing his religion soon though.

MOTHER THOMAS AQUINAS: I see. Well we can never have enough converts, that's for sure. But you can't possibly think of marriage for a long time yet. You'll have to go out and earn some sort of living. And you never know when you might need to help your husband support the children. What does the young man do for a living?

MARY MCGINTY: He's a Co-op milkman, Mother.

MOTHER THOMAS AQUINAS: Indeed.

MARY MCGINTY: But what he really wants to be is a train driver. And that's what he's going to be soon. And then he'll be able to travel all over the place for nothing. And so will I when I'm married to him.

MOTHER THOMAS AQUINAS: Oh, take your head out of the clouds and come back down to earth, you silly girl. I'm certainly not going to accept your decision to leave school and go drifting into some dead-end job and wasting your life. And I'm sure your parents will be on my side. Be a good girl now and come back here in September and into the Secretarial sixth form even if it's only for the one year.

MARY MCGINTY: No, Mother. I don't want to.

MOTHER THOMAS AQUINAS: Never mind what you want or what you don't want. You'll do what I tell you to do.

MARY MCGINTY· No I won't. I don't have to. I'm leaving at the end of this term.

MOTHER THOMAS AQUINAS: Oh I think you'd better leave now, this minute, if that's how you're going to behave. Go on. Get out. Take your things home and don't bother coming back for the rest of

the term. You think you know what's best for
you, you don't want to be helped, well off you go
then. And I hope you end up in the gutter.
MARY MCGINTY *(jumping up and going to the
door)*: Yeah — and the same to you. You fucking
old cunt.

*(Mary McGinty runs away. Mother Thomas
Aquinas gets up and goes to dash after her but
comes back, makes the Sign of the Cross and says
a silent prayer. Mary Mooney comes in.)*

MOTHER THOMAS AQUINAS: Don't stand there
gawping at me like an idiot. Well, I see you've
done all right for yourself exam wise. Not that
there's any reason why you shouldn't have.
You've brain enough inside your head. The
question is where do you go from here? Mr
Emanuelli has told me you're keen to start
studying singing full time as soon as possible. He
seems to think you have the vocal equipment for
nothing less than the grand opera and I'm sure he
knows about such things having been in the
business himself. All I can say is you seem like a
different girl altogether up on the stage, so maybe
it'll be the makings of you. Now, if you were any
other girl with all these O level passes I'd have no
hesitation at all in sending you straight into the
academic sixth form in September. But taking into
account your past behaviour and keeping in mind
that you're aiming for a musical career, I see no
point at all in your remaining at this school. The
best course of action for you, I should think,
would be to go out and get yourself some little job
which would leave you time enough for lessons
with Mr Emanuelli. Unless, of course, your
parents have any objections. Have you discussed
your musical aspirations with them at any length?

MARY MOONEY: No, Mother Thomas.

MOTHER THOMAS AQUINAS: And for heaven's sake why not?

MARY MOONEY: I don't want to be a singer, Mother Thomas.

MOTHER THOMAS AQUINAS: But I spoke to Mr Emanuelli only yesterday and he was quite adamant . . .

MARY MOONEY: I haven't told him yet, Mother Thomas.

MOTHER THOMAS AQUINAS: You let that poor man spend hours of his time instructing you and going to no end of trouble on your behalf and now you want to turn round and tell him he needn't have bothered. Oh, Mary Mooney, isn't that just like your impudence.

MARY MOONEY: I don't get on with him very well, Mother Thomas.

MOTHER THOMAS AQUINAS: Well that's a fine thing to say when he has nothing but praise for you.

MARY MOONEY: I don't want to be left alone with him in his house, Mother Thomas. He's asked me to go there in the holidays.

MOTHER THOMAS AQUINAS: Indeed. It wouldn't be the first time you were alone with a man in his house, would it? *(She opens a drawer and brings out Mary Mooney's diary.)* At least not according to this diary of yours, which you may have back, but you needn't go looking for the two pages of obscenities because they've been ripped out and thrown into the boiler where they belong. You're on the right road to Hell, Mary Mooney.

MARY MOONEY: But I am still a virgin, Mother Thomas.

MOTHER THOMAS AQUINAS: Oh be quiet! You may also take back the Bible that you did not come forward to claim. I went through it very carefully indeed and besides finding several dubious passages underlined in pencil I also came across a Mass card for the soul of a certain Dominic Aloysius Mooney. You can be sure your sins will always find you out.

MARY MOONEY: Please, Mother Thomas, I . . . I . . .

MOTHER THOMAS AQUINAS: Well what is it? We haven't much time. Benediction will be starting in a minute.

MARY MOONEY: Please, Mother, I'd like to be a nun.

MOTHER THOMAS AQUINAS: Oh, would you now.

MARY MOONEY: Please, Mother. I've always wanted to be a nun. Ever since I was six years old.

MOTHER THOMAS AQUINAS: There was never a Catholic girl born that didn't want to be a nun at some stage of her developing years. But you're not a little girl now. You're a big girl with a great deal of experience. Go away now and be thankful you can sing for your supper.

MARY MOONEY: But, Mother, I have to be a nun. I want to be as perfect as I possibly can and be sure of getting a high place in Heaven.

MOTHER THOMAS AQUINAS: You haven't the necessary qualities, Mary Mooney. No. You're much more the type to go into show business.

MARY MOONEY: But, Mother, I want to give my voice back to Our Lord.

MOTHER THOMAS AQUINAS: What, fling it back in his face?

MARY MOONEY: No, Mother. Offer it up to him by singing only for him. Please Mother, could you help me, please? I don't know who else I can go to.

MOTHER THOMAS AQUINAS: I can't believe a creature like you could possibly have a vocation. And I can't imagine what order would accept you.

Certainly this one would not. Although there again . . . I don't know. I suppose we can't all be Maria Goretti. Don't you feel ashamed of yourself when you think of that wonderful virgin martyr?

MARY MOONEY: Yes, Mother Thomas.

MOTHER THOMAS AQUINAS: Saint Maria Goretti was only eleven years old when her purity was put to the test. In nineteen hundred and two. She, too, was left alone in a house with a man. A great lout of a fellow who tempted her again and again but she would not give in to him. And when he found he could persuade her by no other means he threatened her with a shoemaker's awl. But still she would not commit a sin. She would not. So he got mad and took up the weapon and stabbed her with it no less than fourteen times. Mary Mooney, if you really think you have a vocation pray to Saint Maria Goretti for a positive sign. Now, what about Mr Emanuelli? You'll have to tell him what you've just told me.

MARY MOONEY: Oh, I couldn't, Mother. I couldn't face him.

MOTHER THOMAS AQUINAS: Oh, but you'll have to. And I must have a word with your mother. Why does she never come near the school?

MARY MOONEY: She's always tired after work, Mother Thomas.

MOTHER THOMAS AQUINAS: What does your father do?

MARY MOONEY: Nothing, Mother. He's been retired for years.

MOTHER THOMAS AQUINAS: Is he a sick man?

MARY MOONEY: No, Mother. He's just old.

MOTHER THOMAS AQUINAS: Is he a great deal older than your mother?

MARY MOONEY: No, Mother. She's old too. She was nearly fifty when I was born. And now she's going to have another baby.

MOTHER THOMAS AQUINAS: Don't be so ridiculous. She can't be having a baby at that age.

MARY MOONEY: But she is, Mother. I know she is.

MOTHER THOMAS AQUINAS: If she is then she should be going into the Guinness Book of Records. Will you tell her to come and see me before the end of term.

MARY MOONEY: Yes, Mother Thomas.

MOTHER THOMAS AQUINAS: Now go into the chapel. Kneel down in front of the crucifix and offer yourself body and soul to Our Blessed Lord who died for you.

MARY MOONEY: Yes, Mother Thomas.

MOTHER THOMAS AQUINAS: And this is your very last chance, Mary Mooney, I hope you realise. Your very last chance. Go along now.

MARY MOONEY: Yes, Mother Thomas. Thank you Mother Thomas. Thank you very much indeed.

Scene 10

The Classroom.

Mother Peter is at her desk.

MOTHER PETER: When you come back in September you may wear nylon stockings and a smart grey skirt instead of a gymslip. But don't let me see any sign of lipstick or bits of old jewellery. Apart from a holy medal or a crucifix. Those of you going out into the world must remember that the devil will be beckoning to you from every corner. But you can just tell him to go to Hell because you're not going to be fooled by him and his wily ways. You're going to show him a shining example of Christian purity. Always be modest in manner, in speech and in costume. You may often be puzzled when you see decent young men hovering around young women who wear scanty clothes and say provocative things. But you can be sure that such women are really the object of those men's secret contempt. Oh yes, indeed. Remember that God made your body for himself. He lives in it and he may well want to use it for his own work later on when you marry, as a tabernacle for brand new life. All parts of the body are sacred but none more so than the parts connected with the mystery of motherhood. They should be treated with the greatest respect and guarded with absolute modesty. Scrupulous hygiene is, of course, vitally important and you need not imagine you are sinning when you sit in the bath and see yourself or touch yourself with the flannel. Just say a little prayer, think of Our Lady and remember that she had a body just like yours. Oh yes, and beware of indecent articles of news in what may otherwise appear to be innocent publications on sale in any shop. The *News of the World* is the one that springs most readily to mind. If you ever see the *News of the World* lying about on a bus or a train or in any public place don't hesitate to tear it up. And the very same applies to the *Daily Worker*. The rotten old rag of the Communists. Rip it into pieces. It's no easy task to live a good life in the adult world. We must take up our cross every day just like Our Blessed Lord and carry it with us wherever we go. And when God sends us any sickness or trouble we must accept it willingly and say 'Thy will be done. I take this for my sins.' And the best of luck to you. *(She makes the Sign of the Cross.)*

MOTHER PETER AND GIRLS OF 5A: In the Name of the Father and of the Son and of the Holy Ghost, Amen.

Jesus, Mary and Joseph I give you my heart and

my soul.

Jesus, Mary and Joseph assist me in my last agony.

Jesus, Mary and Joseph may I die in peace and in your blessed company. *(Sign of the Cross)*

In the Name of the Father and of the Son and of the Holy Ghost. Amen.

Scene 11

The Back of the Chapel.

A very large crucifix is hanging on the wall with candlesticks and a candle box by the side of it. Mary Mooney comes in, genuflects in the direction of the altar and kneels down in front of the crucifix and prays.

VOICES OFF *(singing)*:

> Tantum Ergo Sacramentum
> Vereremur cernui
> Et antiquum documetum
> Novo cedat ritui
> Praestet fides supplementum
> Sensuum defectui
> Genitori Genitoque
> Laus et jubilatio
> Salus honor virtus quoque
> Sit et benedictio
> Procedenti ab utroque
> Compar sit laudatio
> Amen.

(Mary Mooney stands up, takes a candle, kisses it, blesses herself with it, lights it and puts it into a candlestick. Then she genuflects and goes off in the opposite direction to which she came in,

walking backwards with her hands joined.)

PRIEST *(voice off, chanting)*: Panem de caelo praestitisti eis. Alleluja.
VOICES OFF *(chanting)*: Omne delectamentum in se habentum.

(Enter Mary McGinty. She genuflects in the direction of the altar, goes up to the crucifix and sticks something on it. A very long penis made of plasticine. She runs off.)

PRIEST *(speaking)*: Oremus. Deus, qui nobis per omnia saecula saeculorum. Amen.

(During the above prayer Mother Thomas Aquinas comes in. She genuflects, glances over at the crucifix, sees the plasticine penis and dashes over to remove it. Then she goes off in the opposite direction. She comes back holding Mary Mooney by the scruff of the neck. They genuflect together in the direction of the altar then go off. Three loud bells ring.)

CURTAIN.

THE LAST MEETING OF THE KNIGHTS OF THE WHITE MAGNOLIA

by
Preston Jones

THE LAST MEETING OF THE KNIGHTS OF THE WHITE MAGNOLIA

The Last Meeting of the Knights of the White Magnolia was first performed on 4 December 1973 at the Down Center Stage of the Dallas Theatre Center. Presented by Robert Whitehead and Roger L. Stevens, the play opened at the Broadhurst Theatre in New York City on 21 September 1976 with the following cast:

RAMSEY-EYES BLANKENSHIP	*John Marriott*
RUFE PHELPS	*Walter Flanagan*
OLIN POTTS	*Thomas Toner*
RED GROVER	*Patrick Hines*
L. D. ALEXANDER	*Henderson Forsythe*
COLONEL J. C. KINKAID	*Fred Gwynne*
SKIP HAMPTON	*Graham Beckel*
LONNIE ROY McNEIL	*Paul O'Keefe*
MILO CRAWFORD	*Josh Mostel*

Directed by Alan Schneider

Hampstead Theatre presented the first English production on 7 February 1977 (after four previews) with the following cast:

RAMSEY-EYES BLAKENSHIP	*Frank Singuineau*
RUFE PHELPS	*Leslie Schofield*
OLIN POTTS	*Thick Wilson*
RED GROVER	*Glyn Owen*
L. D. ALEXANDER	*Ian Hogg*
COLONEL J. C. KINKAID	*Ramsay Williams*
SKIP HAMPTON	*Richard Moore*
LONNIE ROY McNEIL	*Ronnie Letham*
MILO CRAWFORD	*Michael J. Jackson*

Directed by Michael Rudman
Designed by Philip Parsons
Costumes by Lindy Hemming
Lighting by Howard Eldridge

CHARACTERS

RAMSEY-EYES BLANKENSHIP Seventy-five. Black custodian of the Cattleman's Hotel. Has lived in Bradleyville since he was ten years old and has known the secondhand existence of a West Texas black. In his own world he is simply known as Granddaddy; in the white world he is Ramsey-Eyes. His full name, Ramsey Washington Blankenship has been used twice — once when he was baptised and once when he was married. It will not be used again till his funeral. Since the death of his wife, Ramsey-Eyes has lived by himself in a small, sagging, three-room house. Most of his children have moved to bigger cities and his grandchildren upset him with their mutterings about social change. As long as Ramsey-Eyes can earn his keep and go fishing every week-end, then he is content. He moves through his old age like a shuffling shadow.

RUFE PHELPS Fifty-five. Refinery worker. As a young man worked in various oil fields around West Texas. However, after he married, he settled down to a more permanent position at the refinery.

OLIN POTTS Fifty-six. Cotton farmer. Grew up on a family farm and stayed there. He married late in life and lives out at his place with his wife and mother. Olin and Rufe are both childless and have kept up a competitive struggle that began in grade school. They went through their softball and rodeo stage and are now hard at each other at checkers, fishing, dove hunting, horseshoes, and dominoes. Their ages and occupations kept them out of World War II and they spent the war years running trotlines and betting on the outcome of battles.

RED GROVER Forty-eight. Owner of Red's Place, a small bar. Originally from Meridian, Mississippi, Red came to Bradleyville following its brief oil boom right after World War II, a conflict he served in totally without distinction. When the 'homecoming G.I.s' defeated the Baptists in the local 'wet, dry election', Red took his savings and put up Red's Place, a bar and package liquor store. When the boom had run itself out and the wells were capped, Red found himself shunned by most of the townspeople and, like most bar owners, developed a deep disgust for his clients. Never taking a wife, Red rides out his sexual desires on skinny-legged barmaids and drunken divorcees and grows more and more bitter as the days and nights drag on.

L. D. ALEXANDER Forty-nine. Manager of A.B.C. Supermarket. Grew up in Bradleyville and married his high-school sweetheart. After his return from World War II, L.D. went to work for A.B.C. Supermarkets. He soon rose to the rank of manager, a modest but respectable position in Bradleyville's middle-class society. L.D. has two children, a boy and a girl. L.D. believes in white supremacy. L.D. is the guy with the green apron and the tag that says MGR. He is usually standing around the checkout stand.

COLONEL J. C. KINKAID Seventy-five. Colonel, U.S. Army (Ret.). Owner of Cattleman's Hotel. Confined to a wheelchair. He was born in 1887 on his father's ranch, and in his youth he enjoyed the soft life that a cattle and cotton empire could provide. In his later years the God of Fortune that looks down and loves us all added a further bonanza to him in the form of oil wells. He attended high school at Mirabeau B. Lamar

Military Academy and went on to Texas A&M, choosing a military career over ranch life. The Colonel served with General John Pershing in the Philippines, in Mexico, and finally in France during World War I. What started out to be a fulfilling military career in the Philippines ended in the trenches in France. 'The Colonel returned from the great war to continue in his father's business interests in and around Bradleyville, Texas, and is interested in many civic organizations,' or so his paragraph reads in the *Texas Who's Who*. Actually, the Colonel returned from France shattered in mind and body. Luckily for the family, an older brother kept the fortune together until the Colonel's son Floyd took up his father's half of the business and simply let the Colonel ramble on into his lost world of memories. Now in his dotage, the Colonel's string is starting to run out.

SKIP HAMPTON Thirty-one. Texaco service station attendant. Born and raised in Bradleyville, graduating from high school and serving in the army during the Korean War. In his entire life Skip has never been able to distinguish himself in any type of endeavour. If you look in his *Senior Year Annual* from Bradleyville High, you'll find under his picture the name Skip Hampton and nothing else. During Korea, Skip drove a supply truck — never getting closer to the front than sixty miles; however, with the passage of time and especially after many drinks, his war record gets bloodier and bloodier. After the war Skip tried several get-rich-quick schemes that always melted in his hands. Then he discovered the bottle. Skip is unmarried and lives with his mother and sister. He pumps gas for a living and has finally been able to distinguish himself in the eyes of all Bradleyville. He is the town drunk.

LONNIE ROY MCNEIL Twenty-one. Pipe fitter at Silver City Pipe Company. Born on a little farm just outside Silver City, Texas, Lonnie Roy had watched his older brothers march off to Korea and envisioned a military career for himself. However, physical defects, asthma, and flat feet kept him out of service. He left high school in his sophomore year and was employed by a pipe-fitting concern. For a while he enjoyed the company of his fellow dropouts and high-school chums — driving around in pickup trucks, smoking cigarettes, and drinking beer — but soon the long arm of the draft board and in one or two cases the state penitentiary in Huntsville cut his peer group down to one. Lonnie Roy found himself enjoying the company of absolutely no one at all until one day Rufe Phelps dropped into Silver City to buy some pipes.

MILO CRAWFORD Twenty-six. Clerk at Bradleyville Grain & Feed. Was born and raised in Bradleyville. He was five years old when his father died, and Milo, as only child, came under his mother's grip. After graduating from high school, Milo was spared the draft when his mother claimed he was her sole support. For many years now Milo has worked at the Bradleyville Grain and Feed Store. Milo has contemplated marriage now and again, but the thought of leaving Mama is too painful for him to get seriously involved with a bride-to-be. Milo has made two great decisions in his life without consulting Mama, one to take up cigarette smoking, and the other to join the Knights of the White Magnolia, both decisions being mild forms of rebellion. To counteract these moves, Mama hides the ashtrays and tries to think up little errands for him to run on meeting nights.

The action takes place in the meeting room of the Knights of the White Magnolia on the third floor of the Cattleman's Hotel, Bradleyville, Texas.

ACT I
Early evening

ACT II
A short while later

Time — 1962

ACT ONE

Early evening. The meeting room of the Knights of the White Magnolia.

The plastered walls are stained and faded, the floor warped and splintered, patched here and there with flat tin cans. Chairs of various ages, colours, and styles are scattered about the room. One is an old wheelchair. At one end of the room is a small podium on a low platform. On the face of the podium is painted a rather smudged white magnolia flower. On the wall behind the podium are two flags, 'The Stars and Bars' and the 'Lone Star', both very old and dirty. Between the two flags hangs a cross made of light bulbs. Stage left is the door into the room. Along the upstage wall is a coat rack. On the floor by the coat rack is an old trunk containing the initiation hats. Hanging on the stage-left and upstage wall are old banners representing the sun, the moon, and the west wind.

Ramsey-Eyes is listlessly sweeping the floor. He is an old black man in very old clothes. As he sweeps the floor he hums and sings snatches of Red River Valley.

After a bit we hear the voices of Rufe Phelps and Olin Potts. Rufe wears khaki work clothes and a baseball cap. Olin wears Levi's, a cotton work shirt, and a straw hat.

RUFE *(Offstage)*: Ah been playin' horseshoes since Jesus H. Christ was a windmill salesman and ah never seen nuthin' like it.

OLIN *(Offstage)*: What the hell are you talkin' about?

RUFE *(Entering)*: Ah wouldn't play horseshoes with you again, Olin Potts, if you was the last man left in West Texas, and that's by-God fact.

RAMSEY-EYES: Howdy, Mr. Rufe. Howdy, Mr. Olin.

OLIN *(Entering)*: Aw hell, Rufe, ah never done nuthin'.

RUFE: Never done nuthin'! Never done nuthin'! Hell, ah spoze cheatin' is nuthin'. Nuthin' to *you*, that is. No, sir, to a fella like *you* cheatin' is jest nuthin' atall.

RAMSEY-EYES: How is you-all this evenin'?

OLIN: Now listen here, Rufe Phelps, ah never cheated!

RUFE: Never cheated! Well, ah don't know what cheatin' is if what you done *wasn't*.

RAMSEY-EYES: Shore been hot today, ain't it!?

OLIN *(Sitting)*: Ah never cheated.

RUFE: Did it!

OLIN: Didn't!

RAMSEY-EYES: You-all is kinda early tonight, ain't you?

RUFE: That last throw of mine was a leaner.

OLIN: Weren't neither.

RUFE: Was too!

OLIN: Weren't!

RUFE: How's come it weren't?

OLIN: Cause for a leaner to be a leaner, it's gotta by Gawd lean!

RUFE: If that last throw of mine wasn't leanin' ah'd sure as hell like to know what it was doin'.

OLIN: It was lyin' flat on its butt in the dirt. That's what it was doin'.

RAMSEY-EYES: Yes, sah, horseshoes is a mighty good game, okay.

(The door opens and Red Grover appears. Red is fat, thicknecked, and cynical. He wears a rumpled

blue suit with a flowered necktie. He carries a paper bag containing four bottles of cheap bourbon.)

RUFE: Hey, Red, when is a leaner a leaner?

RED: Who gives a damn!

RAMSEY: Howdy, Mistah Grover, how is you?

OLIN: That last toss of yours weren't no leaner no way.

RUFE: Was by Gawd too.

OLIN: Weren't.

RED: What you two monkey-nuts fightin' about now?

RUFE: My last throw over to the horseshoes was a leaner and Olin cheated and said it weren't.

OLIN: Well, it weren't.

RUFE: Wouldn't surprise me none if maybe you didn't kick it a little bit.

OLIN: Ah never kicked nuthin'. There was no way to kick nuthin' no ways, 'cause that damned horseshoe weren't leanin'.

RUFE: Was so too. You cheated!

OLIN: Didn't done it.

RUFE: Did too.

OLIN: Didn't!

RED: For Christ's sake, if all you two are gonna do is fight about it, why don't you quit playin'?

RUFE: Well, hell, Red, ah like to play.

RED: Play with somebody else then.

OLIN: Ain't nobody else to play with.

RAMSEY-EYES: Well, iffen you-all is gonna start on wif de meetin' here, ah'll jest go on down to de lobby. *(He exits.)*

RED *(Hearing door close)*: Who the hell was that?

RUFE: Ramsey-Eyes, ah think.

RED: Well, goddamn, ah guess he's gittin' too uppity to talk to people any more. Ah swear, it's gittin' nowadays where by God you gotta talk to

them first.
OLIN: That's about it.

(The door opens and L. D. Alexander enters. L.D. is big and florid. He wears a baggy J. C. Penney Western suit, scuffed black loafers with white socks, and a small white Stetson hat.)

L.D.: Howdy, brothers.
RUFE: Howdy, L.D.
L.D.: Man, it's dark in here. *(Touches switch. After general greeting.)* You bring the re-freshments there, Red?
RED: You bet, L.D. *(He indicates paper bag.)* Best stock ah got in the house.
L.D.: I'll bet. *(He picks a bottle out of the bag.)* Old Buzzard Puke. Yes, sir, Red, this looks like real smooth stuff.
RUFE: Old Buzzard Puke. That's a good one, ain't it, Olin?
OLIN: Shore is.
RED: Ah don't notice you-all passin' any of it up when it comes round.
L.D.: Well, you can bet your butt Skip Hampton won't pass it up.
RED: Hell, Skip wouldn't pass up a drink if he had to squeeze it out of an armadillo's ass.
RUFE: Hey, ah got a good idea. Let's hide the whiskey and play like we ain't got any when Skip comes in.
RED: There ain't any place in this whole world to hide whiskey from Skip. He'd sniff it out if it wuz wrapped in lead.
RUFE: No, no. What we do, you see, is hide these-here bottles and then tell Skip that it was *his* turn to bring the re-freshments. Then he won't know. You see?
OLIN: Hey, that's a good one, Rufe.

RED: Might work at that.

OLIN *(To Rufe)*: How'd you happen to think up a good one like that?

RUFE: Well, hell, Olin, ah think of things sometimes.

(Offstage, ad lib. of Skip and Ramsey-Eyes.)

OLIN: You ain't never thought of nuthin' affore.

RUFE: Now listen here, Olin Potts . . .

(The door opens and Skip Hampton enters. Skip is a pale, thin, blond-headed man. He wears a greasy green Texaco uniform.)

SKIP: Howdy, ever'body.

L.D.: Well, howdy there, Skip, how's the boy?

SKIP: Pretty good.

RUFE: Hey, Skip, didn't you forgit somethin'?

SKIP: No, ah don't think so.

RED: Aw, come on now, Skip. Don't try to kid your old buddies.

SKIP: Ah ain't kiddin' nobody.

RUFE: Old Skip. Always tryin' to kid his buddies.

SKIP: Ah ain't kiddin', ah tell you. What the hell you-all talkin' about?

RED: What are we talkin' about? Well, hell's fire, boy, we're talking about the re-freshments.

SKIP: What about the re-freshments?

L.D.: Where the hell are they?

SKIP: Ah don't know where they are.

RED: You mean to say you didn't bring them?

SKIP: Me? No, ah didn't bring nuthin'.

L.D.: Well, Gawd Almighty damn!

RUFE: Now we ain't got nuthin' to drink.

SKIP: Red always brings them samples from the package store, he always does.

RED: Now, Skip. You know ah told you to pick it

up for me and bring it over here for tonight's
meetin'.

RUFE: Shore he did. He told you to, Skip. Didn't
he, Olin?

OLIN: Shore did.

SKIP: No, you didn't, Red. Ah swear to God you
never. Ah would of remembered. Hell's fire, ah'd
never forget somethin' as important as that.

L.D.: Well, looks like we jest gotta do without
tonight.

SKIP: No, wait. Ah'll go back and git it, Red. Ah'll
jest run over to your place and pick some up!

RED: Too late now. Ah done locked up the
package store.

SKIP: Well, you can open it again, can't you? Give
me the key, ah'll go.

RED: You? Give *you* the key to mah hard liquor.
You gotta be crazy, boy, that would be like givin'
old L.D. here a Charg-a-Plate to a whorehouse.

SKIP: Well, let somebody else go then. How about
Rufe here?

RUFE: Why should ah go do what you was
supposed to do but forgot? *(He and Olin both
giggle.)*

SKIP *(Truth suddenly dawning on him)*: Whatta
you guys tryin' to pull?

L.D.: Well, hell, since old Skip let us down tonight,
ah guess we gotta make do with this. *(He pulls out
the sack.)*

RUFE: Gotcha there, Skip. We really gotcha there.

SKIP *(Dully)*: Yeah, boy, that was a good one.
okay.

OLIN: Rufe thought it up.

SKIP *(Sarcastically)*: Damn good goin' there, Rufe.
(He reaches for the sack.)

RED *(Stopping him)*: Now hold on there. All us
gentlemen wait on refreshments till after the
meetin', don't we, Skip?

SKIP: Sure, sure, oh hell, yes.

(The door opens and Ramsey-Eyes pokes his head in.)

RAMSEY-EYES: 'Scuse me.
RED: What the hell you want, Ramsey-Eyes?
RAMSEY: Ah just come up to say how Floyd done brought his daddy to the meetin'. He's down in de lobby now.
L.D.: Okay, Ramsey-Eyes. *(The door closes.)* Rufe, you and Olin go on down and git Colonel Kinkaid.
RUFE: Okay, L.D.

(They start to exit.)

L.D.: And be careful with him comin' up the stairs.
OLIN: We ain't never dropped him yet.
L.D.: Old Colonel Kinkaid, by God, he's somethin' else, ain't he? Here he is all crippled up and almost blind, but wild horses wouldn't keep him from a lodge meeting. No, sir.
SKIP: How old is the Colonel nowadays, L.D.?
L.D.: Well, let's see, ah reckin he must be at least seventy-five.
SKIP: No kiddin'.
L.D. You bet; hell, all them Kinkaids is tough. All except Floyd, that is.
RED: Oh, that old man ain't so tough.
L.D.: Hell he ain't.
RED: Well, goddamn, L.D., he's got the shell shocks, ain't he? All you gotta do is belch too loud and he starts yellin' about the Germans coming after him.
L.D.: Hell, Red, there were lots of fellers come back from that World's War I with the shell shocks, and even with them he's still more of a

man than that damn Floyd will ever be.

SKIP: That's the damn truth. You know, it's kind of funny what with Floyd and that gnat-titted wife of his, what's her name?

L.D.: Maureen.

SKIP: Maureen, bein' the high by-God so-ciety in this-here town, why ain't Floyd ever joined our lodge?

RED: 'Cause he thinks it's a bunch of bullshit, that's why. All Floyd and old gnat-tits and the rest of the rich bastards in this town wanna do is sit around the goddamned country club and play kneesies. Floyd lets the Colonel come up here to the meetings so's everyone can see how nice he is to his daddy. But you watch, the minute the Colonel kicks off, Floyd's gonna close this-here hotel before the carcass is cold.

L.D.: Oh now, now he wouldn't do a thing like that.

RED: The hell he wouldn't. Floyd may be a bastard, but he's not a stupid bastard. You see how many payin' guests are in this-here fire trap? Probably about five. This mighta been a classy hotel way back yonder when the Colonel had it built, but that Holiday Inn out to the bypass done kicked this dump plumb outta business.

L.D.: That don't mean a goddamn thing. Nobody's gonna close down this place. Hell, Red, this-here Cattleman's Hotel is a by-God landmark in this country.

RED: Oh, hell yes, the whole town of Bradleyville is a by-God landmark, but that didn't stop the state from runnin' the highway around it. Take a look down Main Street for Christ's sake, there's so many damned stores bein' boarded up that the only outfit in town that's makin' any money is the god-damned used-lumber company.

L.D.: Well, ah admit that things is kindly slow but …

RED: Oh, you admit that, do you? *(He starts to laugh.)*

L.D.: What the hell's so funny?

RED: I just happened to think, what if Floyd don't close the place down but turns it into a hotel for Coloreds only? By God, that would damn sure play hell with the old meetin' night.

(L.D. and Skip stare at him.)

L.D.: Well, what the hell!

RED: Oh, I'm jest kiddin', of course. Floyd would never do nuthin' like that.

L.D.: He damn sure wouldn't.

RED *(Still amused)*: 'Course he wouldn't.

(Offstage dialogue before Colonel's entrance.)

COLONEL *(Offstage)*: Watch what you're doin', damnit, you're not totin' a bale of alfalfa!

RUFE *(Offstage)*: Ah'm sorry, Colonel. Confound it, Olin, hold up your part!

OLIN *(Offstage)*: Ah am holdin' up my part. You're the one not doin' nuthin'.

RUFE *(Offstage)*: Now listen here, Olin Potts.

COLONEL *(Offstage)*: Shut the hell up, the both of you. Now open that damn door, Ramsey-Eyes.

RAMSEY-EYES: Yes sah, Colonel. *(He opens the door and goes to the wheelchair to arrange it.)*

(Olin and Rufe carry in the Colonel. The Colonel is dressed in gabardine Western pants, slippers, and a faded, patched World War I officer's tunic. His legs are crippled and he is nearly blind.)

RAMSEY-EYES: Ah got you chair here, Colonel Kinkaid, sah.

COLONEL: Good man, Ramsey-Eyes.

(Olin and Rufe start to ease the Colonel into the wheelchair.)

OLIN: Damnit, Rufe, be careful with his legs.

RUFE: Damnit yourself, ah know what ah'm doin'.

COLONEL *(settling into wheelchair)*: All right, all right, ah'm in, now git away from me, the both of you!

RUFE: Boy howdy, them steps up from the lobby is gittin' hard to climb.

RAMSEY-EYES *(Arranging Colonel's lap robe.)*: Ah'll be right down in the lobby iffen you need anythin'.

COLONEL: Right, Ramsey-Eyes, DISMISSED. *(Ramsey-Eyes doesn't move.)* What the hell you waitin' for?

RAMSEY-EYES: Is you wearin' your dentures tonight, Colonel?

COLONEL: Hell yes, ah'm wearin' my teeth. *(Points to them.)* See.

RAMSEY-EYES: You know what Floyd said 'bout wearin' your dentures.

COLONEL: Ah know what he said; now, damnit, *dismissed!*

RAMSEY-EYES *(Exiting)*: Yes, sah, but Floyd said you gotta wear your dentures.

L.D.: Howdy, Colonel Kinkaid.

COLONEL: Howdy, boys. How you-all tonight?

SKIP: Howdy, Colonel.

COLONEL: Who is it?

SKIP: Skip Hampton, Colonel.

COLONEL: Well, howdy there, Skip. How's your sister?

SKIP: She's jest fine, Colonel.

COLONEL: And your mother?

SKIP: Couldn't be better.

COLONEL: Ah used to court your Aunt Sally. Betcha didn't know that, did you?

SKIP: Yeah, Colonel, you told me.

COLONEL: Slapped mah face so hard one night it knocked me plumb outta the buckboard.

L.D.: Sure, Colonel.

COLONEL: Thought for a second that damned buggy whip ah had in mah hand was a lightnin' rod.

L.D. *(Going behind podium)*: Well, we might as well git started.

RUFE: Where's old Milo Crawford tonight?

L.D.: Milo can't make it. He phoned over to the house and said he hadda take his mama over to the Big Spring.

RED: Jesus Christ — wouldn't you know it.

L.D. *(Banging on podium with his hand.)*: Okay now. This-here meetin' of the Bradleyville, Texas, Lodge of the Knights of the White Magnolia is now in order. Ever'body 'cept the Colonel stand up and repeat the oath.

ALL *(In a rather ragged cadence)*: "Ah swear as a true Knight of the White Magnolia to preserve the merits handed to me by mah forefathers and to hold as a sacred trust the ideals of mah Southern heritage. Ah pledge mah life to the principles of White Magnolia-ism and will obey until ah die the laws of this-here so-ciety."

L.D.: Okay, ever'body can sit down now. *(Olin starts to the door.)* Where the hell you goin', Olin?

OLIN *(Surprised)*: Ah'm goin' on out to git the card tables so's we can commence with the domino games.

L.D.: Well, you can jest sit on back down, 'cause we ain't havin' no dominoes tonight.

OLIN: No dominoes? What kinda meetin' can we have with no dominoes?

COLONEL: Damnit, ah wanna shuffle dominoes!

L.D.: We ain't playin' no dominoes tonight, Colonel.

COLONEL: Why not?

L.D.: 'Cause tonight we're gonna have us a real meetin'!

RED: What the hell you talkin' about?

L.D.: Tonight we're gonna have us a real live initiation.

SKIP: You mean to tell us that somebody wants to join the lodge?

L.D.: That's right.

RED: Well, ah'll be damned.

L.D.: Brother Knight Rufe Phelps here has got us a new man, ain't you, Brother Knight Phelps?

RUFE *(Grinning and shuffling.)*: Yes, sir, ah have.

OLIN: You never told me 'bout no new man whilst we was a-playin' horseshoes.

RUFE: Ah was gonna, till you started cheatin'.

OLIN: Ah never cheated! You're the one that cheats. Any time you throw one four feet from the stake you call it a dadburned leaner!

L.D.: All right now, damnit, let's git on with it! Brother Knight Phelps, tell us 'bout our new brother-to-be.

RUFE: Ah got us Lonnie Roy McNeil. He's old Grady McNeil's boy from over there in Silver City . . .

COLONEL: *Silver City!* Ah won't have him!

RUFE *(Taken aback)*: He's a real nice feller, Colonel.

COLONEL: Don't give a damn; if he's from Silver City he's no damn good!

SKIP: Well, hell, Colonel, it's not like he's from the Congo or somethin'. My God, Silver City's only three miles away.

L.D.: Ah think it's a right good idea that we branch out a little, Colonel. Ah mean, nobody from Bradleyville has joined the lodge for over five years now.

COLONEL: People from Silver City are low-down stinkin' cowards and ah flat will not have them around!

RUFE: Well, hell, ah didn't know *Silver City* was on our list too!

L.D.: Now, Colonel, you know we all respect your judgement in ever'thang but . . .

COLONEL: You damn well better.

L.D.: But maybe we would all understand a little better if we all knew *why* people from Silver City was no damn good.

COLONEL: Because in nineteen hundred and eighteen Staff Sergeant George Plummer from right over yonder in Silver City refused to fight, that's why! Whey-faced little coward jest stood there in the trench with the puttees floppin' around and puke all over his face, hands shakin' and spit runnin' out his mouth. Kept mumblin' over and over, "Who am ah? Who am ah?" Well, ah knew damn well who he was, he was Staff Sergeant George Plummer from over there to *Silver City*. Ah ordered that little son-of-a-bitch to climb up . . . people from Silver City are no damn good. That is an order and that is a fact.

L.D.: Well, hell, Colonel, this-here feller wantin' to join ain't no Plummer, he's a McNeil.

RUFE: That's right, Colonel, he's old Grady McNeil's boy.

COLONEL: He's from *Silver City*, ain't he?

RUFE: Well, yes, but . . .

COLONEL: Well, there you are.

L.D.: Well, actually, he ain't exactly from Silver City, Colonel. Ah mean, not from right there smack in the town. The McNeil place is sorter outside the town, isn't it, Rufe?

RUFE: Well, yeah, kindly out on the rural route there.

COLONEL: Not in the town, huh?

RUFE: No, sir. Now, Lonnie Roy works there in Silver City but he lives sorter out, you know.

COLONEL: Well, ah don't know. You're sure now he's not a Plummer?

RUFE: Oh no, sir, Colonel, he's a McNeil, okay and he's shore wantin' to be a Lodge brother. Ah talked to him day affore yesterday over to the Silver City Pipe Fittin' Company and he said he would come over here tonight for shore.

COLONEL: Which McNeil is that?

L.D.: Grady McNeil's boy, Colonel. From over there to Silver, uh, uh, from over yonder.

COLONEL: That the Grady McNeil that married the oldest Richey girl?

RUFE: No, ah think Lonnie Roy's Mama was a Spencer, weren't she, Olin?

OLIN *(Who is an expert in these matters, therefore he pronounces each name very distinctly.)* She was *Maude Spencer* affore she married *Grady McNeil* over there to, uh, *by* Silver City. I know this 'cause a bunch of my cousins is *Spencers* and *Maude* was the second-oldest girl next to *Winifred Spencer*, who married a P & G soap salesman from Amarillo.

RUFE: By God, that's right. I remember that. Married him kindly on the sly, didn't she?

OLIN: They e-loped up to Durant, Oklahoma. Made her pa mad as hell. He didn't want *Winifred* married to no drummer. Ah remember 'cause her brother *Clete* an' me was pullin' a water well once out to the *Honeycutt* place and . . .

RED: For Christ's sake, let's git on with the meetin'!

OLIN: Ah jest thought you-all wanted to know.

RED: Well, we don't. Come on, L.D., let's git on with it.

L.D.: Yes, well, it sounds like Lonnie Roy's got

himself a real fine background, Brother Knight
Potts.

OLIN *(Smugly)*: Figgered you-all wanted to know.

RUFE: That the same Clete Spencer that drowned
out to Lake Bradleyville?

SKIP: For Christ's sake!

OLIN: No, if you recall, there was two *Clete
Spencers*. You see *Winifred's* daddy married
twice. Now the *Clete Spencer* ah was pullin' the
well with was known as *"Big Clete"* Spencer
'cause he was borned to *old man Spencer's* first
wife, *Bessie*, who was also the mama of *Winifred*
and *Maude*, but the other *Clete Spencer*, who
was knowed as *"Little Clete"* and who drowned
out to Lake Bradleyville, was borned to *old man
Spencer's* second wife, *Mary*, who was also the
mama of . . .

SKIP: Jesus Christ. Sure, Olin, we all know the
story. Now come on, let's git on with the meetin'.

RUFE: You don't want to git on with the meetin'.
You jest want to git on with the refreshments.

SKIP: Ah do not!

RED: The hell you don't. Your tongue's hangin'
out so far now it looks like a necktie.

COLONEL: Onward, onward. Quit dilly-dallying
around. Git the job done. The A.E.F. never
wasted time. Never would have whipped the Hun
if we had. Git the job done.

L.D.: Yes, sir, Colonel. Now, as ah was sayin . . .
*(He is interrupted by a commotion outside the
doors. Shouts and bangs.)*

OLIN *(Leaping up.)*: Oh, my God, what's that?

*(The door bursts open and Ramsey-Eyes appears,
securely holding on to a young man — Lonnie
Roy McNeil.)*

RAMSEY-EYES: Ah got him! Ah got him! He was

tryin' to sneak into the meetin', Mistah L.D., sah, but ah glommed onto him affore he could.

LONNIE: Tell this crazy fool to turn me loose!

RUFE: Let him go, Ramsey-Eyes, this here is Lonnie Roy McNeil.

RAMSEY-EYES *(Releasing him.)*: You mean he belongs up here?

RED: That's right, *he* belongs up here, but *you* don't. Now git your butt back down to the lobby where it does belong.

RAMSEY-EYES: Yes, sah, ah only wishes you-all would tell me who am a Magnolia and who ain't, thass all. *(Exits.)*

COLONEL: What happened, what's goin' on?

L.D.: Nuthin', Colonel Kinkaid. Jest a little mis-understandin', that's all.

SKIP: Ramsey-Eyes jest made a little mistake, Colonel, that's all.

COLONEL: Ramsey-Eyes. He a member now?

L.D.: 'Course he ain't no member, Colonel, he jest caught somebody outside, thinkin' it was an in-truder.

COLONEL: Caught him a spy, did he? Good man, that Ramsey-Eyes. Good soldier.

RUFE: Only it weren't no spy. It was Lonnie Roy McNeil, our new member.

RED: Stupid black, dumb butt!

(They all turn and contemplate Lonnie Roy. He is a thin, big-eyed kid in an ill-fitting suit; his hair is bowl cut and he wears tennis shoes.)

L.D.: Howdy there, Lonnie Roy. Mah name is L.D. Alexander and ah wish to welcome you to the Knights of the White Magnolia.

LONNIE: Jeeezus, that's one mean man you got out there.

L.D.: Ah hell, boy, Ramsey-Eyes ain't one of us.

He jest sweeps up the place, that's all.

LONNIE: Oh well, ah guess that's all right then. You sure now he ain't . . .

L.D.: Hell no! Now come on and meet the fellow knights. This here is Red Grover.

RED: How are you?

L.D.: Rufe Phelps you already know. *(They nod.)* Olin Potts over by the door there.

OLIN: Your mama is *Maude Spencer McNeil*, ain't she?

LONNIE: Yes, sir, she is.

OLIN: Knew it!

L.D.: Skip Hampton.

SKIP: Howdy.

L.D.: And Colonel J. C. Kinkaid.

COLONEL: Retired. Glad to know you, Lonnie Roy. What branch you serve in?

LONNIE: Beg pardon.

COLONEL: Army, Navy, Marines, Army Air Corps?

LONNIE: Oh, that. Nuthin'.

COLONEL: Nuthin'?

LONNIE: I git the asthma sometimes.

COLONEL: Well, what the hell.

LONNIE *(Lifting a tennis-shoe-clad foot.)* An mah feet is flat.

COLONEL: Jesus Christ!

LONNIE: Well, gawlee, ah cain't help it.

L.D.: The Colonel here was in the A.E.F.

LONNIE: The what?

L.D.: The American Army in World's War I.

LONNIE: Ah don't reckon ah ever studied much on them ancient wars and such like.

COLONEL: Blackball the flat-footed asthmatic, *Silver City* son-of-a-bitch!

LONNIE: Hell, ah never meant nuthin'.

L.D.: 'Course you didn't, Lonnie Roy. The Colonel here is jest a little crusty, that's all. He don't mean no harm.

RED: Jest an old war horse, right, Colonel?

COLONEL: Better an old war horse than a young jackass!

L.D.: Now, you jest sit down right here, Lonnie Roy, and we'll git on with the meetin'. Then afterwards we'll all have us a little nip. How's that sound?

SKIP: Sounds damn good to me.

L.D.: Shut up, Skip.

LONNIE: Fine, fine. A little nip would go down real good.

SKIP: Sure would!

RED: Shut up, Skip!

L.D.: Now, Lonnie Roy, affore ah ad-minister the oath of membership, ah want to tell you a little bit about the Knights of the White Magnolia.

LONNIE: Rufe already told me about the domino games. Sounds real good to me.

RUFE: Old Lonnie Roy here really likes them dominoes.

LONNIE: You bet! Moon, Forty-two, ah like to play 'em all.

OLIN: We play mostly Forty-two here, Lonnie Roy.

LONNIE: And when he told me that this-here lodge was for white men only, well, sir, ah was sold. Sold right there on the spot.

L.D.: That's fine, Lonnie Roy, but now let me tell you about the rest . . .

LONNIE: When Rufe come over to the pipe-fittin' company and told me about this-here lodge, ah said right off, "Sign me up," didn't ah, Rufe?

RUFE: Shore did. Ah was over there buyin' some pipe for mah cesspool . . .

LONNIE: You can git it over yonder a whole lot cheaper than here in Bradleyville.

RUFE: That's the damn truth.

L.D.: Well, that's fine, now . . .

OLIN: What you gittin' for pipe over there, Lonnie Roy?

L.D.: Damnit to hell, now you all shut up and let me finish.

OLIN: Well, all ah wanted to know was . . .

RED: Shut up, Olin!

COLONEL: What's happenin'? What's goin' on?

SKIP: *Red* won't let L.D. git on with the meetin'.

RED: The hell you say! Ah never done nuthin'. It was Olin.

OLIN: Ah never done nuthin'.

COLONEL: Shut the hell up, all of you! Now damnit, L.D., git on with the meetin'. By gawd, ah wish ah'd had the bunch of you over there in France. You'd have shaped up then, by Gawd.

L.D.: Yes, sir, Colonel . . . now . . .

COLONEL: You'd have shaped up or ah'da kicked some butts!

L.D.: Yes, sir, Colonel.

COLONEL: No goddamned gabbin' around in the trenches. Find yourself strung out on the wire like a piece of pork. Piece of pork.

L.D.: Please, Colonel. If ah can continue.

COLONEL: Yes, yes, continue. Who the hell's stoppin' you?

L.D.: Nobody, Colonel, it's jest that . . .

COLONEL: You let me know who's stoppin' you, L.D., and ah'll put him up again' the by-God wall.

SKIP: Goddamnit, Colonel Kinkaid, shut up!

(There is a long, stunned silence. All turn and look at Skip.)

COLONEL: Who said that! *(Silence.)* Who said that, ah said!!!

SKIP *(Meekly)*: Ah did, Colonel.

COLONEL: You know the last person who ever dared say that to me?

SKIP: No, sir.

COLONEL *(Animated and cheery)*: General Pershing, that's who. Old Black Jack himself. *(Chuckles.)* We was down in Mexico at the time and ah was a snotnosed shavetail. Well, sir, one afternoon at the officer's mess . . .

L.D.: Please, Colonel, let's save the story till refreshment time, okay?

RED: Shore, Colonel, let's hold her off till then.

COLONEL: Sure, sure, sure. *(Chuckles.)* Old Black Jack himself.

L.D.: Now, Lonnie Roy, as ah was sayin', bein' a member of the Knights of the White Magnolia is actual bein' a member of a brotherhood. Ah mean, you can look on any of us fellers here just like we was your own brothers, your own blood kin.

LONNIE *(Sincerely)*: That there's real nice to know.

L.D.: The Knights of the White Magnolia was founded back in 1902, when Knight Brother Maynard C. Stempco of Austin got fed up to his ears with the way the Ku Klux was runnin' things and broke off to form his own outfit. Well, sir, the idea growed and growed and by the late 1920's there was Knights of the White Magnolia lodges all over Texas and parts of Oklahoma.

LONNIE: My gosh. How's come Mr. Stempco got fed up with the Klan?

RED: 'Cause anybody that's got to put on a white bedsheet to kick a coon's ass has got to be a damn fool, that's why!

LONNIE: Oh, yeah, sure, I see.

L.D.: Why in 1939 we had us a con-vention in Tulsa, Oklahoma, that was attended by two thousand people.

RUFE: The Colonel was there. Weren't you,

Colonel?

COLONEL: Got drunk and threw up all over my wheelchair. Made the wheels sticky.

LONNIE: You still have them con-ventions?

L.D.: Well, uh, now, not in a long time, but we're workin' on it, ain't we, Red?

RED *(Amused)*: Oh hell, yes.

LONNIE: Well, how's come you don't have 'em regular?

L.D.: Stupidity, Lonnie Roy. Pure by-God dumb stupidity. People got to where they didn't want to join up any more. Can you imagine that? They didn't want to be Knights of the White Magnolia. They wanted to be Jaycees or Toast Masters or Elks or Lions or Moose, they wanted to be by-God animals, that's right, animals, but not knights. They turned around and stabbed their granddaddies square in the back. Turned up their noses on their race, started kowtowin' to all them-there mi-norities, and little by little the lodges jest sorter dried up. Nobody wanted to join. No new people. Jesus, but we was big once, Lonnie Roy. Hell, there was governors and senators that was Brother Knights. We had con-ventions and barbecues and parades. Took over a whole hotel there in Tulsa. Gawd, and it musta been somethin' to see. Bands playin' and baton girls a-marchin' along. The Grand Imperial Wizard of the brotherhood rode in a big open carriage pulled by six white horses, and up above the whole shebang was this great old big blimp towin' this-here banner sayin' TULSA WELCOMES THE KNIGHTS OF THE WHITE MAGNOLIA. Gawda mighty, now wasn't that somethin'!

LONNIE: Jeeezus, you mean to say that with all that great stuff, that people quit joinin' up?

L.D.: That's right, Lonnie Roy.

LONNIE: My God, why?

L.D.: Ah don't know, Lonnie Roy, ah honestly don't know. When Red an' me come into the lodge after World's War II, why there musta been fifteen or twenty members. Then fellers jest started a-droppin' out — quit comin'. Oh, ever' now and then somebody would join up, like Skip here, he joined up after Ko-rea.

LONNIE: You was in Ko-rea?

SKIP: Damn right. Blastin' them gooks. Ah was hell on wheels with a B.A.R. Regular John Wayne. Right, Red?

RED: That's what you keep tellin' ever'body.

SKIP: Ah'll never forget the time me an' Dale Laverty was bringin' them Marines down from that-there Chosan reservoir.

RED: For Christ's sake, shut up! We heard that damn story a hundred times.

SKIP *(To Lonnie)*: Ah'll tell you all about it after the meetin', okay?

LONNIE: Swell.

SKIP: It's a hell of a good story.

RUFE: Me and Olin have been members since nineteen and forty-eight, ain't we, Olin?

OLIN: January 24th, 1948. Damn right.

LONNIE: You mean, you fellers is all the members there is?

RUFE: Well, there's Milo Crawford, but he had to take his mama over to Big Spring.

RED: Him and his damn mama. Makes you puke.

LONNIE: What about all the lodges in the other towns?

L.D.: There ain't any more.

LONNIE: You mean they're all gone?

L.D.: Ever' one of em.

RED: We're what you might call the last of the Mohicans, boy.

LONNIE: But how can you-all keep this-here room for your meetin's, don't it cost a lot of money?

L.D.: Nope. You see the Colonel there owns the hotel.

LONNIE: Oh, ah see.

RED: Don't pay no dues to this club, boy. Jest lots of fun and lots of whiskey.

L.D.: But the most important thing is the fact that you're wantin' to join up.

LONNIE: Me? Ah'm important?

L.D.: Shore you are. You see, you can git other smart young fellers like yourself interested in the lodge.

RUFE: Damn right. You may be the start of a whole new movement, boy.

LONNIE: Well, ah don't know many fellers mah age over to home. Most of 'em are either gone off somewhere or are in the army.

L.D.: But you are a start, don't you see? Yes, sir, a start. Hell, we may be beginnin' a whole new ball game here.

LONNIE: Ah could maybe talk to some of the fellers at the pipe company.

L.D.: There you go!

LONNIE (getting excited): And mah daddy knows lots and lots of folks.

L.D.: Damn right! Now you're talkin', boy!

RUFE: By gollies, L.D., maybe we got somethin' here. Maybe we can catch on again.

L.D.: Shore we can. Anythin' can happen. Hell's fire, stuff like this has happened affore. Outfits git kindly down like and jest one little thang gits 'em goin' again, and wham, next thang you know they're back on the top. Bigger and better than affore.

OLIN: You mean big like we was in nineteen and thirty-nine?

L.D.: Sure, why not? Bigger!

SKIP: Oh, for Christ's sake!!!

L.D.: What the hell's wrong with you?

SKIP: You guys are crazy. Jesus Christ, we git one new member in five years and ten minutes later we're bigger than the by-God Woodman of the World.

OLIN: It don't do no harm to plan.

SKIP: Plan! This ain't no plan, it's a dream — a damn-fool dream.

L.D.: You tryin' to say we're damn fools!

SKIP: No, no, ah ain't sayin that. It's only . . .

RED: Only what? If you don't like bein' a member of this goddamn brotherhood, why the hell don't you say so?

SKIP: Ah didn't say that, all ah said was . . .

COLONEL: What's goin' on?

RUFE: Skip Hampton says he don't want to be a knight no more.

SKIP: No, ah never. All ah said was . . .

COLONEL: Shoot the goddamned desertin' son-of-a-bitch!

SKIP: Ah ain't desertin'! All ah said was . . .

COLONEL: Shoot 'em! By God, we shot 'em in France. No reason why we can't shoot 'em right here in Bradleyville.

OLIN: Actual, Skip can't help bein' the way he is, what with his grandmother on his daddy's side bein' a *Bentley*.

COLONEL: A Bentley!

SKIP: Oh, my God!

OLIN: All them Bentleys was mean. Now ah don't want to give no disrespect to your kinfolk there, Skip, but if you'll look back a bit you'll see jest how mean them *Bentleys* was.

SKIP: Who gives a damn!

OLIN: You ought to! Ah mean, if ah had *Bentley* blood in me, ah damn shore would give a damn.

SKIP: Well, ah don't!

OLIN: Well, you ought to!

RUFE: You better listen to Olin there, Skip. When

it comes to kinfolk, old Olin there knows what he's talkin' about.

SKIP: Well, why the hell don't we talk about somethin' else! Jesus, ah'm sick and tired of listenin' to whose Uncle Abraham is married to which Cousin Clarabelle's cross-eyed step-sister.

RUFE: You're jest jealous 'cause Olin here can remember all them names and you cain't remember nuthin'.

SKIP: So he can remember names. So damn what! Let's make him the by-God county clerk and fire the bookkeeper. He can sit on his butt and babble Abernathy to Zackafoozass all day long.

OLIN: Well, now that ain't a very nice thang to say.

RED: Yeah, Skip, why the hell don't you shut up.

SKIP: Shut up, yourself, damnit! Where the hell you git off tellin' people to shut up!

RED: You'd better watch your step there, sonny boy!

L.D.: Now, now, Brothers, let's jest all stand back and cool off a spell. Remember, we got us a new member here. We don't want him to git no wrong ideas about us now, do we?

COLONEL: Shoot him!

LONNIE: My gosh. Do you fellers fight like this all the time?

RED: Only on meetin' nights.

LONNIE: Maybe ah'd better go home and come back next time.

L.D.: No need of that. We're jest horsin' around, that's all. Havin' lots of fun is part of bein' a brother. Why, the best part of the meetin' is comin' up, the initiation, and after that the re-freshments. You don't wanna miss that, do you?

LONNIE: No, ah jest thought . . .

L.D.: Well, hell no, you don't! We gotta initiation for you, Lonnie Roy McNeil, that's gonna be the high by-God point of your life.

LONNIE: You ain't gonna hit me with paddles and such like, are you?

L.D.: Hell no! That there's kid stuff, this-here initiation is based on God and brotherhood.

RUFE: It's a hell of an impressive sight, Lonnie Roy — you see, we light up the cross and . . .

OLIN: No fair tellin'! We ain't started yet.

RUFE: Well, hell, ah didn't *tell* nuthin', all ah said was . . .

COLONEL: Let's git on with it! Good God, you men shilly-shally and fart around worse than the Fifth Marines!

SKIP: Hell yes, let's git started!

L.D.: All right, damnit, we will!

COLONEL: Bumble-dickin' around. That's all you fellers do.

L.D.: Yes, well, all right, Colonel. We will now commence with the ceremony of initiation.

OLIN: Wait a minute. We can't start no ceremony yet.

L.D.: Why the hell not?

OLIN: 'Cause we ain't voted on him yet.

SKIP: Oh, for Christ's sake.

OLIN: We gotta vote! Them there's the rules.

SKIP: We didn't have no goddamn vote when I got initiated.

RED: It's a damn-good thing for you that we didn't.

SKIP: What the hell's that spozed to mean?

RED: Jest what I said, that's what.

L.D.: All right now, that's jest a by-God nuff! Ah want it quiet in here and ah mean dead quiet. *(Silence.)* That's a whole lot better. All right now, Olin, if you insist, we will . . .

COLONEL: Bumble-dick, bumble-dick, bumble-dick.

L.D. *(Patiently)*: Yes, Colonel, that's right. Now . . .

COLONEL: That's what old Black Jack did. Bumble-dicked all over Mexico. Let that fat little greaser Pancho Villa make a damn fool of him. Betcha didn't know that, did you?

L.D.: No, Colonel, we didn't. Now . . .

COLONEL: Well, he did.

L.D.: Please, Colonel, we gotta git on with the vote.

COLONEL: What we votin' on?

L.D.: On Lonnie Roy, Colonel.

COLONEL: Who?

L.D.: Lonnie Roy McNeil, our new member.

COLONEL: We got a new member? Well, it's about time; who is it?

RUFE: Lonnie Roy McNeil, Colonel, Grady McNeil's boy from over there to Silver . . . from over yonder.

COLONEL: Well, ah'll be damned. You don't bumble-dick around, do you, young feller?

LONNIE: No, sir!

COLONEL: That's good. The Germans will get you if you do.

LONNIE *(With deep conviction)*: Well, ah never do.

COLONEL: Come over the top and stick one of them spiky helmets right up your butt.

SKIP: Jesus H. God Almighty, that's the damnedest thang ah ever heard of in my life.

COLONEL: What the hell's wrong with you?

SKIP: Them Germans ain't wore no spiky helmets in fifty years.

COLONEL: Don't mean they ain't gonna put them on again! You-all think the Kaiser's dead, don't you? Well, he ain't! Him and Crown Prince Willie is both livin' on a cattle ranch in Argentina and in secret is storin' up guns in the basements of Catholic churches all over the world.

SKIP: That ain't no Kaiser that's down there in

Argentina. That there's *Hitler!* Hell, we've had a whole new world's war since the damn Kaiser was runnin' around.

LONNIE: That's right. Ah remember readin' about old Hitler in school. Why, he was on the German side in World's War II.

RUFE: Only he ain't down in Argentina, no, sir. Ah read in a magazine over to Billberry's Drugstore how them Russians got old Hitler hid out in a little room over there in Mos-cow.

LONNIE: No kiddin'.

RUFE: Sure. They smuggled him out of Berlin in a hay wagon.

COLONEL: Skinny little son-of-a-bitch couldn't hold a candle to the Kaiser.

RED: Good God! We gonna git on with the votin' or not?

L.D.: Damn right! Now, everybody in this-here membership wantin' Lonnie Roy McNeil to be a brother knight, put up their hand.

OLIN: Hold it.

L.D.: Now what?

OLIN: Lonnie Roy here has got to be out of the room when we make this-here vote. That there's a rule. Ain't it, Rufe?

RUFE: Ah recollect on how it is.

L.D.: Oh, what the hell. Lonnie Roy, would you please leave the room while we have our vote here.

LONNIE: Shore.

L.D.: Won't take a second. We'll be callin' you right back.

LONNIE *(Moving toward the door)*: That's okay, ah'll jest wait outside.

RUFE: Nuthin' to worry about, Lonnie Roy. We jest gotta follow the rules, you know.

LONNIE: Sure, that's okay.

OLIN: Rules is rules.

LONNIE: Fine. *(He exits.)*

L.D.: Okay now, ever'body sit down and we'll com-mence with the votin'. Not you, Olin!

OLIN: How come not me?

L.D.: 'Cause you are the door guard tonight.

OLIN: The door guard?

L.D.: You gotta stand up there and guard the door while we have our vote and initiation so's nobody that ain't a Magnolia will slip in on us durin' the ceremony.

OLIN: Well, ah don't wanna stand up all the time.

L.D.: Well, you gotta.

OLIN: Why cain't I sit down and put my foot up again' the door?

L.D.: 'Cause you cain't, that's why.

COLONEL: You are the sentry, Olin, and sentries don't sit, they stand and they stand tall.

OLIN *(Grumbling)*: Yes, sir.

RED *(Chuckling)*: Rules is rules, Olin.

OLIN *(Mimicking Red's voice)*: Rules is rules, Olin.

L.D.: We will now have our vote.

COLONEL: What we votin' on?

L.D.: On Lonnie Roy, Colonel.

COLONEL: Am ah for him or agin him?

L.D.: You're for him, Colonel.

COLONEL: Hell, ah thought ah was agin him.

(There is another loud commotion outside and Milo Crawford bursts through the door with Lonnie Roy in tow. Milo is mild-mannered, lank, gangly, and very homely. He wears a white shirt, a dark necktie, and an old double-breasted brown suit.)

RUFE: Milo Crawford.

OLIN: Milo.

MILO: Looky here, looky here. Ah caught this-here feller sneakin' around outside the door!

L.D.: Let him go, Milo, this here is Lonnie Roy McNeil. He's a new member.

MILO: A new member?

L.D.: Yes, damnit, a new member!

MILO: Well, gosh, ah didn't know.

RED: Well, you know now, you damned fool! So turn him loose!

MILO *(Releasing him)*: Shucks ah'm plumb sorry, feller. Ah didn't know.

LONNIE: That's okay.

COLONEL: What's goin' on?

L.D.: Nuthin', Colonel.

MILO: Shucks, Colonel, ah didn't know.

COLONEL: Who are you?

MILO: Milo Crawford, Colonel.

COLONEL: Ah thought you took your mama to Big Spring.

MILO: Couldn't get mah danged old pickup started.

OLIN: You try pumpin' her?

MILO: Yeah, but it didn't do no good. Ah jest don't seem to git no gas.

RUFE: Probable the fuel line.

MILO: Speck so.

OLIN: Or the carburetor . . .

L.D.: Well, anyway, since you're here now, go on over there and shake hands with Lonnie Roy McNeil.

MILO *(Shaking hands)*: Pleased to meet you. How's come ah never seed you around affore? You new in town or somethin'?

LONNIE: No, sir. Ah live over to Silver City.

COLONEL: Silver City!

RUFE *(Covering up.)* He's a helluva nice guy, Milo.

OLIN: He's old Grady McNeil's boy, Milo.

MILO: I see.

L.D.: Well, now that we all know each other, let's

please, please, git on with the votin'.

MILO: What we votin' on?

L.D.: We're votin' on Lonnie Roy here.

COLONEL: Who?

RED: *Lonnie Roy McNeil!!*

COLONEL: Ah thought we already done that.

SKIP: We was, but Milo Crawford messed ever'thang up.

COLONEL: Milo Crawford? Ah thought he went over to Big Spring.

MILO: Ah couldn't get mah pickup started, Colonel.

COLONEL: You try pushin' her?

RUFE: Won't do no good to push her if she ain't gittin' any gas.

OLIN: Probable the carburetor.

MILO: Speck so.

RED *(Sarcastically)*: What happened to Mama, Milo? She gotta stay home all by herself tonight?

MILO: No. George and Jane Williams come by and give her a ride.

RED: Ooo-eee, ain't that nice!

SKIP: Let's git on with the votin'!

RUFE: Hell, yes. Let's git on with it.

L.D.: Okay, Okay. Lonnie Roy, would you please . . . *(He indicates the door.)*

LONNIE: Shore thing. *(He goes out.)*

MILO: Where's he goin'?

L.D.: Outside.

MILO: Why?

L.D.: Rules.

MILO: Rules?

L.D., RED, OLIN, SKIP, AND RUFE: Rules!!!

MILO: I see.

L.D.: Okay. Ever'body wantin' Lonnie Roy McNeil for a new member, put up their hand. *(They all do except the Colonel.)* What's wrong, Colonel, why ain't you votin'?

COLONEL: Votin'? What for?

L.D.: Go over and put up the Colonel's hand, will you, Red.

RED: Shore thing. *(He does.)*

COLONEL: What's goin' on? What's goin' on?

L.D.: Nuthin', Colonel. Red's jest helpin' you to vote, that's all.

COLONEL: Oh, well, thank you, Red. Damn nice of you.

RED: Mah pleasure, Colonel.

L.D.: Fine, fine. That's real official-like. Okay, Brother Knight Potts, you can bring on Lonnie Roy now.

OLIN: Okay. *(He opens the door.)* All right, Lonnie Roy, you-all can come in now. Lonnie Roy? Lonnie Roy? *(He steps outside.)* Well, what the hell!

L.D.: What's wrong?

OLIN *(Sticking his head back into the room)*: He's gone.

(They all freeze in place as the lights fade to BLACKOUT.)

ACT TWO

The scene opens in the meeting room seconds later. The characters are found in positions held at the end of Act One. As the lights come up, they remain frozen for a moment before the dialogue begins.

L.D.: What the hell you mean, he's gone?

OLIN: He's gone, he ain't out here.

L.D.: Well, damnit, go look for him. See if Ramsey-Eyes saw where he went.

OLIN: Okay. *(He exits.)*

RED: Well, whattayou know about that.

L.D.: He'll be back, he didn't have no reason to run off or anythin'.

COLONEL: What's happened? What's goin' on?

SKIP: Lonnie Roy's gone, Colonel.

COLONEL: Gone? Gone where?

SKIP: We don't know, Colonel.

L.D.: He ain't gone, ah tell you.

RED: What kinda fellers you bringin' around here, Rufe? Runnin' away from an initiation.

RUFE: Well, hell, Red, ah don't know. He seemed like a nice-enough feller to me.

MILO: Ah didn't like the looks of him the first time ah laid eyes on him.

COLONEL: Shoot the son-of-a-bitch!

(There is a knock at the door.)

L.D.: Ah'll bet that's him now. You see, ah told you he never run off. Come in, Brother Elect Knight of the White Magnolia, *Lonnie Roy McNeil!*

(The door opens and Ramsey-Eyes comes in.)

RAMSEY-EYES: 'Scuse me.

RED: What the hell you doin' up here!

RAMSEY-EYES *(Feisty)*: Mistah Olin Potts done told me to come up hyare and tell you iffen ah seed where Mistah Lonnie Roy McNeil went to!

L.D.: Well, did you?

RAMSEY-EYES: No, sah, but he never went out through de lobby 'cause ah been sittin' down dere by de door.

RUFE: Where's Olin now?

RAMSEY-EYES: He's gone over to see iffen Mistah Lonnie Roy McNeil went down and out de back way.

L.D.: Did the clerk see anythin'?

RAMSEY-EYES: No, sah, he didn't see nuthin' 'cause he's been asleep for 'most an hour. But not me, no, sah, ah been wide awake all evenin'.

COLONEL: Good man, Ramsey-Eyes.

RAMSEY-EYES: Ah been keepin' guard, Colonel Kinkaid, sah.

COLONEL: Damn good man.

RAMSEY-EYES: Thank you, sah.

COLONEL: Back on down to your post now, Ramsey-Eyes.

RAMSEY-EYES: Thank you, sah. Yes, sah. *(Exiting.)* Ah been wide awake all evenin'.

RED *(Muttering)*: Stupid idiot wouldn't recognize Lonnie Roy if he fell over him.

COLONEL: Faithful employee, that Ramsey-Eyes.

L.D.: Sure, Colonel, sure.

COLONEL: Ah would trust that man with anythin' ah owned. *(To Rufe)* General Pershing once commanded Neegrow troops, betcha didn't know that, did you?

RUFE *(Interested)*: No, Colonel, I didn't.

COLONEL: Montana territory, October 1895. Troop of the 10th Cavalry. Neegrow troops. "Buffalo soldiers," the Injuns called 'em.

RUFE: Well, I'll be damned.

SKIP: Aw to hell with it, let's break open the booze.

RED: Gittin' a little shaky there, Skip?

SKIP: No, ah jest don't see any reason not to now.

RED: Whattayou think, L.D.?

L.D.: I don't know. It jest don't figger. You know that kid seemed interested, really interested.

RED: Yeah, well, seein' as how our hope for the future done vanished into thin air, let's drink to the one who got away. *(He takes one of the bottles out of the bag.)* Who's first?

(Skip reaches frantically for the bottle just as we hear a timid little knock at the door and Lonnie Roy sticks his head in the room.)

LONNIE: Votin' all over with?

RED: Where the hell you been?

LONNIE: Ah hadda go pee.

SKIP: Jesus H. Christ on a crutch.

LONNIE: Well, ah hadda.

RED: Looks like we're gonna have an initiation after all, Skip.

SKIP: Aw, come on, Red, jest one shot, jest one.

RED: Sorry, Skip. Rules is rules.

LONNIE: Was ah voted in?

L.D.: You sure was, Lonnie Roy. Ever'body voted for you. Ain't that somethin'?

LONNIE: Well, ah am truly gratified.

L.D.: That jest shows you how much all the brothers think of you.

OLIN *(Entering)*: Ah cain't find that stupid little son-of-a-bitch anywhere!

RUFE: He's here, Olin.

OLIN: Oh, yeah, well. Howdy there, Lonnie Roy.

LONNIE: Ah hadda go pee.

OLIN: Oh. Ah didn't think to look down the hall.

L.D.: Well, ever'thin' is all right now. Now we can have our initiation.

SKIP: It's about by-God time.

L.D. *(Who has been looking behind the podium.)*: Where's the book?

RED: What book?

L.D.: The initiation book. It ain't on the shelf behind the speaker's thing here.

RED: Well, don't look at me. I ain't got it.

L.D.: It's always been on this-here shelf, now it ain't. Now, who took it?

MILO: Ah ain't got it.

OLIN: Me neither.

L.D.: Skip?

SKIP: Are you kidding!

L.D.: Rufe?

RUFE: No, sir.

SKIP: What about the Colonel?

COLONEL: Who? What? What's goin' on?

L.D.: We're tryin' to find the initiation book, Colonel.

COLONEL: Well, go ahead and find it! Who the hell's stoppin' you?

L.D.: We was wonderin' if you had it, Colonel.

COLONEL: Had what?

RED: The goddamned initiation book!!!

COLONEL: Hell no, I ain't got no book!!

L.D. *(In a mild state of panic)*: Well — damn! How we gonna hold a ceremony without a book?

SKIP: Let's jest make one up.

L.D.: What the hell you talkin' about?

SKIP: Make up our own ceremony. *(He stands in front of Lonnie Roy.)* Hokus-pokus Maynard C. Stempco, get ready, get set, Little Clete Spencer — zap! Lonnie Roy McNeil, you are now initiated. Let's have a drink.

MILO: That wouldn't be right. Lonnie Roy wouldn't be a proper member.

OLIN: No, sir, somethin' like that would be agin the rules.

SKIP: What rules?

RUFE: The rules of the order of the Knights of the White Magnolia, that's what rules.

SKIP: Well, hell, there ain't no Knights of the White Magnolia but us. So what difference does it make?

L.D.: It makes plenty of difference. That rule book was writ by Maynard C. Stempco himself, way back in 1902. It's got secret valuable writin's in it.

RUFE: Damn right.

L.D.: We gotta find that book.

RED: You sure it ain't back there on the shelf?

L.D.: It ain't here, I tell you. Only thing on this damned shelf is a box of dominoes.

RUFE: Maybe it's in the room some place.

(They all vaguely look around the room.)

L.D.: Well, look for it!

OLIN: Don't see it.

L.D.: Hell, it ain't in here either. Now hold on just a second, let's jest hold on and think a little bit. Now, who the hell was the last man we initiated?

OLIN: Milo Crawford.

L.D.: Milo, when was you initiated?

MILO: What year is this?

L.D.: It's still 1962.

SKIP: It's been that way ever since January, Milo.

MILO: In nineteen hundred and fifty-seven.

L.D.: You shore?

MILO: Yep, 'cause that's the year my mama had her nervous breakdown.

L.D.: Yeah, well, who did the book readin'?

MILO: You did.

L.D.: Oh yeah, ah spoze ah did.

RED *(Taunting)*: What'd you do with the

book, L.D.?

COLONEL: What's goin' on?

SKIP: L.D. lost the initiation book, Colonel.

COLONEL: That was a damn-fool thing to do, L.D.

L.D.: Ah never lost nuthin'.

RUFE: Well, hell, L.D., you had it last.

LONNIE: Does this mean ah ain't gonna git initiated after all?

L.D.: Of course you're gonna git initiated. Soon as ah can think where ah put that damn-fool book.

RED: Where'd you put it after you used it last?

L.D.: Ah thought ah put it on that shelf behind the speaker's outfit.

OLIN: Well, that jest messes up ever'thin'.

MILO: Shore does.

LONNIE: This mean ah ain't gonna git initiated after all?

SKIP: Hell, let's all have us a little drink, maybe it'll help us remember.

RED: Ah thought you drank to forget.

SKIP: Forget? Shore, ah drink to forget, an' ah got plenty to forget too. You know, the Colonel here ain't the only one that's seen fightin'. Ah seen it too, plenty of it.

RED: Shore you have.

SKIP: Ah have, ah tell you! Plenty of it! Over there in Ko-rea ah was in every combat sector there was.

RED: You never was in shit! That buddy of yours that married your sister told me you guys never got closer to any front lines than fifty miles.

SKIP: That ain't true.

L.D. *(Who has been deep in thought.)* Wait a minute! Wait a minute. Ah remember now! Ah gave the book to the Colonel.

MILO: The Colonel?

L.D.: That's right, he asked me for it and ah gave it to him.

(They all turn and look at the Colonel.)

COLONEL *(After a moment, very quietly)*: Ramsey-Eyes has it.

L.D.: What was that, Colonel?

COLONEL *(Louder)*: Ramsey-Eyes has it!

L.D.: What in the name of Christ is Ramsey-Eyes doin' with it?

COLONEL: He keeps it for me.

L.D.: Well, if that ain't the damnedest thing ah ever heard of in my life. You mean to tell me that you gave the Knights of the White Magnolia secret book to Ramsey-Eyes!

RED: Jeezus Christ!

COLONEL: No, ah didn't give it to him. Ah told you-all, ah jest let him keep it.

L.D.: What the hell for?

COLONEL: 'Cause ah was afraid ah would lose it. Mah memory's been givin' me some troubles lately and ah didn't want to lose it.

L.D.: But why Ramsey-Eyes? Why not one of the brothers?

COLONEL: Because for one thing he is an old and faithful employee, and for another thing ah wouldn't trust any of you bumble-dicks with the rule book if it were writ on the side of an elephant!

RED: Well, ah'll be damned.

COLONEL: Probably.

L.D. *(Resigned)*: Olin, would you please go down to the lobby and ask Ramsey-Eyes for the book.

OLIN: Shore thing. *(He exits.)*

LONNIE: Does this mean ah'm gonna git initiated now?

L.D.: Yes, damnit, yes! Now sit down over there and shut up!

LONNIE *(Sitting)*: Ah never done nuthin'.

COLONEL: Bumble-dicks.

MILO: Gawlee, ah cain't git over it. Ramsey-Eyes,

with the rule book.

RUFE: You reckin he read it?

RED: Hell, no!

SKIP: How you know?

RED: 'Cause he's too damn dumb even to write his own name. Much less *read* anything.

RUFE: Well, at least we know where it is.

MILO: Yes, that's true. You know, even in the darkest moments you can always find a little good.

RUFE *(Impressed)*: By God, that's damn truthful, Milo.

MILO: Thank you.

RUFE: You orter write that one down some place and send it in to a magazine or somethin'.

MILO: Think so?

RUFE: Hell, yes. Whattayou think, Red?

RED: Who gives a damn!

SKIP: Why don't you write it on the shithouse wall over to Red's place?

L.D.: Shut up, Skip.

COLONEL: "Shut up, Kinkaid," that's what old Black Jack said when we was out there in Mexico. Hot as hell one day there in the officers' mess. Wind blowin' the tent sides back and forth. Flap, flap, flap . . .

OLIN *(Entering)*: Well, here it is. He had it in an old seegar box in a closet.

L.D. *(Taking the book.)* That's the damnedest thing ah ever heard in my life.

RED: Crazy old fool.

L.D.: Okay, boys, let's git at it. *(Walks to the podium and opens the book.)* Okay. Now, Red, you come up here and stand by me. Now, Milo, you stand by the station of the moon. Olin, you stand by the station of the sun, and, Rufe, you stand by the station of the west wind. Let's see now, what part can we give the Colonel?

COLONEL: Don't want no part. Ah don't feel good. Ah got me a headache.

OLIN: You want ah should go down and git you an aspirin, Colonel?

COLONEL: Don't want no part.

RED: Forget him. Let's git on with it.

COLONEL: Ah was havin' me a cup of coffee with the Major when old Black Jack come in. Well, sir, as luck would have it, he come in jest as I was sayin' to the Major, "Ah don't think we're ever gonna catch that fat little greaser if we stay out here in this damn Meheeko for five hundred years . . ." and the General he says to me he says . . . *(Voice trails off.)*

L.D.: Lonnie Roy, you stand in front of Red and me.

LONNIE: Yes, sir.

L.D.: Okay, Skip. You hand out the written parts.

SKIP: Right.

LONNIE *(To Red)*: Boy, this is excitin', ain't it?

RED *(Muttering)*: If you like hunred-year-old snatch, it's a gas.

(L.D. takes some cards out of the book and hands them to Skip. Skip walks around handing out the written roles while L.D. takes the initiation hats out of the trunk. The hats are fez-type with ribbons on the back and emblems on the front. A half moon, a sunburst, a cloud with streamers for the west wind, a lamp for wisdom, a series of fountain-type lines for the truth, and a bolt of lightning for the wizard.)

L.D.: Now, Brothers, here are the *Chapeaux de rituale.* Milo, you are the moon. Olin, you are the sun. Rufe, you are the west wind. Skip, you are Wisdom the Guide to the Mystic Mountain.

SKIP: Hot damn.

L.D.. Red, you are the Golden Fountain of Truth and ah am the Imperial Wizard.

(The knights put on their hats and move back to their stations looking over their roles. As they are doing this, the Colonel says his lines.)

COLONEL: Flap, flap, flap. Horses standin' round hip-shot, slappin' at flies with their tails, lots of flies buzzin' around.
OLIN: Hey, L.D., somethin's wrong with my hat.
L.D.: Spin it around, Olin, you got it on backward.
RUFE: Hey, look at old Milo Crawford there.

(Milo's hat is much too big and is almost down over his ears.)

L.D.: Milo, put that thing on the back of your head, you look like hell.
SKIP: Hey, Red, that thing you got on your head look a whole lot like somethin' ah got growin' on my butt.
RED: Go to hell!
L.D.: Shut up, Skip!
RUFE: Ah cain't read my part.
L.D.: Why the hell not?
RUFE: It's got a big splotch or somethin' right in the middle of it.
L.D.: Well, read around the goddamn splotch!
RUFE *(Dubiously)*: Okay.
L.D.: Okay now, here we go. *(He starts to read.)* "You are now on a journey, initiate Lonnie Roy McNeil. A journey to seek the Golden Fountain of Truth that flows deep in the darkness of the Mystic Mountain."
LONNIE: Gawlee.
L.D.: During your journey, initiate Lonnie Roy McNeil, you will converse with the great heavenly

sages, and as you heed their advice, your reply will be "Stempco, Stempco, Stempco." Do you understand?

LONNIE: Stempco, Stempco, Stempco. Yes, sir.

L.D.: But you are not alone, initiate Lonnie Roy McNeil. By your decision to become a Knight of the White Magnolia you have wisdom by your side to guide you toward truth.

SKIP *(Reading)*: "Ah am wisdom. Ah am with you always as your friend and companion. Fear not as we begin our journey, for ah am here with you to place your footsteps on the right path toward truth."

LONNIE: Stempco, Stempco, Stempco.

L.D.: Your first journey, initiate *Lonnie Roy McNeil*, is to the pale-blue grotto of the moon.

(Skip leads Lonnie Roy over to Milo.)

MILO *(Reading)*: "Ah am the moon. By night ah cast beams down upon you, lightin' the way along your journey toward the truth."

LONNIE: Stempco, Stempco, Stempco.

L.D.: You now travel, initiate Lonnie Roy McNeil, to the blazin' realm of the sun.

(Skip leads Lonnie Roy to Olin.)

OLIN: "Ah am the sun. Ah bring my warmin' rays and glorious beams to warm and comfort you durin' the day as you journey toward the truth."

LONNIE: Stempco, Stempco, Stempco.

L.D.: You now travel, initiate Lonnie Roy McNeil, to the long low plains of the west wind.

(Skip leads him to Rufe.)

COLONEL: Flap, flap, flap . . .

RUFE *(Reading with great difficulty)*: "Ah am the west w____. Ah blow my balmy bree____ er ____ the ——ren desert an—— the sails of your craf____ cross the sea of ignor____ on your journey toward the truth." Hell, L.D., it don't make no sense readin' around this-here splotch.

L.D.: It sounded jest fine, Rufe. Anyway, we got the idea.

COLONEL: Flap, flap, flap . . .

L.D.: You now arrive, initiate Lonnie Roy McNeil, at the Mystic Mountain, wherein lies the Golden Fountain of Truth and the great white marble temple of the Imperial Wizard.

(Skip brings Lonnie Roy to the podium, and has him kneel down.)

RED *(Starting to read)*: "Ah am the Golden . . ." *(Just as he reads the Colonel says the role from memory.)*

COLONEL: "Ah am the Golden Fountain of Truth. I welcome travelers to my magic waters. Your journey has been long and hard, but rejoice now, pilgrim, your reward is at hand."

LONNIE: Stempco, Stempco, Stempco.

L.D.: By God, Colonel, that was real fine. How was it, Red?

RED *(Grinning)*: Letter-perfect.

L.D.: Jesus, Colonel. You think you can remember the part of the Imperial Wizard too?

COLONEL: Shut your mouth, Lieutenant Kinkaid. You keep talkin' a lot of bull and I'll have you on the horseshit detail for the rest of the campaign.

RED: Offhand, L.D., ah'd say that wasn't it.

L.D.: Yes, well, maybe ah'd better read it. "Ah am the Imperial Wizard. You have been guided by wisdom and aided by the sun, the moon, and the west wind to taste now the living waters of the

Golden Fountain of Truth.'' Oh hell!

RED: What's wrong?

L.D.: It says here that ah am now to give the initiate a drink of clear water from a silver cup. Ah forgot all about that.

OLIN: Ah could go down to the lobby for a Coke.

RED: How about a shot of booze?

MILO: That's what you gave me when ah was initiated.

RED: Did you take it?

MILO: Of course ah took it.

RED: Does your mama know about this?

MILO: Ah do lots of things my mama don't know about.

RED: Shore you do.

L.D.: Okay, okay, let's do this right now. Give Lonnie Roy the bottle, Red.

RED: Okay. *(Opens the bottle, hands it to Lonnie Roy.)*

L.D.: Let's see. Uh . . . Living waters of the Golden Fountain of Truth. Drink deeply, knight initiate Lonnie Roy McNeil, your quest has been rewarded.

(Lonnie Roy takes a long pull.)

RED *(Grabbing the bottle)*: Not too damn deeply.

SKIP: How about a shot for his faithful companion?

L.D.: Shut up, Skip. Now that you have known wisdom and tasted truth, knight initiate Lonnie Roy McNeil, you are ready to receive the final rites of membership. Light up the cross, Olin.

OLIN: Okay. *(He flips on the switch by the door. The cross comes on but the bulbs are so covered with dust, dirt, and fly specks that they are barely visible.)*

L.D.: What's wrong with that damn thing?

OLIN: Sure seems dim-like.

RUFE: I'll jiggle it a little bit and maybe it'll come on better. *(He walks over to the cross and looks at it.)* Well, no damn wonder!

L.D.: What's wrong?

RUFE: Well, it's all covered with dust and stuff.

L.D.: Well, git somethin' and clean it off.

RUFE: Turn off the light, Olin. *(He pulls a chair over and stands on it to clean the bulbs with his handkerchief. Milo, Red and Olin gather around to help him.)*

COLONEL: When General Pershing was a lieutenant, he was instructin' all them smarty-assed Kay-dets there at the West Point and they didn't like him. No, sir, they did not like him one little bit. So when they found out that he commanded them Neegrow troops, they started callin' him Black Jack.

MILO: . . . Spit on the base affore you screw it back in.

RED: Somebody orter spit on your base.

COLONEL: But he fixed 'em. He jest held on to the name, you see. Made it famous, by God. Yes, sir, you can have your goddamn Ike's and Doug's, give me old Black Jack Pershing anytime. Yes, sir!

OLIN: Don't touch them wires there . . . they'll shock the hell outta you.

RUFE: How can they shock me? You got the switch turned off, ain't you?

OLIN: Shore I got it off, but don't you know electricity lingers.

RUFE: Electricity lingers . . . that's the dumbest thing I ever heard in mah life.

L.D.: For Christ's sake, ain't you all finished yet?

RUFE: All done, L.D. Okay, Olin, you can fire it up again.

(Olin does — the cross gleams more or less like new.)

L.D.: That's a lot better. Okay, Olin, you can turn off the room lights now.

(Olin does. They all stand in the dim glow of the cross.)

LONNIE: Gee, that's pretty.

OLIN: Ain't that somethin'!

MILO: It looks like a church or somethin'. You know?

COLONEL: What's that glow up there? What is it?

L.D.: We got the cross on, Colonel.

COLONEL: Used to fire them lights up in the sky over the trenches. Light things up real bright like, then commence to shootin'. Hated them damn lights.

RED: You and General Pershing right, Colonel?

COLONEL: General Pershing? He told me to shut up one time. You know, he never said anythin' to me again, not one word, 'cept maybe to give an order or two. Ah don't think he liked me.

L.D.: Shore, Colonel, shore. Now, Brother Knights, we come to the most important part of our initiation. This-here part ah'm about to read to you, Lonnie Roy McNeil, is the real meanin' of White Magnoliaism . . . *(The cross makes a few sputtering noises and goes out, plunging the room into darkness.)* What the hell? Turn on the lights, Olin.

OLIN: Ah'm gittin' there.

(The lights go on.)

L.D.: Rufe, seek if you can fix that damn thing.

RUFE: Hell, ah don't know what's wrong with it, L.D. It must have a short in it or somethin'.

L.D.: Well, quit foolin' with it. We'll go on without it.

COLONEL: Don't like the goddamn dark!

RED: Git on with it, L.D. Ah'm gittin' tired of standin' here.

SKIP: Me too. Can't we git Lonnie Roy sworn in sittin' down? *(He sits down.)*

L.D.: Hell no, Skip!

MILO: Confound it, Skip, you're gonna ruin the whole darn thing.

SKIP: Hell with it. Ah done my part. Guided old Lonnie Roy here plumb to the Mystic Mountain an' ah'm bushed. Besides that, my piles itch. *(He squirms around in the chair.)*

L.D.: Goddamnit, Skip, stand up!

COLONEL: Gits goddamn dark in the trenches, ah can tell you. The rats come out in the dark and eat up ever'thin' they can git their teeth into.

RUFE *(Sits down)*: Aw, the hell with it!

MILO: Now, come on, fellers, it won't hurt you none to stand up a little while longer so's we can git Lonnie Roy sworn in proper.

COLONEL: Them rats was fat too. Big and fat, that's 'cause there was so many bodies to eat on, you see, and the fellers used to say that if one of them rats breathed on you that you would die! That's right, they would come up at night and breathe on you, then they would commence eatin' on your body. That's right. That's right!

OLIN: Hey, Colonel, take it easy. Boy, ah don't know, L.D., he's really got snakes in his boots tonight.

L.D.: He'll be okay, jest leave him alone, Olin.

LONNIE: What's wrong with him? He crazy or somethin'?

L.D.: No, no, of course not, he jest has these spells. Now, please, will ever'body sit down.

OLIN: Me too?

L.D.: You too.

OLIN: About by-God time.

RED *(Moving off platform)*: Ah wish to hell you'd make up your damn mind.

L.D.: Well, it is made up. Ah want ever'body sittin'.

(Lonnie Roy makes a move for the chair.)

Damnit, Lonnie Roy, not you!

LONNIE: Mah knees hurt.

L.D.: Well, that's too bad. *You* gotta kneel down there.

LONNIE: Yes, sir.

SKIP: For Christ's sake, let's git this damn thing over with and have a drink!

RED: Why the hell don't you shut up, you goddamn little lush. You'll get a drink when ever'body else does and not until then!

SKIP: Ah'm not a lush, damn you, ah'm not! Who the hell do you think you're talkin' to anyway?

RED: Oh sure, ah plumb forgot. You're a hero, ain't you? A Korean war hero.

SKIP: Ah seen plenty of stuff over there, lot more than the Colonel ever seen; ah been in battles, big battles.

RED: Shoreshore. The battle of the Tattoo Parlor and the Beer Hall. Face it, Skip, you're nuthin' but a phony, a boozer and a phony.

SKIP: Ah'm not, damn you! Ah'm not!

L.D.: All right now, all right, that's jest a goddamn nuff! This part I'm about to read is real important and ah want it quiet in here!

(The cross light comes on again, this time very bright and vivid, then it goes off.)

RUFE: Mah Gawd, did you see that!

COLONEL: What was that? What was that flash?

L.D.: Nuthin', Colonel, just that damn-fool cross

actin' up again.

(Cross sputters on and off.)

COLONEL: A creepin' barrage. *Five-nines* and *seventy-sevens*, blowin' up all around us! Throwin' up bodies of Frenchmen that was killed over a year before. Old bodies and new bodies jumbled together in the air.

SKIP *(Getting up and moving away)*: Mah God, listen to that! For Christ's sake, somebody shut him up!

(Cross sputters on and off.)

COLONEL *(His voice rising to a high whine)*: Hangin' on the old bob wire like pieces of pork. Fellers out there with half their guts shot away, sharin' a shell hole with a year-old corpse, out there all night screamin' and cryin' on the old bob wire.

RUFE *(In a hushed voice)*: Mah God, ah ain't never heard him talk this crazy-like affore.

(The cross light flares on and off again.)

COLONEL: Stop that, stop doin' that! Cain't you see ah'm old now? Ah'm old, ah'm an old man! Ah'm not like ah was. Ah was young then. Ah was young when ah was in France. Ah could be with wimmen. Walkin' down them streets of Bar-le-Duc like some kind of young god, American Doughboy, six foot tall. Oh, God. Oh, mah God. What's wrong with me?

SKIP *(Going to him)*: Colonel Kinkaid? Colonel Kinkaid, for God's sake, stop it! Snap out of it!

COLONEL: Who is that? Who's got hold of me? Is that you, George?

SKIP: No, Colonel, it's . . .

COLONEL: Is that you, George Plummer? Remember when we was at the Argonne. Them dirty bastards killed you there, didn't they, George Plummer? You was afraid and that goddamned whiz-bang hit and tore off your head, and your body jumped up and run off like it was still alive, flappin' its arms and runnin' and the boys next to me shootin' at it, shootin' at it, shootin' at it for the hell of it, shootin' and laughin' and your head rollin' around on the duckboards at the bottom of the trench like some kind of ball.

SKIP: He's gone crazy, it's like he was still over there. Still fightin' that old war.

RED: Doesn't sound too heroic when it's the real thing, does it, hot shot!

(Cross sputters on and off.)

RUFE: Maybe we better git him outta here.

L.D.: Olin, you better go on down to the lobby and git Ramsey-Eyes to phone over to the Colonel's house and tell Floyd to come on over here and pick up his daddy.

OLIN: Shore thing. *(He exits.)*

(Cross sputters on and off.)

COLONEL: Killin' people all around me! Throwin' the bodies up in the air! Up in the air.

L.D.: Shore, Colonel, shore.

LONNIE: We gonna have the rest of the readin' soon?

L.D.: The what? Oh, shore, shore, Lonnie Roy, of course we are.

LONNIE: Shore seems like a long time.

COLONEL: The padre come along and put that

head in a sack. It musta been a flour sack or somethin', 'cause when he walked, it let out little puffs of smoke and the blood run out over his shoes and over his . . . over his puttees. One of the boys yelled out, "Hey, Padre, you're gettin' maggots in the gravy." Hey, Padre, you're gettin' mag . . . mag . . . oh, mah God!

SKIP: Jesus Christ, now that's enough. *(Backing away.)* That's enough!

RED: Maybe a shot of whiskey would help him.

L.D.: Damn good idea, Red. Bring that bottle over here.

RUFE: Why don't you jest leave him be?

L.D.: Ah'll hold his head back and you give him a drink.

RED: Okay. *(L.D. holds the Colonel's head back and Red puts the bottle to the Colonel's lips. The Colonel thrashes about violently and spits the fluid out all over Red's shirt.)* Look here what he done to my shirt.

COLONEL: Let me go, let me go. Ah ain't crazy, damn you! It's jest them shells. Oh, Jesus, they're comin', the Germans. Oh, Jesus God, ah can see their shadows up agin the wire.

RED: Goddamn crazy old fool, look what he done to my shirt!

OLIN *(Entering)*: Ramsey-Eyes is phonin' over to Floyd's now.

RED: Damnit to hell, this is a bran'-new shirt.

RUFE: Serves you right. Ah told you to leave him alone.

RED: Keep your damn trap shut, Rufe. Who the hell asked you anythin'.

OLIN: Now hold on here. There ain't no call for you to go yellin' at Rufe.

RED: Ah'll yell at anybody ah damn well want to!

SKIP: To hell with this, ah need a drink! *(He grabs bottle.)*

RED: Put down that bottle, Skip.

SKIP: Go to hell, ah need this!

RED: Gimme that bottle or ah'll break your goddamn neck!

SKIP *(Pulling an object from his pocket and concealing it with his hand)*: If you think you can git by this-here knife, you jest come on ahead!

LONNIE *(Jumping away)*: Jesus God, he's got him a knife!

L.D.: Don't be a damn fool, Skip. Come on and give us the knife, then you can have all you want to drink.

SKIP: Ah got all ah want right now. *(He takes a long drink.)*

RED: You rotten little bastard! You stinkin' two-bit lush!

SKIP: Stay where you are, Red, or ah'll cut you! Ah ain't kiddin' now.

RUFE *(Backing away)*: Watch him, Red, watch him.

MILO: Maybe we'd better adjourn this-here meetin' and finish off the initiation next time.

COLONEL *(Grabbing hold of Lonnie Roy, who has backed into his wheelchair)*: Help me, help me. God in heaven, help me.

LONNIE *(Screams and struggles to get loose)*: He's got me! He's got me! Old crazy man's got me! Old crazy man's got me, help, help. *(He tears loose from the Colonel and bolts out the door. The Colonel slumps over in his chair.)*

L.D.: Stop him, Olin, don't let him get away!

OLIN: Come on, Rufe.

(They dash out the door after Lonnie Roy.)

RED: To hell with him. Help me git the knife away from Skip.

L.D.: Come on now, Skip. Give me that knife.

SKIP *(Hands L.D. a small tyre gauge and grins)*: What knife?

L.D.: Damn tyre gauge!

RED *(Advances on Skip swiftly)*: You son-ot-a-bitch! *(He grabs the bottle from Skip and smashes him viciously in the stomach. Skip doubles up and falls to the floor.)*

SKIP: Oh, my gut. Damn you, Red, ah think ah'm gonna puke.

RED *(Pulling him up)*: Not in here you ain't. *(He opens the door and pushes Skip out.)* Git your ass on down the hall. *(Red comes back in and closes the door.)* Half a bottle. That damn little sot drank half a bottle.

MILO: Well, ah think it's time for me to be gittin' on home now.

L.D.: No! By God, you stay right where you are, Milo.

MILO: Gee, L.D., it's gittin' late and you know my mother waits up for me on meetin' nights.

L.D.: Screw your mother! You're stayin' right here till Olin and Rufe git back with Lonnie Roy.

MILO *(Shocked)*: What did you say about my mother?

L.D.: Nuthin', Milo. Ah mean, ah didn't mean to say it.

MILO: You had no call to say somethin' like that. No call at all, now, by gollies, you apologize, L.D. You jest apologize for sayin' that!

RED: Go to hell! L.D. here ain't apologizin' for nuthin'.

L.D.: Now wait a minute, Red . . .

MILO: Well, he better! He jest better or ah'm walkin' out that-there door an' never comin' back!

RED: Well, go ahead and walk damnit. Who the hell needs you. Stinkin' little mama's boy!

L.D.: Now hold on a minute, Red. Wait, Milo,

don't go.

MILO: Well, ah'm goin'. Ah'm goin' right now!

RED: You bet your ass you are. Gitt!!!

(Milo exits, then returns suddenly.)

MILO: Ah never did like you, Red Grover, never! You're nuthin' but a lard-butted booze drinker. *(He exits.)*

RED *(Laughing)*: "Lard-butted booze drinker." By God, ah've been called worse.

L.D.: You had no call to do that.

RED: Do what?

L.D.: Treat Milo thataway.

RED: Well, hell, L.D., you're the one that told him to go hump his own mother.

L.D.: Ah didn't mean that, but you did. You meant to run him off.

RED: So damn what. Ah never liked the gutless little s.o.b. anyway.

L.D.: But we need him. We need ever'body, don't you see? Jesus, we're breakin' up. Jest when things are startin' to look good, we start breakin' up.

(Rufe and Olin enter.)

RUFE: Well, he's gone.

L.D.: You couldn't catch him, huh?

OLIN: The way that boy was runnin', he's probable back in Silver City by now.

RUFE *(Sitting down)*: Olin and me is gittin' too old to run all over Bradleyville after half-initiated kids.

OLIN *(Seeing Colonel)*: What's wrong with the Colonel?

L.D. *(Rushing to Colonel)*: Oh, mah God! Colonel Kinkaid, are you okay? Colonel Kinkaid?

(Olin and Rufe gather around.)

OLIN: Is he dead?

L.D. *(Feeling Colonel's pulse)*: No, his heart's still beatin', but, mah God, he looks terrible. Olin, you and Rufe better git him on down to the lobby and wait with him till Floyd gits here.

RUFE: Okay, L.D. Come on, Olin. We'll wheel him to the stairs and carry him on down from there. *(He wheels the Colonel out the door. L.D. watches them for a moment and then closes the door.)*

RED: Well, sir, that about does it.

L.D.: Yeah, ah guess the meetin's over all right. *(Starting to collect hats.)* Now, look here, that damn-fool Milo Crawford ran outta here with his moon hat on.

RED: No, ah don't mean the meetin'. Ah mean the whole shootin' match. There ain't gonna be any more meetin's.

L.D.: You're crazy!

RED: Ah am, huh?

L.D.: Yes. We ain't through by a long shot.

RED: Sure we are, L.D. That old man down there's gonna die. Ah can tell by lookin' at him, and with him dead there goes the old meetin' room. Like ah told you before, Floyd ain't gonna give nuthin' free to nobody.

L.D.: So what? That don't mean nuthin'. We can meet somewheres else. Hell's fire, the brotherhood means more than jest a beat-up old room in a flea-bag hotel.

RED: The *brotherhood?* Oh, mah God! The *"brotherhood!"* Jesus Christ, L.D., wake up. Git back on the goddamn planet. The *brotherhood* ain't any more. The *brotherhood* ran outta here with Lonnie Roy and Milo. The *brotherhood* fell on its ass with Skip over there. The *brotherhood* got carried outta here with a dyin' old man. There ain't gonna be no stinkin' Knights of the White Magnolia cause the Knights of the White Magnolia idea is gone, finished, all washed up. Did you really listen to that crap we were readin' tonight? The Gospel according to Maynard C. Stempco. The sun, the moon, and the west wind? Well, L.D., old pal, lemme tell you as far as this-here lodge is concerned, the sun's done set, the moon's gone down, and the west wind's got a big splotch on it.

L.D.: That ain't true! The ideas that this-here lodge was founded on have a hell of a lot of meanin'.

RED: Meanin'? Meanin' to who? For God's sake, take a look around you, L.D., whatta ya see? Domino players, stumble bums, mama's boys, pimple-faced kids, and crazy old men.

L.D.: And you? Just where the hell do you fit in?

RED: Me? Ah don't fit in nowhere. Ah'm just a lard-butted booze drinker. Remember? *(He picks up the sack of whiskey.)* So I guess that jest leaves you, L.D. The only true believer, L.D. Alexander, supermarket manager and keeper of the White Magnolias. Let me tell you somethin', Brother White Knight, Imperial Wizard, you don't put down the sons-of-bitchin' freedom riders and minority bastards with all this crap any more. You got to look for the loopholes, pal. Let 'em all squawk about lunchrooms and schools all they want. In mah place ah simply reserve the right to refuse service to anybody. You look for the loopholes, pal. Well, so long, L.D. If ah don't see you down to the bar, ah'll save a seat for you on the back of the bus. *(He pitches the half-empty pint to him and exits, leaving the door open.)*

(L.D. watches him off and glances dejectedly around. Crosses to the door and closes it, then to

*the Stempco portrait and contemplates a moment,
then he crosses to the truth banner, and after a
moment rips it down and tosses it into the trunk.
He takes off his hat and throws it into the trunk as
well. The sound of a train passing through town
makes him pause. The door opens and Skip comes
in.)*

SKIP: Jesus, ah think he busted mah gut. Ah been
pukin' up Dixie Dinette chiliburgers by the
goddamn bucketful.
L.D. *(Giving Skip the bottle)*: Here, maybe this will
help.
SKIP: Oh, God, thanks. *(He drinks.)* Where the
hell is ever'body?
L.D.: Gone.
SKIP: Gone? Gone where?
L.D.: Quit. Walked out.
SKIP: Quit? Who quit?
L.D.: Lonnie Roy, Milo, and Red.
SKIP: What about the rest of the guys?
L.D.: Finished. It's all finished.
SKIP *(Getting up)*: You mean Colonel Kinkaid
quit too?
L.D.: You might say so, yes.
SKIP: Well, ah'll be damned.

(Olin and Rufe re-enter.)

RUFE: Well, Floyd finally got here.
OLIN: He said he was gonna take his daddy
straight over to Doc Crowley's. He was mad as
hell at us for lettin' the Colonel get into that
shape.
RUFE: That's right. He says he's gonna shut down
the meetin' room.
L.D. Let him go ahead. It don't matter no more
anyway.

OLIN: Well, hell, L.D., if we cain't come up here no more, where we gonna hold our meetin's?

L.D.: Whattayou care? What the hell do you come to the meetin's for anyway?

OLIN: Well, hell, L.D., me and Rufe like to play the domino games and Skip there, he, well, uh . . .

L.D.: Shore, shore, we all know why Skip comes up here.

SKIP: Now wait a minute. Ah never done nuthin'.

RUFE: Well, hell, L.D., we cain't jest quit.

L.D.: Who says we cain't? Ah'm tired of tryin' to keep ever'thin' goin' any more. Watchin' things bust apart. Things ain't the same no more. Damn, damn, things is changin'. Damn. Oh, to hell with it. *(He walks to the podium and picks up the initiation book.)* This-here lodge, this-here society, this-here brotherhood, this-here ever'thin' is now adjourned! *(He takes the book and slowly walks out.)*

OLIN: Well, what the hell do you think about that?

RUFE: What did he mean, "This-here brotherhood is now adjourned"?

SKIP: Ah think we jest knighted our last Magnolia, boys. All the rest of the brothers done flew the coop.

RUFE: You mean that we're all the members there is?

SKIP: That's right. Who would have thought that one day old Olin Potts there would be the Grand Imperial Wizard of the White Magnolia? Stempco! Stempco! Stempco!

RUFE: Doggone it, ah'm sure gonna miss our old meetin' nights.

SKIP: Oh hell, yes, me too. Especially this last one. *(He rubs his stomach.)*

RUFE: Now there won't be nuthin' to do.

OLIN: Aw hell, Rufe, there's always somethin' to do. We could go over there to the new bowlin' alley and give that a try.

RUFE: Yeah, I spoze we could. Well, ah gotta be gittin' on back home now or Sara Beth will be mad as hell.

OLIN: Not half as mad as old Mabel's gonna be at me.

RUFE: What the hell you talkin' about, Olin? You know damn well Sara Beth can git a hunred times madder than Mabel ever could.

OLIN: Now listen here, Rufe Phelps, that ain't true.

RUFE:The hell it ain't. Old Sara Beth gits up in the morning mad at the rooster an' goes to bed at night cussin' the owl.

(The exit arguing. Skip watches the exit and finishes the rest of the bottle. He flips the bottle cap. Ramsey-Eyes enters.)

RAMSEY-EYES: Meetin' all over with, Mistah Skip?

SKIP: Yes, Ramsey-Eyes, the meetin' is all over.

RAMSEY-EYES: Ah'll jest straighten thangs up and lock de door.

SKIP: You jest do that little old thing, Ramsey-Eyes. *(He looks at the empty bottle.)* Christ, ah wish ah had another drink.

RAMSEY-EYES: Mistah Red Grover is over to his saloon. Ah seed him go over dere when he left the hotel here.

SKIP: Hot damn! Ah'll bet he'll give me a drink, sure enough, ah jest bet he will. Thanks, Ramsey-Eyes. Good night. *(He exits.)*

RAMSEY-EYES: Good night, Mistah Skip. *(He closes the door and snaps the cross light switch a couple of times. When it doesn't work, he moves to the cross and raps the wall next to it with the broom handle. The cross lights up. He chuckles and moves back to the door, turning off the overhead lights. A piece of paper catches his eye. He picks it up and moves to the light of the cross to read.)* "Ah am de moon. By night ah cast beams down upon you, lightin' your way along your journey toward de truth." *(He chuckles.)* "Ah am de moon." Oh Lawdy. "Ah am de moon." *(He chuckles again.)*

(The cross lights fade to BLACKOUT.)